WHAT PRESENT AND FORMER POLITICAL PRA

What's particularly valuable about this handb
ities of lobbying from the perspective of the ̶l̶o̶b̶b̶y̶i̶s̶t̶ ̶a̶n̶d̶ ̶t̶h̶o̶s̶e̶ ̶b̶e̶i̶n̶g̶ ̶l̶o̶b̶
bied. It gets deep into the psychology of this relationship that is the essence
of lobbying.

—*Tom Brice, Former State Legislator and Lobbyist*

Having served in the Alaska legislature for over 30 years, I highly
recommend this book from both a personal and professional perspective
for its insightful guide to lobbying and navigating the often wild and wooly
goings-on in Juneau.

—*Senator Johnny Ellis, Member of the Alaska Legislature, 1987-2016*

In a business where knowledge and information reign supreme, it's simply
too risky to ignore this excellent approach to lobbying lest you give ground
to a more informed and adept opponent.

—*Thor Stacey, Contract Lobbyist, Thor Stacey & Associates*

The lobbyist is the sales department for their members or clients. This book
will help you make your first lobbying sale, to maintain positive relationships to make further sales, and to become a successful lobbyist.

—*Dennis DeWitt, DeWitt & DeWitt, LLC,*
Government Relations Consulting

This hands-on approach is invaluable for those lobbying from a wide range
of organizations—professional associations, non-profits, citizen activist
groups, businesses, and local governments.

—*Ron Clarke, special staff assistant to two governors, legislative aide and*
caucus press secretary, legislative liaison and assistant director with two
state agencies, and non-profit executive director

This handbook incorporates decades of observing and interviewing elected
officials, legislative aides, executive branch staff, lobbyists, and journalists,
as well as the author's experience as a volunteer lobbyist.

—*Rynnieva Moss, Alaska Senate Rules Committee Aide*

This excellent, holistic approach to lobbying in Alaska covers the importance and the do's and don'ts of dealing with the governor's office, as well as state agencies and the legislature.

—*Darwin Peterson, Long-time Legislative Aide and Governor Bill Walker's Legislative Director*

As part of its extensive coverage of political advocacy, this book shows the importance of dealing with state agencies. It provides a comprehensive explanation of how to navigate the state bureaucracy and those officials to deal with to be most effective.

—*Leslie Houston, former Deputy Commissioner, Department of Corrections*

This handbook is a must for all senior state agency managers. I wish it had been available when I was a new division director.

—*Britteny Cioni-Haywood, former Director of the Alaska Division of Economic Development*

This is an excellent job of demystifying Alaska's public policy process. It's what legislative liaisons, those seeking state budget funds, and all those involved in representing a cause, should know about lobbying.

—*Micaela Fowler, Office of Management and Budget, and former Legislative Liaison, Department of Commerce*

For the novice and those needing to retool their approach, here you'll find indispensable guidance on the lobbying process and where and how to apply the skills necessary for success.

—*Dave Donaldson, former Alaska Public Radio Network Political Reporter*

Even though this handbook focuses on Alaska, the principles of lobbying it covers are universal and part of any advocacy campaigns. I'll use this book to explain to my clients what I do and why, and how they can help.

—*Andréa Cristina Oliveira Gozetto, Government Relations Specialist, São Paulo, Brazil*

How to Lobby
Alaska State Government

Clive S. Thomas

Text © 2019 University of Alaska Press

Published by
University of Alaska Press
P.O. Box 756240
Fairbanks, AK 99775-6240

Cover and interior design by UA Press.
Graphics by Amber Granados Wise.

Spine photo of the Alaska Capitol building in Juneau: Shutterstock

Library of Congress Cataloging in Publication Data

Names: Thomas, Clive S., author.
Title: How to lobby Alaska state government / by Clive S. Thomas.
Description: Fairbanks, AK : The University of Alaska Press, 2019. | Includes
    bibliographical references and index. |
Identifiers: LCCN 2019003136 (print) | LCCN 2019006932 (e-book) | ISBN
    9781602233966 (e-book) | ISBN 9781602233959 (pbk. : alk. paper)
Subjects: LCSH: Lobbying—Alaska—Handbooks, manuals, etc. | Alaska—Politics
    and government—Handbooks, manuals, etc.
Classification: LCC JK9574.5 (e-book) | LCC JK9574.5 .T47 2019 (print) | DDC
    324/.409798—dc23
LC record available at https://lccn.loc.gov/2019003136

Printed in Canada

★ CONTENTS ★

★ INTRODUCTION ★

Tips on Using this Handbook

So you want to lobby Alaska state government. But, as a novice, or someone from out of state, you need help on how to go about it. Or you've lobbied before, but it didn't work out quite the way you'd hoped, and you're looking for advice on rethinking your approach.

Or maybe you're a seasoned lobbyist who'd like to look at your business in a different way. Or perhaps want a quick and easy way to give your clients or members a grounding in lobbying, so they can help but don't get in the way of your lobbying effort.

Whatever your reason, the hands-on approach in this handbook will be useful.

In these pages you'll find a guide to the essentials of organizing and implementing a lobbying campaign in Alaska. As a foundation for this we explain: how to think politically; the structure and operation of state government, including the all-important budget process; the psychology and needs of the public officials you'll be lobbying; and how Alaska government really works.

To give all this practical value, besides the author's own experiences as a volunteer lobbyist, the book includes the experiences and insights of more than 250 practitioners— lobbyists, legislators, legislative aides, governors and their staffs, bureaucrats, political journalists, and others involved in the political goings-on in Alaska state government. Many of these, as well as those who provided feedback and suggestions as the book was written, are listed in Appendix 5.

Because the basic principles of lobbying are the same from Argentina to Australia to Arizona to Alaska, much of the information here can be applied far beyond Alaska. You can mount an effective lobbying effort by integrating the basic principles explained here with the politics and power structure of any democratic government, whether a national, regional, state, provincial, or local government.

TRUTH IN ADVERTISING—NO GUARANTEE OF SUCCESS

Lobbying is an art, not a science. A lobbying campaign is shaped by the personalities, issues, and circumstances, particularly the political power structure, at any one time.

Consequently, like any guide to lobbying, even one that draws on the experiences and expertise of the most effective lobbyists, using this handbook is no guarantee of success. The uncertainties of politics mean that sometimes even the most well-organized and well-financed interest groups in Alaska, as elsewhere, lose their lobbying battles, including the oil industry and other business interests.

So, the information presented here is not a set of strict rules to follow to the letter. Rather, it provides guidelines for effective lobbying. This handbook will make you aware of the factors that can lead to lobbying success and the ones that will undermine your effort.

> *Lobbying is an art, not a science—there's no right way to conduct a campaign, nor one best path to guarantee success.*

When you organize and implement your own campaign you'll make your own judgments as to how to use the information presented here. As do all lobbyists, you'll develop your own style of political advocacy.

TIPS ON USING THIS HANDBOOK

There are several ways to use this handbook depending on your present level of knowledge of state government and lobbying. But whatever your level, there are aspects of the format that will be useful to all readers.

Finding the Information You Need

Using the Contents, turn to the chapter you need, and you'll find a list of the topics by sections covered in that chapter. Each section of each chapter is numbered for finding specific information on the topic you're considering.

Whatever your level of knowledge of lobbying, this handbook is organized to meet your needs.

Choosing Chapters to Meet Your Needs

It's recommended that the newcomer to lobbying read the book in sequence from Chapter 1 to 16.

If you need advice on rethinking a campaign, or are a seasoned lobbyist looking for different perspectives, you can, of course, pick the chapters and their sections that most interest you. But even in this case, you may get new insights by reading particular chapters, such as Chapter 10 on group influence, Chapters 11 thru 15 on organizing a lobbying campaign, and adjusting it to changing circumstances.

Executive directors of associations and their staff who want to bring their members up to speed to aid in their lobbying effort, might use Chapter 1 on the fundamentals of lobbying, Chapter 5 on the psychology of public officials, Chapters 6, 7, and 8 on how the Juneau political scene really works, and Chapter 14 on face-to-face meetings with public officials.

Three of the appendices will be useful to those not familiar with the layout of the state capitol, the location of state offices, and places to stay and eat in downtown Juneau. Appendix 4 explains where to get more information on Alaska politics and lobbying.

Clive S. Thomas
Pullman, Washington and Juneau, Alaska,
September 21, 2019

THIS CHAPTER COVERS

1. What are Interest Groups, Interests, Lobbying, and Lobbyists?

2. How Some Novices Approach Lobbying

3. Public Ambivalence to Lobbying, Past Abuses, and Present Realities

4. Delving into the Misconceptions and Realities of Lobbying

5. What Shapes the Lobbying Environment?

6. Strategies and Tactics

7. Giving Policy-Makers a Reason to Help You

8. The Importance of Group Unity

9. Integrating all Parts of the Policy Process in a Lobbying Campaign

10. Link with the Rest of the Handbook

★ CHAPTER 1 ★

The Fundamentals of Lobbying

If you want to know what lobbying is all about,
I can sum it up in five words:
contacts, trust, information, management, and compromise.

—Bob Manners,
Executive Director and Lobbyist,
National Education Association-Alaska,
1977-2002

Bob Manners would admit that there were many more aspects to his job as a lobbyist during the years he represented schoolteachers and other K-12 employees. But these five basic elements are a foundation for what's covered in this handbook.

1. WHAT ARE INTEREST GROUPS, INTERESTS, LOBBYING, AND LOBBYISTS?

Most of us know the answer to this question. But there are aspects to it that are not well known.

Interest Groups and Interests

An **interest group** is: *An association of individuals or an organization, which, based on a shared value or concern, works to influence public policy in its favor.*

Interest groups are wide-ranging as organizations, their level of lobbying sophistication and influence, from those representing oil companies to environmentalists to grassroots community groups.

Not all those involved in lobbying are strictly interest groups with dues-paying members. Many are organizations, like businesses, universities, think tanks, philanthropic foundations, and particularly governments and their agencies. These are usually called **interests**, and likely outnumber formal interest groups in Alaska as elsewhere.

Lobbying and Political Advocacy

Lobbying involves: *An individual, group, or organization working to influence policy makers on an issue or issues.*

Some people distinguish between lobbying, which they see as conducted by professional lobbyists where an economic interest is involved, and **political advocacy** conducted by citizen groups where the goal might not involve money. If the actions are to influence public policy, the distinction is one of labeling and not a practical reality. So we use the terms lobbying and political advocacy, and lobbyist and political advocate, interchangeably in this book.

Lobbying doesn't begin and end with the legislative session—it's a year-round activity.

Lobbyist

A **lobbyist** is: *A person designated by an interest group or interest to work to influence public policy on their behalf by directly contacting public officials.*

Not all lobbyists are those identified in the media, which usually focuses on high-profile lobbyists who make big bucks from wealthy special interests. There's a wide range of lobbyists, from the highly professional to volunteers who lobby for various social causes.

Those Usually Considered not to be Lobbyists

Should individual citizens who give testimony at committee meetings, participate in public hearings, or meet with public officials to push their own cause, be included as lobbyists? There's no right or wrong answer to this—it's a judgment call.

In this book we don't include these people as lobbyists. For the most part, they provide input into the policy process only occasionally, perhaps only once. They might, for example, express an opinion representing only themself, or as an association member making a visit to a legislator to back up the work of their lobbyist.

The Process and Frequency of Lobbying

Lobbying is usually conducted through an organized campaign; but not always. Some lobbying involves an individual lobbyist working to push or kill legislation. Or it may involve keeping in contact with public officials for when the lobbyist needs to actively lobby to promote the interests of their client, group, or organization.

Contrary to what many people think, the contact that lobbyists have with public officials involves less than half their time. The major aspect of a lobbyist's work is monitoring political activity that may affect their issue, and organizing and planning their campaign.

The Constitutional Right to Lobby

The right to "petition the Government" (in effect, to lobby) is guaranteed by the First Amendment to the U.S. Constitution. This right is also guaranteed in all state constitutions, including Alaska's (Article 1, Section 6).

Most Americans view this guarantee as their fundamental right as citizens. As a result, tens of millions of Americans don't hesitate to lobby politicians of all types.

2. HOW SOME NOVICES APPROACH LOBBYING

Armed with their political birthright, many people lobbying for the first time, who perhaps have a skeptical attitude toward politicians and how things get done in government, often don't understand the basics of lobbying. Let's use an example of a group called the Firearms Safety Coalition, or FSC.

FSC is a new group formed in response to the accidental death of a four-year old girl shot by her friend when playing with her father's revolver. The group wants to enact legislation requiring all school children to take a firearms safety course, for the state to develop and distribute pamphlets about gun safety to all those purchasing firearms, and to designate a week each year as firearms safety week.

While the members of FSC are well-meaning and very committed, their leaders have little experience dealing with government and none in lobbying. As a result, consciously or subconsciously, they approach lobbying in the way set out in Box 1.1.

A Recipe for Failure

The problem is, far from getting FSC what it wants, these attitudes and this approach are a sure guarantee of failure. The realities of lobbying are much different.

The rest of this chapter points out the problems with FSC's approach by explaining the fundamentals of lobbying and how to begin to think like a lobbyist.

3. PUBLIC AMBIVALENCE TO LOBBYING, PAST ABUSES, AND PRESENT REALITIES

Because of past abuses by lobbyists and the common belief that big, powerful interests often get their way at the expense of the public interest, few aspects of American and Alaska politics generate a more negative public reaction than the mention of interest groups and their lobbyists. Lobbyists rank below politicians in their public image, on a par with used car salespeople and ambulance-chasing lawyers.

At the same time, Alaskans join interest groups by the tens of

BOX 1.1
AN EFFECTIVE APPROACH TO LOBBYING?

- Our goal is right and necessary, and in the public interest.

- We're all passionate about what we want—totally committed.

- Everyone will see how needed and important our goal is, so no one can possibly oppose our cause.

- It's hard to believe our issue wasn't dealt with a long time ago.

- Every part of our proposal is essential, so we need to make sure it's not changed in any way.

- We need to go down to Juneau and get it on the books right away, before the legislature adjourns in April.

- Two of our members know some lobbyists who've worked in Juneau for years. They can tell us the right way to lobby.

- A lot of our members are willing to help, so we can talk to all legislators to get their help.

- It's time those politicians did something for the people instead of always helping big special interests.

- We elected those people down there and they need to do what we want. We'll remind them they work for us!

- If any of those legislators won't support us, we'll spread the word that they're just out for themselves, not the public. We'll tell them we'll work to get them defeated in the next election.

- All those who support us can send hundreds of e-mails, messages on Twitter, and keep their phones ringing for days. And we can hold protests, even a sit-in at the capitol. That'll make them take notice and support our cause.

thousands and Americans by the tens of millions. This ambivalence is well summed up in a 2008 headline in the *Alaska Journal of Commerce:* "Lobbyists: Are they Alaska's heroes or villains?"

Special Interests versus Stakeholders

There is no definitive answer to this question. It largely depends on which values and causes a person or interest supports. To groups pushing an issue, theirs is a just cause, lobbying is a positive thing, and their lobbyists are "heroes." They often describe themselves as "stakeholders," not "special interests." In their eyes "special interests" are organizations whose lobbyists are "villains," have self-serving members, and who act against the public interest.

But in their lobbying efforts, those "special interests" have the opposite perspective. They see their opponents as "special interests" represented by "villains."

Lobbying Today and the Consequences of Past Abuses

Despite the widespread public skepticism of lobbying, reinforced by stories in the media of lobbying scandals, contemporary lobbying is far cleaner than any time in the past. Certainly, because the stakes are often so high, sometimes with millions of dollars at stake, there'll always be lobbyists who break the law. But the vast majority act well within the law, a fact not interesting enough for the media to report.

Nevertheless, past and continuing concerns about abuses, including some in Alaska, have led the federal government and all fifty states to regulate lobbying. These abuses have also given lobbyists a bad name. As a result, many groups and organizations, and many lobbyists themselves, avoid using the term "lobbyist." Instead, they use various euphemisms to avoid soiling their public image. These are misleading labels, such as "government relations director" or "government affairs specialist." But a lobbyist by any other name is still a lobbyist.

I'd always been suspicious of lobbyists until I got elected to the legislature. Then I learned their value.

4. DELVING INTO THE MISCONCEPTIONS AND REALITIES OF LOBBYING

Another consequence of negative attitudes to interest groups and lobbyists, is there are several misconceptions about lobbying. Given this, one way to view the role of interest groups and lobbyists is to compare the misconceptions with the realities. Ten of these contrasting perspectives are set out in Box 1.2 on the next page.

Understanding these differences is important for both developing the right state of mind as a lobbyist, and for approaching the practical aspects of lobbying. This comparison is a first step in showing why the approach to lobbying in Box 1.1 is misguided.

5. WHAT SHAPES THE LOBBYING ENVIRONMENT?

Many factors shape the political environment where lobbying takes place. But five are most significant:

- The organization of state government.

- The human element.

- Political power.

- Compromise and transactions in policy-making.

- The reality of public policy-making.

The major terms used in connection with the lobbying environment are set out in Box 1.3, following Box 1.2 on page 16.

The Organization of State Government

As lobbying is conducted primarily in the legislative and executive branches of state government, existing laws, rules, and procedures, are the major elements shaping the lobbying environment (some court decisions also affect this environment; but judiciary cannot

BOX 1.2
TEN MYTHS, HALF-TRUTHS AND REALITIES ABOUT LOBBYING AND LOBBYISTS

1. Lobbying is a complex business that can only be understood by political insiders

In some lobbying campaigns, the strategies and tactics get complicated and require much planning, management, and constant refining as political circumstances change. But, at bottom, there's nothing complicated about lobbying, and there are no secrets about what constitutes successful lobbying—it's all about political power.

2. Lobbying is an underhanded, sleazy, and sometimes corrupt business

As we saw in section 3, today, this is far from an accurate picture of the reality of lobbying.

As Bob Manners said, trust is an essential element in lobbying. Without trust, a lobbyist will likely not remain a lobbyist for long. Besides, these days with lobbying disclosure laws and media scrutiny, public officials—elected and appointed—don't want to be associated with a suspect or tainted lobbyist.

3. Special interests act against the public interest

This can certainly be the case and the media regularly report examples. But interest groups do not always act against the public interest. Many public interest groups promote public goals, such as the group Common Cause, which advocates for a cleaner, more open government.

4. Lobbying success is all about money. It favors the rich and powerful, not the little guy

True, money is a great asset. It's one of the major factors in lobbying success, and big economic interests are often more successful than those with fewer resources. Again, however, public interest groups and those advocating for the poor and underprivileged do score victories.

5. Lobbyists explain only one side of the issue

A lobbyist's job is certainly to push the cause of his or her client or organization. But for a public official to trust them, a lobbyist can't just tell their side of the story. Any credible lobbyist presents the other side too. In doing so, they'll point out why the opponent's position is the wrong course to take politically.

6. There's one right way to lobby on all issues

Those not well versed in lobbying and its many options, such as those representing FSC in the example in section 2, often think there's only one "right" way to lobby. This is not the case.

The way a group should lobby depends on many factors. These include: the type of group (business, public interest, community group, etc.); the group's issue; group resources; how the group is perceived by policy makers; and the current political climate, among other factors.

7. All lobbying takes place in the legislature

Again, because most of us get a lot of information from the media, and it covers the more interesting aspects of politics, their focus is mainly the legislature. But much lobbying focuses on the governor and state agencies. Plus, some groups' strategies involve using the courts.

8. The large numbers myth

A large membership can be a major lobbying asset. But sometimes the perception of such a group may be negative with policy makers, as with trade unions in recent years. This can undermine success. In contrast, smaller membership groups, like physicians and lawyers, are effective because they have other assets that promote success.

9. High visibility isn't always an indication of influence

Some groups and organizations, such as school teachers, business groups and environmentalists, have a high profile in Juneau. Sometimes these are successful—but not always. While they are both high-profile and very vocal, as of 2019, right-to-life groups have had little success in restricting abortion in Alaska. In contrast, many groups with a low or no visibility, such as beauticians and marine pilots, can be very successful.

10. Governments don't lobby

Ask most Americans what are the major lobbies or interests, and they'll likely say business, trade unions, environmentalists, senior citizens, or other large organizations. It's unlikely they'd list government as a major lobby.

In fact, the various agencies of federal, state, and local governments are significant lobbying forces. They lobby for funding to provide new programs and maintain existing ones. In Alaska, these lobbies include the University of Alaska, state departments, and state boards and commissions.

However, because government agencies are not defined as interest groups in Alaska law, they don't have to register. This is in contrast to businesses, unions, and other familiar lobbies. Consequently, lobbying by government is not clearly visible. But however you look at it, governments do lobby, and often very effectively.

BOX 1.3
THE POLICY PROCESS AND OTHER KEY TERMS DEFINED

Politics: Results from the clash between individuals or groups over values or beliefs, their needs and desires. Sometimes, these conflicts become intense, as with oil development versus environmental protection.

The public policy-making process: Usually shortened to the policy process. We define this as how conflicts over political issues are resolved or, in some cases, not resolved so that the status quo remains.

Public policy: Is what emerges from the policy process. It may be a new or reformed law or regulation, or taking no action at all—maintaining the status quo. The American (and so the Alaskan) system of government is organized to favor the status quo.

The legislative process: This term appears to apply only to action in the legislature. But the law-making process involves the executive branch, too. Consequently, it's another term for the policy process.

The bill process: Consideration of specific proposals to be enacted into law or to amend an existing law. These are proposed by both the legislature and the executive branches. Consideration of bills is the major part of the policy process.

be lobbied in the ways used to influence the other two branches). This involves understanding the organization of the legislature and executive branches: how a bill becomes law; and the budget process,

among other aspects of government operations.

It's not necessary to memorize all aspects of state government and the minutiae of its day-to-day operations. You just need a basic knowledge of government operations, as explained in Chapter 3.

The Human Element is Dominant

Although the workings of government are important, the fundamental factor shaping the lobbying environment is the **human element**. Lobbying boils down to human beings interacting with other human beings where the stakes are often very high. For instance, this could be giving a billion-dollar tax break to the oil industry, or affecting peoples' future through the amount of money allocated per student for K-12 education, or the funding of the University of Alaska.

The Ideal versus the Reality of How Public Officials Act

Given this, it's important to be clear about what we may see as the ideal way public officials *should* act versus the reality of how they *do* act. We may believe that, as public servants, they should put aside their personality quirks, foibles, and their own interests, and make the public's interest paramount. But it doesn't and likely can't ever work that way.

> *Good lobbyists are students of human nature—they know how to deal with each politician on their own terms.*

Public officials are human beings like the rest of us, with all this implies. They have: needs, hopes and fears, attitudes toward a variety of things, plus a range of personalities (placid, short-tempered, hyper, friendly, jolly). These aspects of human nature inevitably come through in their roles as public officials—they are who they are! This is a fact we must accept and deal with public officials accordingly. Added to this, what exactly is in the "public interest" sounds a simple enough question, but there's no definitive answer.

Different people see the public interest differently. It depends largely on a person's values and political perspective.

As a result, to be a successful lobbyist requires understanding the mindset of public officials. You need to put yourself in "their shoes" to deal with them effectively.

Political Power

Continuing in the vein of the ideal versus reality, for better or for worse, political decisions and the policies that result, are driven by power. As many people associate power with "abuse," or being "excessive," among other negative connotations, it re-enforces public skepticism of politics.

Beliefs about Politics versus the Reality

A common belief is that politics should be driven by what's right, good, and fair. Realizing the public's negative feelings about power, many politicians deny that power drives their actions. They often claim their decisions are, in fact, based on what's good, right, and fair.

The problem is, like the idea of the "public interest," people disagree over these values because they are just that—values. The result is conflict, often intense conflict, such as over abortion. The only way to resolve these conflicts is by reaching some form of accommodation through the exercise of power: people using what they can bring to bear to get their values into public policy or preventing those of which they disapprove. Consequently, like views about interest groups, people support or oppose the use of power depending largely on whether it promotes policies they or their group supports or opposes.

Whether viewed positively or negatively, power is the common denominator, and the motivating force of politics and policymaking. A politician without power is like a lion without teeth.

What's the Difference Between Political Power and Political Influence?

To be more precise about power, we define it as:

The ability to direct and shape the political behavior of others or the course of political events. This involves, making a policy maker or other political operative do something they'd not do otherwise.

Obviously, if those being pressured would take the action voluntarily, there would be no need to bring pressure to bear.

In everyday speech, **power** and **influence** are often used interchangeably, though some people distinguish between them. Some see power as more extensive than influence, more direct and obvious, sometimes heavy-handed. In contrast, influence is viewed as subtler, often imperceptibly applied. Other people see influence as more extensive than power because of its subtlety.

Consequently, the distinction between them is too hazy to be useful in practice. For this reason, in this book we use them interchangeably. Now and again we use the colloquial terms for power and influence—political clout and political juice, or simply juice.

The Need for Compromise

In the separation of powers system operating at the national and state levels, power is dispersed, spread among several parts of the political and government system. No single part of the system, not the legislature, the governor, state agencies, political parties, or interest groups, can get all they want in a public policy or other political outcome.

With only limited power, to get some of what they want, all those involved in politics and the policy process must **compromise**. This is another of Bob Manners's essentials of lobbying.

The Transactional Nature of Policy-Making

Another way to look at this process of compromise, is that politics and lobbying involve **transactions** that are the result of negotiations. Because none of those working to resolve a conflict have all the power, this requires both sides giving up some of what they want and agreeing to things that were not part of their original goal.

As a fundamental aspect of politics, it follows that compromise through concluding transactions—making bargains—is also a practical reality that shapes a group's lobbying effort. As a representative of their organization, a major part of the lobbyist's job is to get the best compromise, the best deal they can.

The Realities of Public Policy Making

Together with the importance of the human element and the role of political power, delving into the various aspects of the reality of the policy process is a major focus of this handbook. By way of introduction, Box 1.4 identifies ten aspects of this reality. Clearly, the policy process is not efficient. But its goal is not efficiency—it's to maximize representation. And to involve all those who want a say in a policy, to vet new proposals and revisit existing policies. This slows down the policy process, sometimes considerably.

Taking Stock of FSC's Approach to Lobbying

Having looked at the misconceptions and realities of lobbying and the major aspects of the lobbying environment, let's take stock of the advocacy approach of the Firearms Safety Coalition (FSC) outlined earlier.

It appears they've not considered that lobbying doesn't just involve the legislature. If they ignore affected state agencies, they'll undermine their chances of success. They also assume they have strength in numbers, but this may not work to their advantage. Their leadership is also mistaken in believing there's only one right way to lobby.

Another weakness of FSC's approach is, given the way power is distributed, it's pointless to meet with all 60 legislators. FSC needs to deal with those with the juice to advance their issue. Even if they contact a few legislators, even with a cause as laudable as gun safety, they'll see that not everyone will support them. This means they'll need to compromise and won't get all they want. It may also come as a surprise that good ideas are not always considered solely on their merits.

> *No need to visit all 60 legislators—you'll waste a lot of time. Most won't have either the influence or the desire to help you.*

Not only that, because the policy process is both messy and often long and tortuous, it's unlikely FSC will achieve its goal in one legislative session or even two, certainly not with the speed they hope.

BOX 1.4
TEN REALITIES OF THE POLICY PROCESS

- The separation of powers principle of American government doesn't mean the legislative and executive branches function independently from one another. They are separate branches with their own power bases that share power. As the most influential parts of the policy process, ultimately they must cooperate to finalize laws and other policies.

- While the legislature and the governor must cooperate to finalize policies, their separate power bases mean they are often in conflict. This could be over general policy goals, ideology, the specifics of the budget, or a particular policy. This power struggle, its characteristics, and how it is resolved, is a central aspect of the policy process.

- The major influences on policy-making are located in relatively few places. Power lies mainly in the governor's office; with the majority party or caucus in both houses of the legislature; in some circumstances, in state agencies; as well as certain interest groups.

- Even in a democracy, the policy process is not a level political playing field. Those with extensive resources generally have more influence in getting their issues addressed.

- Because political considerations, such as personal ambition, ideology, and benefit to a narrow constituency or interest, tend to dominate, many issues supported by a majority of the public or a coalition of interest groups, are not always considered on their merits and fail to be enacted into law.

- There are no certain outcomes in policymaking because of the fluidity of the process. The location of power in several places, changing political alliances, and a host of factors outside of government, result in a degree of unpredictability in any attempt to enact or block a policy proposal.

- There is no finality to politics and the policy process. Policies are constantly revisited mainly because:

(continued . . .)

BOX 1.4 CONTINUED

o   Those who didn't get what they wanted one year, try again the
     next year.

o   Values change. As a result, attitude to issues, like the death
     penalty, aid to the poor, regulating business, among many other
     policies, are reconsidered.

o   The influence of various political forces, such as particular
     interest groups, and various politicians, wax and wane. This
     often leads to policies being revisited.

•   Because of the last point, the policy process is best seen as
    a continual cycle that not only considers new proposals, but
    reconsiders existing laws and regulations.

•   The policy process is very messy—not streamlined and generally
    inefficient in dealing with problems and issues.

o   The parts of the process are not well coordinated.

o   There are often roadblocks to getting things done.

o   Drawn-out, highly conflict-ridden, negotiations to resolve an
     issue.

o   Sometimes, actions create unintended consequences.

•   For a combination of these realities, there is no objective way to
    judge the effectiveness of the policy process overall. But there are
    ways to determine the effectiveness of particular policies.

6. STRATEGIES AND TACTICS

Working to deal with the fluidity of the policy process involves
another of Bob Manners's keys to effective lobbying—management.
An important part of management is developing a lobbying plan. The
plan sets out the strategy and tactics the group will use to promote
its goal and reduce the uncertainties that might undermine success.

Whatever the type of group or organization and regardless of its goals, all lobbying campaigns involve four elements:

- Gaining access to policy makers.

- Building a relationship with them.

- Providing information (in some cases educating them) on an issue or cause (another of Bob Manners's essentials of lobbying).

- Attempting to influence their actions.

Distinguishing between Strategies and Tactics

Many people use the terms strategy and tactics interchangeably and they do overlap; but there is a difference between them.

Strategy

This is an overall plan for gaining access to policy makers and lobbying them to exert influence. A strategy will include:

- The goals to be achieved and what are and are not acceptable fallback positions.

- Identifying which power points in the system will affect a group's issue.

- Who will contact policy makers—hired lobbyists, group staff, or group members, among other general decisions.

Tactics

These are the specific ways the strategy is implemented on a day-to-day basis. These include:

- Who specifically will contact which public officials and when.

- How they will be contacted—through direct contact, phone,

letter, e-mail, public opinion messages (POMs—sent from one of the Legislative Information Offices—LIOs—around the state), or social media, and in what combination.

- What aspects of the group's message will be delivered in each contact with an official.

- What support materials to deliver to which policy-makers.

- Which groups to ally with, if any, to advance an issue.

Tactics may also include a media and public relations campaign, rallies, and protests.

Lobbyists and Strategies and Tactics

The main link between the group and the public official is, of course, the lobbyist. Besides contacting public officials directly, a lobbyist will likely be involved in one or more of the following:

- Monitoring political and government activity as it affects the group's issue.

- Advising on strategy and tactics.

- Developing and coordinating the group's lobbying effort.

To be effective, a lobbyist must have the other two of Bob Manners's five elements for successful lobbying: a network of contacts and trust.

Developing a contact network is essential for getting information about what's going on politically, but also for planning lobbying strategies and tactics.

In the uncertain world of politics and policy making, lobbyists must establish trust with public officials. They must be considered honest, provide reliable and not misleading information, and able to keep a confidence, among other aspects of trust.

The next three sections explain key aspects of lobbying strategy and tactics. They are so important, we'll return to them many times in this handbook.

7. GIVE POLICYMAKERS A REASON TO HELP YOU

This is an aspect of the importance of the human element. As lobbying involves transactions, public officials, particularly elected ones, will often want something out of a deal, although they will rarely say this directly. So, to get a policy maker to be willing to use their political capital, the group should try to give him or her a reason to want to help them. Among other things, the benefit to a policy maker might be to help on their re-election campaign, or provide information unavailable elsewhere.

Whatever the benefit, being aware of this need and having something to offer in a political transaction, is a major asset to any lobbying effort.

Another Weakness of FSC's Approach

Never threaten a politician. They'll cut you off forever. Some may even work to destroy your chances of success.

In this vein, FSC's approach is even weaker for not realizing the various aspects of the psychology of public officials. The organization's approach involves a sense of entitlement, in some ways arrogance, and the use of threats. The group's leaders appear oblivious to how those they lobby may react both as policy-makers and as human beings.

FSC failed to follow one of the major tenets of lobbying: to put themselves in the shoes of policy-makers. By not doing so, they can't begin to give those they lobby a reason to want to help them.

8. THE IMPORTANCE OF GROUP UNITY

A major goal in developing strategies and tactics is to ensure group unity. This is essential, because sending mixed, conflicting, or several different messages to public officials will likely lead them to do nothing—not help advance your cause.

In part, the reason is they won't want to alienate some group members who hold a different perspective. More importantly, a public official's credibility with their colleagues will be negatively affected if they work to advance a cause with no clear goal and upon which the group is divided.

This is certainly not to say that a group cannot have disagreement on political actions and debate them vigorously. But this should be done in private—a group shouldn't wash its political laundry in public. Many a lobbying campaign has failed because it lacked unity.

To ensure unity, a group must have a clear goal and obtain support for it within the organization. Then, those group representatives contacting public officials will convey one message supported by the entire group or organization's membership.

9. INTEGRATING ALL PARTS OF THE POLICY PROCESS IN A LOBBYING CAMPAIGN

Most lobbying campaigns involve the legislature, the governor's office, at least one state department, perhaps a board or commission, and usually working with groups supporting you. It may also include other tactics, such as garnering public support. Your lobbying plan, in laying out your strategies and tactics, needs to include dealing with all these.

The need to integrate these various aspects of government and other elements in your campaign, is probably the most challenging part of lobbying. It requires constant vigilance and tenacity, particularly when things go wrong and you're depressed and want to give up.

10. LINK WITH THE REST OF THE HANDBOOK

To go into depth on the topics in this chapter, the book is divided into two parts.

The first part, Chapters 2 thru 8, expands on the lobbying environment. The second part, Chapters 9 thru 16, cover the essentials of planning and implementing your lobbying campaign.

The foundation for approaching all aspects of political advocacy is grasping the basics of political savvy and how to think and act like a lobbyist. We begin our in-depth look at lobbying by going into detail about what's involved in developing this mindset.

THIS CHAPTER COVERS

1. Understand the Difference Between the Organization and the Power Structure of State Government

2. Develop and Convey the Right Attitude

3. Put Yourself in Their Shoes

4. Establish a Relationship of Mutual Benefit

5. Be Open-Minded and Willing to Compromise

6. Learn How to Use Information

7. Build a Contact Network

8. Don't take Situations at Face Value in Politics— Develop a Healthy Skepticism

9. Develop an Ability to Think Beyond the Obvious

10. The Importance of Management and Planning

11. Recognize the Need to Make Decisions in a Fluid Environment with Incomplete Information

12. Understand the Importance of Timing

13. Political Savvy, Trust, and Credibility

14. Is Lobbying for You?

15. The First Steps in Thinking and Acting Like a Lobbyist

★ CHAPTER 2 ★

The Basics of Political Savvy: Learning to Think and Act Like a Lobbyist

Some people are born with political smarts, some can learn them, others couldn't think that way to save their life.

—Walter J. Hickel,

Alaska Governor,

1966-69 and 1990-94

Those in trades or professions—be they carpenters, lawyers, or computer programmers—have a particular way of thinking in approaching their job. So it is with lobbyists. Successful lobbyists need to be politically savvy to work in a fluid and uncertain political environment to achieve the results they want.

Maybe you're already politically savvy and have developed the mindset of a lobbyist. If not, this chapter explains twelve essentials to start you on the right road.

1. UNDERSTAND THE DIFFERENCE BETWEEN THE ORGANIZATION AND THE POWER STRUCTURE OF STATE GOVERNMENT

Many people coming to lobbying for the first time assume they need to contact the governor, a legislator, or a commissioner (the head of a state department) to succeed in lobbying. In other words, they see the officials at the top as most powerful, while those in the middle and at the bottom of the organization as less so, or not influential at all.

Don't assume that those at the top in state government can help you the most.

Political Savvy

This is not the case. Understanding why and acting accordingly is fundamental to effective lobbying, and key to appreciating the importance of several other aspects of thinking politically.

The reason the top dogs may be less useful than those lower down the organization, stems from the difference between power and authority. Certainly, the two are closely linked; but an official's authority may not be identical to their power in certain circumstances.

Authority

Authority is: *The formal vested right to take action*, and is placed in a position or office. For example, whether it's the office of governor, or a judgeship, the position of a teacher, or a manager of a business, each is given rights by a constitution or statute, the rules of a school, or the operational structure of a business, to take action to perform the functions of their office or job. These include, for example, a governor's right to veto bills passed by the legislature, and a manager's right to fire an employee.

The authority structure of an organization usually resembles a pyramid, with the company president, executive director, or governor at the top. Coming down the pyramid, people have various levels of authority affecting the operation of the organization, from division managers down to support staff.

Power and Political Power

Power is a much more complex concept than authority; scores of books and articles have been written on it. As we learned in Chapter 1, **power** is: *The ability to direct and shape the political behavior of others or the course of political events. This involves making a policy maker or other political operative do something they'd not do otherwise.* In everyday life, especially in government and politics, the authority a person has doesn't automatically translate into power.

Turning Authority into Power

People with authority must turn the resources of their office—the type and extent of their authority, control over financial resources, and personnel, among other things—into forms that can achieve their goals. This requires political skill—political acumen—in dealing with those who can help or hinder achieving those goals.

Wherever they are on an organizational chart, people possess this skill in varying degrees. As Governor Hickel says at the beginning of this chapter, some people are effective political operatives, others have some ability, while others have little or no political acumen.

Authority as an Indicator of Power

In many circumstances, the authority structure is a good indicator of the power structure. The governor, for instance, has extensive authority. This includes appointing senior executive branch officials and judges, and control over the allocation of certain funds. Authority is also the basis of the power of the leadership in the legislature, and senior people in the administration, such as commissioners.

Variations between Authority and Power and Degrees of Influence

However, those with the most extensive authority do not have power in all situations. Even the power of the governor will vary from circumstance to circumstance as different factors come into play. And just because someone has little authority doesn't mean they won't have considerable power in certain situations. In fact, because of their political skill, some people lower down the chart are much more effective in getting things done. Box 2.1, on the next page, provides an example of the variation between authority and power.

Added to this, no one has all the power: it's dispersed, distributed in many places, and held by many people. The result is political power is nebulous, it varies from situation to situation, and from issue to issue. By contrast, authority is not subject to variation in different circumstances.

BOX 2.1
AUTHORITY VERSUS POLITICAL ACUMEN

One of the most effective and powerful Alaska politicians in the 1970s and early '80s was Senator Frank Ferguson of Kotzebue. His highest legislative position was as chair of the Senate Community and Regional Affairs Committee. He never held the top job of President of the Senate, nor chaired the influential Senate Finance Committee.

Nevertheless, Senator Ferguson exerted considerable power, influencing action across state government, including securing extensive benefits for rural-bush areas. In particular, he was a prominent player in putting together the agreement between the legislature and the governor to adjourn the legislative session. For many years, his chief aide, Mike Scott, was also very powerful, often referred to as "Alaska's twenty-first senator," and more influential than many members of the legislature.

Both men were powerful because they had extensive political skills, more so than many with much more authority.

Types of Power

Power comes in several forms. Those set out in Box 2.2 are especially important in politics. The more of these a person can draw upon, the more influential they will be—and vice versa.

The Major Lesson

The major lesson about power and authority is being able to distinguish between them and apply this to lobbying. The person at the top—the governor, commissioner, or legislator—may not be the best person to contact first about your issue. It's usually better—more effective—to deal first with a middle level agency person, a special assistant in the governor's office, or a legislative staffer.

Even after reading this, it may still be hard to get used to the authority structure not always being the power structure. So, you may still be tempted to want to talk to the governor or a commissioner, rather than someone lower down. With very few exceptions, this is a mistake. It may undermine your lobbying campaign.

BOX 2.2
FIVE TYPES OF POLITICAL POWER

Logic: Using reasoned argument to convince a policy-maker to take a particular course of action.

Overt: Bringing pressure to bear in the form of a sanction, often involving a threat. This might be a lobbyist threatening a legislator that his or her organization won't provide financial support for the next election as they have in the past. The exercise of this type of power is often referred to as "strong-arm tactics."

Perceived: Power perceived as potentially detrimental. For instance, legislators are aware that a state agency can undermine a proposal it sees as bad policy or detrimental to its interests.

Inducement: Offering an incentive to achieve a goal. This often provides a mutual benefit, such as when a legislator offers to support a colleague's bill in exchange for support of his or her bill.

Subliminal: Where a person is not aware of being influenced. They naturally act in response to situations that are part of their acculturation. This includes various forms of deference to superiors and those one respects. Subliminal power in politics is minor compared to the other four types of influence.

Political Savvy

2. DEVELOP AND CONVEY THE RIGHT ATTITUDE

You must convey a positive attitude to public officials, from legislators and their staffs, to those in the governor's office, to agency personnel. Don't be obsequious; but treat them with respect. However much you may dislike politicians and bureaucrats, perhaps even those you need to deal with, you can't let this come through.

One of the worst things you can say is: "I am a member of the public who elected you, so you work for me." Although most elected officials see their job as primarily representing their constituents, like most of us, they won't appreciate being treated as your servant. You'll likely annoy them and they'll freeze you out politically—not help you, and direct their staff to do the same. Remember, they hold all the political marbles—you need them more than they need you.

3. PUT YOURSELF IN THEIR SHOES

Never forget public officials and others involved in the policy process are human beings just like you. Unlike most of us, however, politicians have both private and public lives. On a private level they must deal with their families, manage their finances, and perhaps face health issues. As public officials, they have values, motives, goals, agendas, likes, and dislikes. All these factors shape their actions.

Consequently, as with any relationship, to really understand a public official, put yourself in their shoes. Be aware of the pressures and constraints that are part of their job—such as being pulled in many directions by constituents, clienteles, and colleagues. In the case of legislative aides and the governor's staff, their main job is to support their bosses' goals and work to deflect attempts to undermine these goals. Plus, many politicians' needs and actions are driven by their desire to be re-elected.

Also keep in mind that public officials don't only deal with major policy decisions and high-profile concerns. They also deal with: mundane things day-to-day, like constituents' problems and issues. In the case of bureaucrats, they deal with: their clienteles' needs; personnel concerns; managing budgets; and juggling their schedules.

Try to imagine these situations and reflect on how they'd shape your attitude and actions if you were in their shoes.

4. ESTABLISH A RELATIONSHIP OF MUTUAL BENEFIT

Given the largely transactional nature of politics, most politicians expect something in exchange for their help or support. And so a lobbyist should show how their request will benefit the public official.

Creating a relationship of mutual benefit will likely give the policy maker a reason to help you, more so than if you just expect something but offer nothing in return. Viewed from a power perspective, this relationship is one of inducement, as set out in Box 2.2, where both parties gain through a quid pro quo. Box 2.3, on the next page, lists several ways in which a lobbyist can help a public official.

If you don't explain it (which you should), most politicians will want to know how supporting your issue will benefit them and their constituents.

Political Savvy

5. BE OPEN-MINDED AND POLITICALLY FLEXIBLE

Approach lobbying with an open mind—be flexible and pragmatic—for three major reasons:

- The need for compromise. All public officials must compromise to get some of what they want, as do all those involved in lobbying.

- The shifting political sands of the policy process require that a lobbying plan must include provisions to deal with change.

- If you don't acquire these first two elements of thinking politically, your lobbying effort will almost certainly fail.

Remember, no one has a monopoly on truth, especially in politics, including you and your organization. Although you may think yours is the worthiest cause in the world, some public officials and interest groups will see it differently, as it may clash with their values, causes, and immediate political goals.

No compromising means no deal for you—you'll get no pie instead of some of it.

BOX 2.3
WAYS TO HELP PUBLIC OFFICIALS

Political Savvy

- Aid in advancing their political agenda: something that directly benefits their constituents and/or provides support on one or more of the official's pet issues.

- Helping constituents or groups in their district to solve a problem.

- Get the word out that the policy-maker endorses an issue with widespread public support. This might include publicizing it in a group's newsletter, at a group meeting, or at a conference.

- Name recognition is important to elected officials. So get their name out there by inviting them to speak at a group meeting, or just introduce them with time to say a few words.

- Holding a "thank you" reception.

- Contributing money to their election campaign, and/or working on their campaign.

- Providing information they can't get elsewhere.

- Making a contact for a public official.

A way to look at helping public officials is you "ease their pain." You help with a concern where they don't have the information or the time to deal with it themselves; or, for a variety of reasons, they don't want to be seen dealing with it.

One thing to be very careful about in working to establish mutual benefit, is giving politicians gifts or buying them meals. State law restricts such activities. Know these rules beforehand.

Don't Fall in Love with Your Issue

A good piece of advice here is: "Don't fall in love with your issue."

While you can be passionate about your cause, don't be so wedded to it that you're not willing to compromise.

If you're in love with your issue, it will cloud your judgment, like being in a romantic relationship often does. Stand back and take a holistic view of the political situation and be rational about how to deal with it—look at things pragmatically. This includes that, in some situations, you'll be better off pulling the plug on your campaign than alienating those you may need in the future.

Furthermore, if you are inflexible, not only will your lobbying effort likely fail, in the process you'll get a reputation for being a political zealot who doesn't understand the basics for political success. As a result, public officials will avoid you.

6. LEARN HOW TO USE INFORMATION

The primary job of a lobbyist is providing information to policy makers. It's a major tool in helping an advocate achieve their goals. But, as important as the information, how it's presented determines its effectiveness. Before explaining the use and abuse of information, let's distinguish between **factual information** and **political information.**

Factual Information

While technically not all this type of information is facts, it's a good generic term. It covers a wide range of information, including:

- Details of policies, laws, and regulations.

- Survey research about public support or opposition to policies.

- What's happened in the past on issues and policies in Alaska, in other states, or at the federal or local government levels.

- The projected costs of certain policies.

- Information on policy makers, their personal and professional backgrounds, political orientation, policy goals, and the constituencies they represent, among other things.

Without factual information, public officials cannot plan or make policy proposals and lobbyists can't present their case.

Political Information

This is information about strategizing to get a policy enacted or defeated:

- Who's for and against a proposal and why, how their minds might be changed, and what's the chances of success?

- How can the various interests be accommodated and aligned to smooth the way for the passage of a proposal?

CONFIDENTIAL Political information is necessary because a majority is needed in the legislature to get something passed (21 votes in the House and 11 in the Senate), secure the governor's support, and, in many cases, that of a state agency. Consequently, it's essential to know where all interested parties stand to be sure to get the necessary support.

A major reason for gathering political information is that, in certain circumstances, it facilitates exerting pressure—power—on other policy makers to get a desired result. For instance, it might be the governor using the threat of the veto—a sanction—of a legislator's bill if he or she doesn't support a particular bill the governor wants.

A lot of political strategizing takes place behind closed doors. The obvious reason is that, for a strategy to succeed, opponents must be kept in the dark. For all those involved, this requires trust and confidentiality; otherwise the goal may be thwarted. This is one of the many reasons why trust and confidentiality are so prized in politics.

The Use and Abuse of Information

What's important to know about using factual and political information?

Factual Information

To be credible and taken seriously, be well-informed about your issue. This includes: what may be happening to it in the current leg-islature; its status with the governor; and the state agency or agencies concerned. So it's essential to keep on top of what's going on each day. Doing research and monitoring the legislature and executive branch can be a full-time job. For this reason, organizations that can afford it, hire lobbyists and others to help in this task.

Presenting Your Message Effectively: You'll likely want to provide as much information on your issue as you can, which may add up to volumes of material. But a public official who's short of time won't want or need all this.

Initially, the official will be interested in the answers to four questions:

1. What do you want?

2. Why do you want it?

3. How much will it cost?

4. How will it affect me, and our office politically? How will it affect my constituents or, for a state agency, our clientele?

Be very brief. Write the answers to all four questions in half a page or a page at most, the political equivalent of an executive summary. This will be very helpful to the official and to you. It will show you're able to put yourself in their shoes—you understand and respect their time constraints.

If they need more information, they'll ask for it. Having done your homework, you'll have anticipated their additional questions and prepared concise, useful responses.

Political Information and its Pitfalls

Because of the paramount need for trust and confidentiality in acquiring and using political information, a public official or staffer who doesn't know you will likely be very cautious and non-committal when you first approach them. As they get to know you and you build up trust and credibility, it will be easier to work with them.

A policy maker will want some political information from you, particularly regarding which legislators are for and against your issue, and suggestions on the strategies and tactics to use to achieve your goal. Beyond this, as Box 2.4 points out, there are pitfalls in using political information.

Political Savvy

7. BUILD A CONTACT NETWORK

You can get some factual information from government documents, other printed sources, and the Internet. Some political

BOX 2.4
THE PITFALLS OF USING POLITICAL INFORMATION

Some professional lobbyists trade in political information: they use it as a means of access and influence. Knowing what colleagues, allies, and opponents are thinking can be useful in establishing successful courses of action.

These professionals can get this information from their contacts, observing who's coming and going to particular offices in the legislature, what's said and not said and the body language in committee hearings, among other sources. As a novice, not tuned to the ins and outs of legislative life, this insider information is unlikely to come your way.

Even if you get wind of some political information, to use it as a bargaining chip or to get in someone's good graces, is a very risky business.

A lot of political information is gossip. It may not be true and likely can't be verified. If you pass it on and it's inaccurate, it undermines your credibility and trust in the eyes of those to whom you gave it. Trading in political information is best left to the professionals.

That is not to say political information isn't potentially useful. It's just that for the part-time or amateur lobbyist. It's generally best to keep your eyes and ears open but your lips tightly shut.

information is available from the media, both mainstream and social media, and political blogs. But most political information can be gotten only from people in the know.

Lobbying success depends heavily on personal contacts. If you don't establish relationships with legislators, staffers, people in the governor's office, and agency personnel, as well as fellow lobbyists, interest group representatives, and others in your area of policy, you won't be able to function as a credible lobbyist. Building a contact network and good relationships can't be done overnight. Establishing trust and creating a track record takes time and energy.

Remember, however, that given the transactional nature of politics, having good contacts is a two-way street—when your contacts need information you help them. Also remember, you must be sure you can trust those in your network, and determine the value of each contact as to the veracity of information they provide.

To be effective, every lobbyist needs a contact network.

Political Savvy

8. DON'T TAKE SITUATIONS AT FACE VALUE IN POLITICS— DEVELOP A HEALTHY SKEPTICISM

Sometimes things are what they seem in politics and the policy process. For instance, lobbying to provide more funds for animal shelters, or improve safety in the logging industry, are unlikely to be driven by political subterfuge or ulterior motives. This is not necessarily so with many aspects of public policy-making.

Examples of situations where the motives for a political action may be more than meets the eye are:

- A legislator or governor may have to pay off political debts incurred to get elected.

- A current or previous occupation or other experience may influence a politician's actions. For example, a trade union member or small business owner will understand the operation, concerns, and needs of that business or profession. As a result, they are often sympathetic to those perspectives, and may be open to lobbying by these people.

- A high fiscal note (the estimated cost of a bill), drawn up by a state agency, may indicate the administration's desire to kill a proposal.

- A lobbyist whose client opposes an issue, doesn't deal directly with opponents of the measure. Instead, the lobbyist works behind the scenes to kill it.

Dealing with Political Unknowns

Consequently, those involved in politics and the policy process must constantly be aware that things may not be what they appear in a policy proposal; or a politician saying one thing, but their actions indicating something different.

To deal with these situations, part of the mindset of politicians is a healthy skepticism. They use their intuition, their contacts, and other sources, to try to find out what's behind it.

As a novice you need to develop this mindset. This doesn't mean distrusting everyone and questioning their motives. Even in politics, assume people have good intentions until they prove otherwise. But be wary—develop a questioning approach to political situations.

However, even with such a mindset, being able to use it to dig below the surface on an issue is not easy for a novice. This is another reason to build a contract network to get the information to apply your healthy skepticism.

In politics, things are often not what they seem—so dig below the surface.

9. DEVELOP AN ABILITY TO THINK BEYOND THE OBVIOUS

In a similar vein to not taking things at face value in politics in general, but applied specifically to planning your campaign, there

Political
Savvy

may be formidable opponents or strong allies you have not considered. Box 2.5 provides some examples.

Besides not taking things at face value, you need the political savvy to cast a wider net, to consider the potential broader implications of your proposal. Not seeing the bigger political picture may not only cause you to overlook potential opposition, but deprive you of potential support. These oversights could sink your campaign.

10. THE IMPORTANCE OF MANAGEMENT AND PLANNING

Contrary to what many people believe, lobbyists and interest group leaders don't spend all their time dealing with legislators and other public officials. They spend at least half their time, in some cases much more, planning their lobbying effort.

They don't operate by the seat of their pants, which is a road to failure. To be successful, you must be good at organizing and deploying your group's resources.

BOX 2.5
THINKING BEYOND THE OBVIOUS IN IDENTIFYING ALLIES AND FOES

Two Examples of Overlooking Potential Allies

Odd Political Bedfellows

Sometimes groups that are generally at odds, such as a business association and a trade union, find common ground on an issue and work together. This might be the case where they have a common interest in dealing with high healthcare costs, certain aspects of occupational safety, and government subsidies for technical training programs. In these cases they bury their differences and work together to achieve mutual benefits.

The lesson: when identifying support on your issue, think beyond the logical allies, consider the common goals you may have with other groups. You can get ideas on likely allies from people in your contact network.

(continued . . .)

BOX 2.5 CONTINUED

Don't Reinvent the Wheel on Your Issue

Whatever your issue, chances are it's been considered before in various ways, perhaps in Alaska, but almost certainly in other states. Some of these situations and the organizations involved will be obvious, others may not be.

For example, a citizen group seeking state funding to improve its local transit system might be unaware that other communities have tried to do the same, but failed. Identifying and contacting these could be a good source of information. It could help garner potential support, save a lot of trouble in planning the lobbying effort, and make the resulting campaign more effective.

Two Examples of Unanticipated Opposition

Unexpected Fallout

Take, for instance, a proposed law to impose longer prison sentences for possessing and selling drugs. Besides expected support from the "get tough on crime" lobby and opposition from criminal justice reform advocates, unanticipated opposition may come from the court system, the Department of Public Safety, and the Department of Corrections.

They will likely not weigh in on the pros and cons of the bill. However, they may oppose it because it will increase their costs by having to hire more prosecutors, public defenders, and judges, needing more state troopers, finding more prison space, and hiring more prison guards.

An Unfounded Assumption

Another example is a proposal to prohibit the sale of soda pop and candy in K-12 schools for health reasons, particularly fighting obesity.

It is reasonable to assume this cause will be strongly supported by school administrators. They appear as shoo-ins on the pro side, so much so that they are not contacted early on in the campaign. Instead, the proponents focus on how to deal with obvious opponents, such as soda pop distributors.

Big mistake. Even though school administrators may be supportive of the proposal as parents or advocates of student health, they may be opposed because the new law could reduce school revenues in an already tight budget situation.

The lesson? Assume nothing and never take anything for granted.

Among other things, management involves: developing a lobbying plan; taking steps to ensure group unity; choosing a lobbyist; preparing materials to use when lobbying; and, if you aren't located in Juneau, carefully planning your visit to the capital city. Most planning and other preparations need to be completed long before the legislative session begins.

But this is not a typical management situation, where you have control over virtually all parts of a project to get the desired result.

11. RECOGNIZE THE NEED TO MAKE DECISIONS IN A FLUID ENVIRONMENT WITH INCOMPLETE INFORMATION

In part, success at lobbying requires the ability to operate in a fluid political environment where you don't have all the information you need. This reality has two significant implications.

First, it's why you need several of the elements of political savvy. It's why planning is essential; why a lobbyist must be pragmatic, especially being willing to compromise; the need to understand the real intent behind a proposal; and developing a good sense of timing (covered in element 12 below).

Second, in this fluid environment, the situation can change rapidly. Political alliances may break apart or be formed; the substance of a bill may change in a committee hearing; a legislator whom you thought was on your side no longer supports you; or some outside force, such as the earthquake in Anchorage in 2018 (which redirected some state spending), can change the political landscape for a group or organization.

This requires immediate awareness of the situation and, if action is necessary, a rapid response by the group and particularly their lobbyist.

When you're lobbying, you've got to be prepared for things to change at any moment— usually when you least expect it.

12. UNDERSTAND THE IMPORTANCE OF TIMING

Having a good sense of timing is an important element in the lobbyist's mindset. Without it, the impact of the message may be lost.

Any good political operative knows there's a right time to deliver a message—when it's most likely to get serious attention by a policy maker. This might be just before a committee hearing or a vote on the floor of the House or Senate; in an office meeting; or when an agency person is developing their budget that affects your issue.

By implication, there are times when it's ineffective or inappropriate to deliver a message. The message may have little or no impact in the policy-maker's mind.

For instance, those not aware of the importance of good—most appropriate—timing, may visit a legislator early in the session, lobby on their issue, think it's fixed in that legislator's mind, and go home feeling good. Given all the matters a typical legislator attends to, the issue and its pros and cons may be forgotten by the time it reaches a crucial stage of consideration. Follow-up is essential. Contact the legislator or their staff regularly (but not too much) to jog his or her memory, and ask what they need from you to help your issue advance.

13. POLITICAL SAVVY, TRUST, AND CREDIBILITY

Gaining access to public officials is one thing, building up a credible and trusted relationship is quite another— it takes lots of time and effort.

In combination, many of the 12 elements of political savvy are what it takes to build the trust and credibility required to be a successful lobbyist. By possessing these qualities, it tells public officials you know how the system works, understand what it takes to mount a serious lobbying effort, and respect their needs and strictures.

Obviously, you can't become politically savvy overnight, especially if you've not been involved in politics before. But you can review the 12 elements before you lobby to see how to approach acquiring and developing these skills. Most public officials will give you credit for trying if you are a thoughtful, respectful novice, and likely help you become more politically aware.

How Not to Lobby

The immediate benefits of being familiar with the elements of political savvy are insights into what not to do when you lobby. These include don't:

- Go into a meeting with the wrong attitude.

- Lobby by the seat of your pants.

- Deluge a public official with information.

- Insist on going first to the top dog, among other mistakes.

Lobbying success involves not making major mistakes, as well as doing the right things.

14. IS LOBBYING FOR YOU?

Deciding whether you want to be a lobbyist is not necessarily a straight up "yes" or "no." You may want to be involved in some ways and not in others. Here are six questions to ask yourself to see if you have the interest and temperament to lobby.

- Am I a people person?

- Do I feel comfortable with the elements of a political mindset? Can I develop one?

- Can I work in a real-life political environment?

- Can I adapt quickly to change?

- Can I deal with conflict, being told "no," and disappointment?

- Do I have management skills?

The first four questions you can answer based on what we've said already. The following comments on the last two may help you decide "yes" or "no" on becoming a lobbyist.

Dealing with Conflict and Disappointment

Conflict is a constant in politics. Most conflicts are low-key. Examples are disagreements over how the effectiveness of state spending should be evaluated, or building a new facility versus renting office space for state operations. On other occasions, emotions boil over and intense conflicts occur. This is especially so on issues such as budget allocations, and dealing with crime and social issues, such as abortion.

In these circumstances, conflicts can erupt into strong language that you witness, or are the target of, perhaps because you've been too persistent on an issue (though professional lobbyists are more likely to be punching bags in these situations than volunteer lobbyists).

Lobbying is not for the faint of heart—it takes a lot of people skills, determination and stick-to-it-tiveness.

At other times, in various ways, you may be told "no" on something you're pushing. Although politicians don't tend to say "no," instead they may say: "Let me think about that," or, "I'll take that under advisement," or simply not deal with your issue, which may include avoiding you.

You may lose on your issue, for all sorts of reasons, despite putting all your effort into it. Losing can be a major downer, even for professional lobbyists.

The question is: can you handle these situations?

Political Management

As an element of political savvy, political management includes:

- Having a mind for detail.

- Being able to plan and organize a campaign.

- Being systematic in approaching issues and political situations.

- Depending on the organization, having a pragmatic political attitude, and understanding what's possible and not possible in political advocacy.

Whether you like to lobby or not, if you have a small operation, you'll likely be both manager and lobbyist. In large organizations, these jobs can be split. If you are in such an organization and don't like dealing with public officials directly, management may fit you perfectly.

15. THE FIRST STEPS IN THINKING LIKE A LOBBYIST

These are the first steps in beginning to think like a lobbyist— equipping you with the tools of the lobbying trade. If you are a novice, some of these elements may seem rather abstract. They will make more sense as we consider the various aspects of the lobbying environment and the hands-on aspects of lobbying in the rest of the book.

Chapter 5 on the psychology of public officials, Chapter 6 on where power lies in Juneau, and Chapters 7 and 8, on the realities of the policy process, will increase your practical understanding of the power dynamics in lobbying. First, though, these chapters will make more sense by explaining how state government is organized and how the budget process works.

49

THIS CHAPTER COVERS

1. The Big Picture of Alaska State Government

2. The Legislature

3. The Governor and the Governor's Office

4. The Lieutenant Governor

5. Departments, Boards, and Commissions

6. The Courts

7. The Basics of the Bill Process

8. The Federal and Local Governments, and Inter-governmental Lobbying

9. Political Parties

10. The Majority and Minority Caucuses

11. Interest Groups and Lobbyists

12. The Media and Public Opinion

13. A First look at the Policy-Making Process

14. The Initiative, Referendum, and Recall

★ CHAPTER 3 ★

The Organization of Alaska State Government and the Policy-Makers

To be an effective lobbyist you need to know the ins and outs of the organization and procedures of state government, and who's involved in it.

—Thor Stacy,
Contract Lobbyist,
Thor Stacy & Associates

As one of Alaska's up-and-coming lobbyists, Thor Stacy puts it perfectly: an important aspect in becoming politically savvy is familiarity with the organization and operation of state government, and those involved in the policy process. This chapter covers all this except the state budget, which is dealt with in the next chapter.

1. THE BIG PICTURE OF ALASKA STATE GOVERNMENT

Box 3.1, on the next page, sets out the structure of state government. It shows the major parts of the organization of the legislature and the executive branch. The box doesn't show details on the judicial branch of Alaska government. This is because the courts are not a part of the day-to-day policy-making process.

BOX 3.1
THE ORGANIZATION OF THE LEGISLATURE AND EXECUTIVE BRANCH IN ALASKA

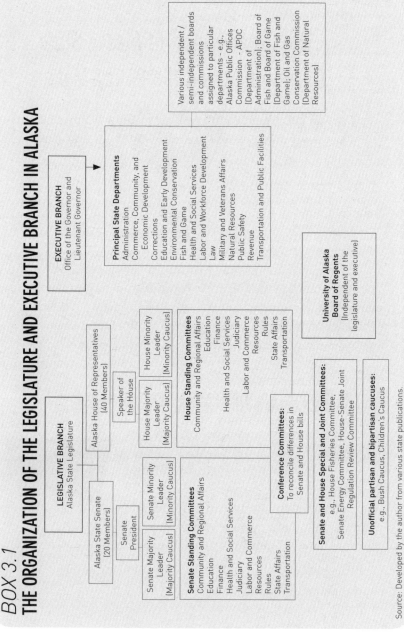

EXECUTIVE BRANCH
Office of the Governor and
Lieutenant Governor

Principal State Departments
Administration
Commerce, Community, and
    Economic Development
Corrections
Education and Early Development
Environmental Conservation
Fish and Game
Health and Social Services
Labor and Workforce Development
Law
Military and Veterans Affairs
Natural Resources
Public Safety
Revenue
Transportation and Public Facilities

Various independent /
semi-independent boards
and commissions
assigned to particular
departments – e.g.,
Alaska Public Offices
Commission - APOC
[Department of
Administration]; Board of
Fish and Board of Game
[Department of Fish and
Game]; Oil and Gas
Conservation Commission
[Department of Natural
Resources]

LEGISLATIVE BRANCH
Alaska State Legislature

Alaska House of Representatives
[40 Members]

Speaker of
the House

House Majority
Leader
[Majority Caucus]

House Minority
Leader
[Minority Caucus]

House Standing Committees
Community and Regional Affairs
Education
Finance
Health and Social Services
Judiciary
Labor and Commerce
Resources
Rules
State Affairs
Transportation

Alaska State Senate
[20 Members]

Senate
President

Senate Majority
Leader
[Majority Caucus]

Senate Minority
Leader
[Minority Caucus]

Senate Standing Committees
Community and Regional Affairs
Education
Finance
Health and Social Services
Judiciary
Labor and Commerce
Resources
Rules
State Affairs
Transportation

Conference Committees:
To reconcile differences in
Senate and House bills

Senate and House Special and Joint Committees:
e.g., House Fisheries Committee,
Senate Energy Committee, House–Senate Joint
Regulation Review Committee

Unofficial partisan and bipartisan caucuses:
e.g., Bush Caucus, Children's Caucus

**University of Alaska
Board of Regents**
(Independent of the
legislature and executive)

Source: Developed by the author from various state publications.

2. THE LEGISLATURE

Article II of the Alaska Constitution sets out the authority of the legislature. The 20 members of the Senate are elected for four-year terms, the 40 members of the House for two years. Each legislator has an office and at least two staff (also known as aides). The legislative leadership often has as many as five. Some staff working for legislators in the majority party, or caucus, are also committee aides, such as for the Transportation Committee or the Education Committee.

The House and Senate Finance Committees are the most significant as they consider all bills to approve their funding. Their chairpersons are among the most influential legislators. The Rules Committee and its chairperson also wield considerable influence. The committee schedules bills for consideration in floor sessions (meetings of both bodies in their respective chambers).

The legislature also has expert help, such as the Legal and Research Services unit which provides bill drafting and legal research for legislators.

Important aspects of the operation of the legislature are explained in Box 3.2 on the following pages.

Government Organization

3. THE GOVERNOR AND THE GOVERNOR'S OFFICE

Governors are elected for four-year terms. They may serve two consecutive terms, but then sit out one term before running again. Article III of the Alaska Constitution gives them extensive authority, including: preparing the state budget; appointing heads of government departments with approval of the legislature; and appointment of judges. Governors also have

Alaska's governors have extensive constitutional authority, but are not always the dominant political force on issues.

ALASKA STATE CAPITOL

BOX 3.2
THE LEGISLATURE: BASIC TERMS, ORGANIZATION, AND OPERATION

Legislatures meet for two years and are designated by numbers beginning with the First Alaska Legislature in 1959 and 1960, following the granting of statehood. So, the legislature that met in 1981 and 1982 was the Twelfth Legislature, the one in 2019 and 2020 the Thirty-First Legislature.

First and Second Sessions, Special Sessions, and the Interim

The first year of the legislature is designated the **First Session** and the second year the **Second Session**. By statute, each legislative session lasts for 90 days from January to April; but constitutionally, it can last for up to 120 days, and often extends beyond the 90 days.

In addition, **Special Sessions** are often called by the governor or the legislature. These are limited to consideration of individual bills or specific subjects, such as criminal justice reform, or imposing new taxes to deal with state revenue shortfalls.

Bills and the organization of the legislature (which party or caucus is in control) roll over (continue) from the First to the Second Session. At the end of the Second Session, all bills and the organization of the legislature are terminated. Everything begins anew after the November election.

The nine months or so when the legislature is not meeting is called the **interim**, whether between the two sessions of the legislature, or between legislatures.

The Organization of the Legislature

After an election, the legislature organizes in both houses into a **majority** and a **minority**: a House majority, a Senate majority, a House minority, and a Senate minority. Generally, the majority is composed of members of one party, or a coalition that has more than 20 seats in the House and more than 10 in the Senate.

As explained in section 10 below, power in the legislature lies with the majority caucuses, that often include both Republicans and Democrats.

Legislative Committees

There are several types of committees. Most are shown in Box 3.1. The major type, the ones that do most of the work, are **standing committees**. These hear bills and make recommendations on them. They will be the major committees with which you deal.

Also listed in Box 3.1 are **conference committees**. These are ad hoc committees formed for the sole purpose of reconciling differences between the House and Senate versions of a bill. They are disbanded once their tasks are completed.

Several house and senate **special committees** and **joint committees** also exist, or are created from time to time. These will generally be of less importance to you and your issues. Some examples are given in Box 3.1.

Bill Numbering, Authors and Sponsors, and Committee Substitutes

After they are drawn up, bills are given a number preceded by **SB** (Senate Bill) or **HB** (House Bill) to indicate the house in which they were introduced. For example, a bill introduced in the House to legalize casino gambling, might have the designation HB 146. A Senate bill to require cyclists to wear crash helmets, might be SB 231.

The First Page of a Bill

The first page of a bill lists the legislator who sponsored (authored) it, plus other legislators who are co-sponsors—those who officially support the bill. Bills from the executive branch are introduced by the Rules Committees in each house. Their first page has the words, "By the (House or Senate) Rules Committee by Request of the Governor."

Amended Bills

Often, a standing committee will amend—change—a bill or combine one or more bills on the same subject. The changes result in a "Committee Substitute" and has **CS** in front of its number. So, a committee substitute for SB 242 would then become CS for SB 242. If a subsequent committee amends the bill, the new version is a CS for a CS for SB 242.

Fiscal Notes

Each new bill requires a statement of anticipated itemized costs. Called a fiscal note, these are prepared by the state agency or agencies most affected by the bill.

(continued . . .)

Government
Organization

BOX 3.2 *CONTINUED*

The Daily Schedule

During the 90-day session, the House and Senate meet in floor sessions in their respective chambers. In the early days of the session they meet three or four times a week, five days a week toward the end of the session.

Floor sessions start between 10AM and 11AM., again, depending on the point in time of the session and the number of items to be considered. Sessions are announced by bells or chimes, and sometimes tunes, playing throughout the Capitol and adjacent buildings.

Legislators' and Committee Schedules

Before the floor sessions, legislators are usually in their offices to hold meetings with colleagues, constituents, and attend standing committee meetings. Committees also meet in the afternoons.

At the End of the Session

All these schedules usually go out of the window during the last week to ten days of the session.

This is especially true in the Second Session, as pressure builds to finish business and get the budget and other bills finalized and passed. During this time, committees may meet at any time. Floor sessions are called at all hours of the day, and often go late into the night, sometimes into the early hours of the morning.

line-item veto authority. This allows them to delete particular items in budgets, or delete them and insert lower amounts.

The governor's staff ranges in number depending on the governor. Box 3.3 sets out the typical organization of the governor's office.

Three of the governor's staffers are particularly important: the chief of staff; the legislative director; and the Director of the Office of Management and Budget (OMB).

BOX 3.3
THE ALASKA GOVERNOR'S OFFICE: TYPICAL ORGANIZATION AND STAFF POSITIONS

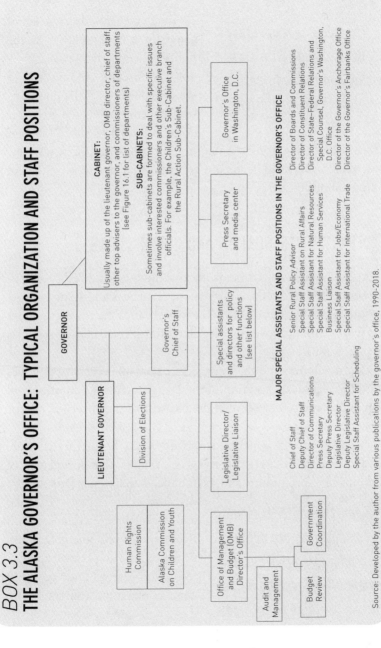

GOVERNOR

LIEUTENANT GOVERNOR

Division of Elections

CABINET:
Usually made up of the lieutenant governor, OMB director, chief of staff, other top advisers to the governor, and commissioners of departments (see Figure 16.1 for list of departments)

SUB-CABINETS:
Sometimes sub-cabinets are formed to deal with specific issues and involve interested commissioners and other executive branch officials. For example, the Children's Sub-Cabinet and the Rural Action Sub-Cabinet.

Governor's Office in Washington, D.C.

Governor's Chief of Staff

Press Secretary and media center

Special assistants and directors for policy and other functions (see list below)

Legislative Director/ Legislative Liaison

Human Rights Commission

Alaska Commission on Children and Youth

Office of Management and Budget (OMB) Director's Office

Government Coordination

Audit and Management

Budget Review

MAJOR SPECIAL ASSISTANTS AND STAFF POSITIONS IN THE GOVERNOR'S OFFICE

Chief of Staff
Deputy Chief of Staff
Director of Communications
Press Secretary
Deputy Press Secretary
Legislative Director
Deputy Legislative Director
Special Staff Assistant for Scheduling

Senior Rural Policy Advisor
Special Staff Assistant on Rural Affairs
Special Staff Assistant for Natural Resources
Special Staff Assistant for Human Services
Business Liaison
Special Staff Assistant for Jobs/Economy
Special Staff Assistant for International Trade

Director of Boards and Commissions
Director of Constituent Relations
Director of State–Federal Relations and
   Special Counsel, Governor's Washington,
   D.C. Office
Director of the Governor's Anchorage Office
Director of the Governor's Fairbanks Office

Source: Developed by the author from various publications by the governor's office, 1990–2018.

Government Organization

4. THE LIEUTENANT GOVERNOR

The lieutenant governor deals mainly with state elections, and the codification of state regulations.

The lieutenant governor is not generally a major player in the policy process. They may or may not have a close relationship, or see eye to eye, with the governor. Consequently, often, the governor does not involve the lieutenant governor in policy issues. Sometimes, though, when the two have a close relationship, the lieutenant governor may be given significant policy responsibilities.

5. DEPARTMENTS, BOARDS, AND COMMISSIONS

At the head of departments are commissioners, aided by a deputy commissioner. In the commissioner's office is a legislative affairs person (legislative liaison) who tracks legislation for the department and works with the governor's legislative director, and other agencies on policy issues.

Commissioners and their immediate staff are political appointees (with the technical exception of the Departments of Education and Fish and Game). They serve at the pleasure of the governor, and/or the commissioner.

Departments are organized into divisions, headed by a director and usually a deputy director. For example, the Department of Commerce, Community and Economic Development has several divisions including: Banking and Securities; Insurance; and Economic Development. Division directors are also political appointees who come and go with changes of administrations.

Departments, boards and commissions are not just administrative bodies, they are often involved in the thick of politics.

Boards and Commissions

There are over a hundred boards and commissions in Alaska. Examples are listed in Box 3.1. Boards typically have governing bodies with chairs and permanent staff headed by a director or executive director. For example, the Alaska Public Offices Commission (APOC—which deals with lobbying regulations and campaign finance), has a five-member board, a director, and a small office staff.

With a few exceptions, board members are appointed by the governor. Appointees have fixed terms, ranging from three to seven years. Most have expertise related to the authority of the board, and are often appointed on the recommendation of the interests they represent. For instance, members of the Board of Nursing will likely have received the endorsement of the nursing community.

Other boards and commissions have a combination of professionals in the field and public members, such as the Judicial Conduct Commission (which considers complaints against judges). Still others are composed almost entirely of laypersons, such as the Board of Regents, which oversees the University of Alaska.

Various members of boards and commissions and their staff work with the legislature, the governor's office, and state agencies on legislative, budget, and regulatory issues.

6. THE COURTS

Courts are not part of the day-to-day policy making process, for two major and related reasons.

First, their major function is to administer criminal and civil law. As such, the judiciary is an independent branch of government that acts impartially in interpreting the law, free from political pressures, particularly from the legislature, the governor, and interest groups.

Government
Organization

Second, for this reason, judicial ethics prevents judges from engaging in a conversation with anyone attempting to lobby them to shape the outcome of a court case.

Even so, the courts do, in effect, make public policy through decisions on issues, such as privacy and prisoners' rights. Plus, the court system's administrative director lobbies the other two branches of government to secure the court system's funding and other benefits.

7. THE BASICS OF THE BILL PROCESS

Most of us learned in high school civics that a bill has three readings. This involves its introduction, consideration by committees, it's voted on by the full House and Senate, and then signed by the governor. There are other aspects of law-making, but the three readings are the essence of the formal process.

The actual process is more complicated. In most cases it involves much politicking, with clashes of interests and power relationships coming into play. Chapters 7 and 8 on the way the policy process really works, go into the political aspects of bill making.

The large majority of bills never make it into law.

8. THE FEDERAL AND LOCAL GOVERNMENTS, AND INTERGOVERNMENTAL LOBBYING

The federal government owns 55 percent of Alaska's land, and regulates many policy areas, such as environmental protection and fishing beyond the 200-mile limit. It's a major funding source for many state services, including transportation (close to 90 percent), social programs, and those for Alaska Natives.

In many cases, to receive these funds, the state is required to provide matching funds—paying part of the cost of these programs. This "federal match" is particularly important for receiving Medicaid funds (a medical assistance program for low-income and others with special needs).

To facilitate contact with Alaskans, the federal government has several offices in the state, such as for the Forest Service and the Bureau of Indian Affairs. Also, because the state has a major interest in many federal matters, it has an office in Washington, D.C. (the governor's office), to work with Alaska's three-member Congressional delegation to secure funds and favorable policies for the state.

Negative Attitudes toward the Federal Government

Despite the extensive funds received by the state, among many Alaskans there's a negative attitude to the federal government. They believe that the national government stymies Alaska's development by too many regulations, and control over so much of the state's land area.

This perspective, often referred to as "federal overreach," is largely that of many Republicans and Libertarians, who tend to favor economic development over protection of the environment.

Local Government

Some groups and organizations lobby boroughs and cities because their issues are affected by local governments. These include: mining interests that need to deal with residents who oppose their operations; schoolteachers; and business groups.

Intergovernmental Lobbying

In many cases groups lobby at all three levels of government—state, federal and local—including Alaska Native interests, environmental groups, and the University of Alaska. This so-called intergovernmental lobbying is increasing as more groups and organizations are affected by all three levels of government.

Government Organization

9. POLITICAL PARTIES

As elsewhere in the country, there are two major parties in Alaska—the Democrats and Republicans. There's also third parties, such as the Alaska Independence Party (AIP) and the Green Party; but their support is insignificant compared to the major parties.

Yet, generally, even the two major parties are not the most important part of the policy process in controlling what legislation gets passed. This is despite virtually all legislators being Republicans or Democrats, and some members of each party working to promote policies in line with their party's platform.

Part of the reason is that less than 50 percent of Alaskans identify with a political party—the lowest in the nation. It is also due to many legislators from rural-bush areas being very pragmatic, less wedded to one of the major parties, to secure benefits for their constituents.

10. THE MAJORITY AND MINORITY CAUCUSES

A **caucus** is: *A group of people within a larger body, in this case the legislature or a political party or a combination of the two, which unites to promote a particular political agenda.* Because of the weakness of parties, power lies with the majority caucus in each house of the legislature. These control and drive the policy process. Each house also has a minority caucus, but these have little influence in policy-making.

While the majority caucuses are usually composed of a majority of one party—Republicans or Democrats—they are often bipartisan coalitions of members of both parties. Bush Democrats often join Republicans to form or bolster a majority caucus. From time to time there are also coalitions of urban and bush legislators. This was the case with a loose-knit coalition, the Bipartisan Working Group (BWG) in the Senate from 2007-12; and a stronger, more cohesive coalition in the House from 2017-20.

Even when most majority caucus members are from one party, it's usually referred to as "the majority." Though when the majority is of one party, it's often referred to as the Republican or Democratic majority. Minority caucuses are

Power in the legislature lies mainly with the majority caucuses, not with political parties.

rarely coalitions. Nevertheless, they are referred to interchangeably as the minority or Republican or Democratic minority.

Other Caucuses

Besides party caucuses, there are several that are bipartisan, based on regions, such as Anchorage or the Bush. Others form around issues, such as the Fish Caucus and the Children's Caucus.

11. INTEREST GROUPS AND LOBBYISTS

The public and the media often refer to both interest groups and lobbyists in a generic way, as if all interest groups and all lobbyist are the same. There are, however, different types of each. The distinction is important for understanding the way they operate in Juneau.

Types of Interest Groups

There are four types of interest groups. One is composed of individual members. A second does not have individual members; they represent organizations, like school districts and oil companies. Then there are groups with both individuals and organizations as members. The fourth type is what are called **institutional interests**, because they are not interest groups, but institutions of various types, like businesses and governments. Examples of these four types are set out in Box 3.4 on the following pages.

To see the range of interest groups operating in Alaska, who they employ as lobbyists, and how much they spend, visit the Alaska Public Offices Commission (APOC) website. But these are not the only interest groups and lobbyists that operate in Juneau.

BOX 3.4
EXAMPLES OF INTERESTS AND INTEREST GROUPS IN ALASKA

Individual Membership Groups

Alaska State Employees Association—ASEA: A long-time active lobby in Juneau. It has competed with the Alaska Public Employees Association (APEA) in representing state and local government employees.

National Education Association—NEA-Alaska: Represents K-12 employees, mainly schoolteachers; a long-time major lobby in Juneau.

Alaska Bar Association—ABA: With over 4,000 members, it represents lawyers to state government on various issues involving the qualifications and legal liabilities of lawyers, among other concerns.

Alaska Wildlife Alliance—AWA: Founded in 1978, it advocates for healthy ecosystems, scientifically and ethically managed to protect wildlife for present and future generations. AWC depends on grassroots support and the political activism of its members.

Association for the Education of Young Children-Southeast Alaska— AEYC-SEA: This citizen group is the local chapter of a state and national organization working to improve funding for, and the quality of, day-care and early childhood education. It relies largely on volunteers to advocate to state government.

Organizational Interest Groups

Alaska Municipal League—AML: Represents most boroughs and cities. It lobbies on general issues affecting local government, such as funding, and employee benefits, among other issues.

Association of Alaska School Boards—AASB: Represents Alaska's school boards, including Rural Education Attendance Areas—REAAs. It has a major presence in Juneau.

Alaska Oil and Gas Association—AOGA: Is a major lobby in Juneau representing most oil and gas companies operating in the state.

Alaska Federation of Natives—AFN: Its mission is to enhance and promote the cultural, economic, and political voice of the Alaska Native community. The Federation's membership includes: 178 villages; 13 regional Native corporations; 12 regional non-profit corporations; and tribal consortiums.

Combined Individual and Organizational Membership Groups

Alaska State Chamber of Commerce—ASCC: Bills itself as "the voice of business" in Alaska, seeking to promote a positive business environment. It has a major lobbying presence in Juneau. Its membership includes: individuals; businesses; local chambers of commerce (including chambers from Seattle and Canada); as well as other organizations.

Alaska Outdoor Council—AOC: An association of individual members and clubs dedicated to preserving outdoor pursuits— hunting, fishing, trapping, gun ownership, and public access to, and conservation of, the habitat upon which AOC members depend. The Council is the official state representative of the National Rifle Association (NRA). It has a major on-going presence in Juneau.

United Fishermen of Alaska—UFA: Works to promote and protect the common interests of Alaska's commercial fishing industry. Its members are individuals, businesses, and other fishing organizations. It has a constant presence in Juneau.

Institutional Interests

Alaska Department of Education and Early Developments—DOEED: With K-12 education accounting for 25 percent of the state spending, the Department works to maintain its budget and deal with various federal and state regulations relating to education. This often includes utilizing its constituent groups, such as the PTA, and working with other interest groups, including AASB and school administrators.

University of Alaska—UA: Includes various interests, such as faculty, students, administrative and maintenance employees, some of which have their own political representation. As an institutional interest, the UA's Statewide Office has a continual presence in Juneau, mainly for budget purposes. Plus, its individual campuses lobby on their own, sometimes at cross purposes with the Statewide organization.

(continued . . .)

Government Organization

BOX 3.4 CONTINUED

North Slope Borough—NSB: Has hired a contract lobbyist for many years, and uses its own staff to promote and protect its political interests. It is particularly concerned with maintaining its authority to tax the Trans Alaska Pipeline (TAPS) and North Slope oil production facilities for local revenue.

ExxonMobil Corporation: Has operated in the state/territory for over 90 years. Works to protect its interests on its own behalf, including hiring one or more lobbyists, as well as through membership in AOGA.

Alaska Airlines: As a Seattle-based company and the state's major air carrier with a monopoly in many communities, it has hired a contract lobbyist for many years to promote good relations with state government, among other political goals.

Government Organization

Types of Lobbyists

There are also four types of lobbyists. Some work on a contract for one or more clients. Another type lobby only for the organization that employs them. Third are those representing government agencies. And fourth, volunteer lobbyists who represent various causes.

Interest groups and lobbyists are essential and ever-present parts of legislative life.

We go into detail on all four types and the importance of the differences between them in section 8 of Chapter 5 on the mindset and role of policy-makers.

How Many Interest Groups and Lobbyists are there in Juneau?

Answering this question is difficult because not all groups and lobbyists are required to register. About 300-350 of both interest groups and lobbyists register, as required by Alaska law.

Governments, including state agencies and local governments, as well as many cause groups, are not required to register. Based on surveys by the author, an estimate of interests and interest groups not required to register each year is in the 300-range.

So, there are likely almost twice as many groups and interests, as well as lobbyists, operating in Juneau than APOC's records indicate.

12. THE MEDIA AND PUBLIC OPINION

Because of Alaska's small population, those in the media (newspapers, including those on-line, magazines, TV, and radio) covering Alaska politics and the goings-on in Juneau, is very small. Few journalists have politics as their sole beat—responsibility—for their organization.

In a typical legislative session, only a half dozen or so reporters are based in Juneau to cover legislative activities. These include: the *Anchorage Daily News*; the *Juneau Empire*; KINY radio in Juneau; the Alaska Public Radio Network (APRN); the Associated Press (AP); and KTUU and KTVA TV in Anchorage. A few other organizations have a reporter in Juneau during the hectic days at the end of the session.

Gavel Alaska, a public television and web service is broadcast by KTOO-FM and TV in Juneau, provides live and recorded daily coverage of the legislature. This includes: senate and house floor sessions; committee meetings; press conferences; and other legislative events.

These news sources are supplemented by political blogs that combine news with opinion. Examples include: *The Midnight Sun*; *Alaska Politics & Blogs Daily*; *Must Read Alaska*; and *The Mudflats*.

Public Opinion

At first glance, the idea of public opinion seems simple enough; but what exactly is meant by "the public's opinion" is difficult to determine specifically. Is it the message sent by an election; the information gathered in public opinion polls; the desires of those who contact politicians; public attitudes reflected in some media stories; or what?

How the media and public opinion do or do not translate into influence on policy-making, is considered in section 7 of Chapter 7 on the realities of the law-making process.

In most cases, the influence of the media and public opinion on public policy is far from clear.

13. A FIRST LOOK AT THE POLICY-MAKING PROCESS

As defined in Chapter 1, the policy process is: *The course of action taken by government to resolve conflicts over political issues. Or, in some cases, issues are not resolved, so that the status quo is maintained.*

There are several stages to this process best viewed as a cycle. In most cases, the core of the cycle is the bill process.

The cycle begins with getting the issue considered, a bill is drafted, followed by its consideration, enactment, and implementation. If there is concern with the law after its enactment, whether from those who opposed it or those who didn't get all they wanted, they'll regroup and present a new proposal. So the cycle begins again.

A major aspect of the politics of the policy cycle is the budget developed by the governor and its consideration by the legislature. Policy making also includes: decisions of executive agencies; formulating positions on various issues involved in state-federal relations; in some instances court decisions; and other activities.

We look at the political realities of the policy cycle and policy making in detail in Chapters 7 and 8.

14. THE INITIATIVE, REFERENDUM, AND RECALL

The Alaska Constitution includes provisions for the initiative, referendum, and recall, collectively known as provisions for direct democracy. On occasion, these are used as part of the policy process by being placed on the ballot. As such, they can be used as an interest group tactic.

Government Organization

The recall is a blunt policy instrument to remove an elected official from office. There have been several attempts to recall state elected officials, but none has been successful. The initiative and the referendum are more finely tuned and has been used on many occasions; most often to bypass the regular policy process when the legislature or the governor is perceived as being unresponsive or unwise on an issue.

An initiative is a proposed law placed on the ballot by a citizen petition. A referendum can also be placed on the ballot by citizen petition to repeal a law recently enacted. An initiative may not be used to amend the Alaska Constitution. And there are other restrictions on both the initiative and the referendum, including a prohibition of their use to enact or repeal appropriations.

Because of the extensive resources needed to mount an initiative or referendum campaign, they are rarely promoted and managed by one group alone. This is even the case for well-established groups with major resources. The use of direct democracy usually involves a coalition of groups, or a citizen group organized for the purpose. This means it is unlikely that you'll use these provisions.

Mounting a referendum or initiative campaign is not a realistic option for the vast majority of interest groups.

Government Organization

THIS CHAPTER COVERS

1. Major Budget Terms

2. Putting the State Budget Together

3. The State Budget is a Political Document

4. Components of the Budget

5. The Year-Round Budget Process

6. The Budget Cycle and the Budget Calendar

7. Major Public Officials and Agencies involved in the Budget

8. State Revenues

9. Budget Spending

10. State Politics and Budget Politics

★ CHAPTER 4 ★

Making Sense of the State Budget

The budget should reflect reality: why various programs exist; how much they actually cost; and how well they perform.

—Karen Rehfeld,
Former Director,
Alaska Office of Management and Budget—OMB

For many people, and perhaps for you, trying to make sense of the various aspects of the budget are daunting. Reduced to its basics, however, the state budget and the budget process are not difficult to understand.

1. MAJOR BUDGET TERMS

There are dozens of specialized terms used in connection with the budget. The major ones are set out in Box 4.1 on the next page. Of these four are particularly important, as they'll be referred to several times in this book. The most obvious one is budget. The other three are: fiscal year (FY), operating budget, and capital budget.

2. PUTTING THE STATE BUDGET TOGETHER

To garner support, many politicians running for office, especially Republicans, compare a household budget to the state budget. Their message is that the state must live within its means like a family: prioritize expenditures that are essential and eliminate those not

BOX 4.1
MAJOR BUDGET TERMS

Appropriation: A specific statutory authorization to spend money for a stated purpose. Appropriations must be made by law before a state agency can spend funds.

Budget: A formal plan of the allocation of funds for government expenditure for a fiscal period, including the means of financing the expenditures.

Budget Amendment: A proposal to change the dollar amount or scope of an activity or project after the budget has been submitted to the legislature. The governor is required to deliver budget amendments to the legislature by the 30th day of the legislative session.

Capital Budget: A plan for the distribution of state funds for items with a value of over $25,000 and an anticipated life of more than one year—such as, buildings, land purchases, and one-time studies. Capital appropriations lapse only if funds remain after the project is completed.

Constitutional Budget Reserve (CBR): A fund created by constitutional amendment intended as a "rainy day" fund to supplement expenditures in years of insufficient revenue. The constitution requires a supermajority of the legislature (three-fourths of members in each body) to approve an appropriation from the CBR for expenditure. Repayment to the fund is to be made in years of a revenue surplus, but this is not always done.

Entitlement Program: A government program, such as food stamps, student loans, or the Permanent Fund Dividend (PFD), which, if a citizen meets the eligibility criteria and applies for the program, they are "entitled" to receive the benefit. Entitlement programs are a major part of the Alaska state budget. See also **formula program**.

Federal Receipts (or Federal Matching Funds/Federal Match): Funds received by the state from the federal government to support state programs. Some federal programs require the state to appropriate a percentage of "matching funds"—often called a "federal match"—before the funds can be released to the state.

Fiscal Note: A statement itemizing the cost of proposed legislation. They are usually prepared by the state agency whose function relates to the subject of the bill.

Fiscal Year (FY)/Budget Year: In Alaska this runs from July 1 of one year to June 30 of the next. Fiscal years are designated by the year in which they end. Thus, FY20 began on July 1, 2019 and ends on June 30, 2020. In contrast, the federal fiscal year runs from October 1 to September 30.

Formula Program: A program with eligibility requirements that guarantees a specific benefit. In contrast to entitlement programs for individuals, formula programs appropriate money to organizations and specific groups. For example, the Base Student Allocation (BSA) for K-12 is part of the Foundation Formula determining the amount a school district and a school receive each year for each student.

General Appropriation Bill: Makes appropriations for the estimated expenses of state government for a fiscal year. It is introduced at the request of the governor.

General Fund Account (usually called the General Fund or GF): The major state account into which revenues are paid and expenditures made. It's used to finance the operations of state agencies.

Line Item: A specific expenditure (e.g. personnel, supplies, contractual services, travel, grants, etc.) included in the budget by a state agency, the governor, or the legislature.

Line-item Veto: A provision allowing a governor to eliminate or reduce a proposed expenditure in the legislative budget on a line-by-line basis.

Office of Management and Budget (OMB): The division of the governor's office responsible for preparing and monitoring the governor's budget.

Operating Budget: A one-year plan for funding the operations of state programs and other functions of government. It usually include items with an anticipated life of less than one year, such as employees' salaries, utility bills, aid to schools and communities, and various entitlement programs. Operating appropriations are made for a fiscal year. Any unspent or unobligated funds revert to the GF, or lapse, at the end of the fiscal year.

Reappropriation: Funds not used for their original purpose, and assigned to another purpose by a new appropriation.

Supplemental Request (usually referred to as a supplemental): A request from a state agency for additional funds to its appropriation for the last fiscal year. Usually due to unforeseen costs, new circumstances, or because the legislature partially funded the program in the initial budget. Supplementals require an appropriation by the legislature.

The State Budget

To understand state politics and lobbying, first get a handle on the basics of the budget and its revenues and expenditures.

The State Budget

necessary. This approach resonates with many Alaskans and they vote for candidate with such a common sense view of developing a budget.

In practice, the state budget is put together in a much different and far less systematic way than a household budget.

The Priorities of Politicians

Unlike a household, whose priorities are essential expenditures, such as rent, food and gasoline, putting together the state budget usually doesn't revolve around the essentials or the urgency of some expenditures. In effect, putting together the state budget is the reverse of drawing up a household budget. Initially, most politicians have a wish list and then seek the money to pay for it.

Some want to expand existing programs and fund new projects. Others see certain past expenditures as unnecessary, and want the money used for other programs. Still others oppose some items being included in the budget, even though they are essential to the functioning of state government. Even those who want to cut the budget overall, have a wish list of expenditures they want to keep, particularly those that benefit their constituents.

What all this adds up to, is that some necessary expenditures, such as funds for a backlog of deferred maintenance for state and university buildings, may not be included in the budget, while a pet project pushed by legislators and the governor may be. Nevertheless, there must be money to cover programs and services, such as prisons and education, many of which are required by the state constitution or statute. These expenditures take up about two thirds of the budget.

As a result, not all the state budget is up for grabs. In the final budget, because expenditures are determined by available revenue, some desired items on politicians' wish-lists will not be funded. All the same, the final budget reflects the politics in the state at any one time.

3. THE STATE BUDGET AS A POLITICAL DOCUMENT

In an ideal world, as Karen Rehfeld states at the beginning of this chapter: The budget should reflect reality: why various programs exist; how much they actually cost; and how well they perform. The problems is, while there are ways to assess parts of the budget by these criteria, there are no agreed upon standards for determining its overall efficiency and effectiveness.

The Political Realities of the Budget

Besides wanting the programs that benefit them, many members of the public believe that the budget should be assembled based on what's "best for the state" or what's "right" or "fair" to produce the "best" public policies possible.

But these criteria are all values—they are in the eye of the beholder. Consequently, people disagree and conflict over the criteria that should determine the budget, and thus its contents to produce the "best public policies."

These disagreements and conflicts dictate that the only way to resolve them, to develop the budget, is through political means. Consequently, the budget is a political document put together by a political process. This involves transactions, compromise, often major conflicts, where the final outcome depends largely on how much power the contending parties can bring to bear.

Even so, politicians who support a budget often claim it's "in the best interests of the state" to demonstrate their strong commitment to all Alaskans. They also often argue that it's "good" public policy. Those who oppose all or parts of that budget, will likely argue that it only helps special interests, and is "bad" public policy. Box 4.2, on the next page, shows how the interests of politicians shape the budget.

The State Budget

The Budget is also a Policy Statement

The budget is first and foremost a political document—the most important policy statement in state government.

As development of the budget is based on politics, in effect, it's a policy statement. It sets out what government intends to do and how much is allocated to each item. Another aspect of this policy is indicated by what parts of existing programs and services will receive less funds. And, by implication, what government doesn't intend to do because these items are not included in the budget.

These decisions reflect contemporary politics. They are shaped by the policy goals of those officials and other influences—particularly the majority caucus in the House and Senate, the governor, interest groups and the federal government—who wield power at the time.

BOX 4.2
THE INTERESTS OF POLITICIANS AND THE BUDGET

As in many aspects of politics, in writing the budget it's important to watch what politicians do, not what they say. We can see this by reflecting further on Karen Rehfeld's quote.

Likely most politicians, both governors and particularly legislators, have a general desire for the budget to reflect the reality of needs and available revenues.

Yet, when it comes to specifics and a politician's best interests, in many cases, these criteria are subordinated to political benefit. Their major considerations will be: does a program reward their supporters; help their constituents; aid their re-election; give a boost to their desire for higher office; or promote their ideological goals; among other things.

As a result, other than the governor, a commitment to act in the "best interests of the state" goes out of the window. Instead, the budget is littered with all sorts of expenditures that are of dubious value to Alaska. They may even be to the detriment of the state, but are good politics for those who secured them.

4. COMPONENTS OF THE BUDGET

The major parts of the budget are the operating budget and the capital budget, which make up the bulk of the state's spending plan for the fiscal year. There is also a separate budget for the Alaska Mental Health Trust Authority, which includes operating and capital funds; but we don't consider that budget in this handbook.

The operating budget gets priority of available revenues because it covers necessary and on-going expenditures. Next comes money required to match federal payments, so the state can receive these for various programs. The funds that are left go to the capital budget, which varies in size depending on available revenues. Each year the governor also presents a bill for supplementary cost overruns for the last fiscal year, and to reappropriate funds not spent.

5. THE YEAR-ROUND BUDGET PROCESS

Because the media tend to focus on the budget during the legislative session, it is easy to get the impression that the only time the budget is dealt with is during that time.

In fact, the budget process goes on year-round. Its consideration by the legislature is only a part of the process, and in many ways not the most important influence on the outcome of the size and allocations within the budget.

For the first six months—July to mid-December—the budget is assembled by the governor and the administration. It's not until December 15 that the governor issues the budget for the legislature and the public to see. Then, the budget is considered by the legislature during the session (and perhaps in a special session). Following this, it goes to the governor for his or her consideration. The governor may approve parts of it and reduce or eliminate other expenditure by using the line item veto.

The State Budget

6. THE BUDGET CYCLE AND THE BUDGET CALENDAR

At any one time, the state is dealing with budgets for three fiscal years. For example, in October 2018, it was auditing the funds spent in FY18 (July 1, 2017 thru June 30, 2018). It was spending FY19 funds (July 1, 2018 thru June 30, 2019), and putting together the budget for upcoming FY20 (July 1, 2019 thru June 30, 2020).

Because budget years overlap, the process is best understood as a cycle repeating itself year after year. Box 4.3 illustrates the typical state annual budget cycle. Box 4.4, on the following pages, shows the month-by-month involvement in the process by both the executive and the legislature. Even though it's not until December that the legislature begins to consider it, when it's being put together individual legislators often work to get their projects into the budget.

7. THE MAJOR PUBLIC OFFICIALS AND AGENCIES INVOLVED IN THE BUDGET

Because of its crucial importance, all legislators and senior members of the executive branch are concerned with the budget and participate in its development. There are, however, some key individuals who are particularly involved with the budget.

The chairs of the House and Senate Finance Committees are not only major influences on the budget, but on all legislation.

The Office of Management and Budget—OMB

To aid in putting together and shepherding the budget through the legislature, monitor its implementation, and evaluate its effectiveness, governors appoint a Director of the Office of Management and Budget (OMB), who serves at the will of the governor. OMB is part of the Governor's Office and has a staff of analysts to aid the director.

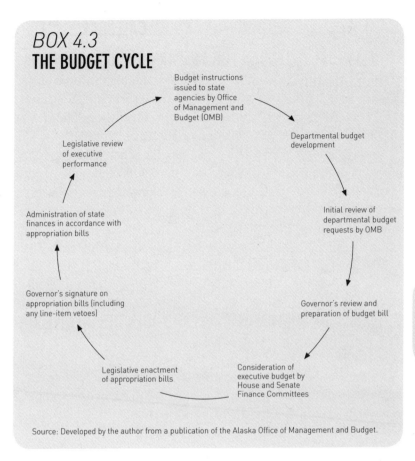

BOX 4.3
THE BUDGET CYCLE

Budget instructions issued to state agencies by Office of Management and Budget (OMB)

Departmental budget development

Legislative review of executive performance

Initial review of departmental budget requests by OMB

Administration of state finances in accordance with appropriation bills

Governor's signature on appropriation bills (including any line-item vetoes)

Governor's review and preparation of budget bill

Legislative enactment of appropriation bills

Consideration of executive budget by House and Senate Finance Committees

Source: Developed by the author from a publication of the Alaska Office of Management and Budget.

The State Budget

The Legislature

In the legislature, the chairs (often co-chairs) of the House and Senate Finance Committees and their Committee members are key participants in the budget process. Some committee members chair subcommittees on parts of the budget, such as transportation and education. All members of the House and Senate finance committees are influential legislators.

Aiding the legislature with the budget is the Legislative Finance Division. The Division conducts research, fiscal analyses, and budget reviews at the request of the House and Senate Finance Committees.

BOX 4.4
THE ANNUAL CALENDAR FOR PREPARING AND APPROVING THE STATE BUDGET

MONTH	EXECUTIVE BRANCH ACTIVITY	LEGISLATIVE BRANCH ACTIVITY
July	1. Record new budget authorization from fiscal year just ended. 2. Begin closeout of past fiscal year.	1. Legislative audit review of prior year's budget activity commences based upon federal audit requirements and legislative priorities. This activity continues throughout the year.
August	1. Closeout past fiscal year. 2. Develop interagency payment rates (e.g., for computer services) for upcoming fiscal year for use in budget preparation.	
September	1. Begin development of budget request for upcoming fiscal year. Identify needs and priorities. 2. OMB budget instructions issued.	1. Legislative Budget and Audit meets to consider audits and authorization of new federal revenues. LB&A meets as needed throughout the year.
October	1. Agencies negotiate budget requests with OMB and the governor. 2. Develop expenditure projections for current year and quantify any prospective supplemental appropriations needed.	
November	1. Complete budget documentation. 2. Fall revenue forecast made public.	
December	1. Public release of governor's proposed budget for upcoming fiscal year.	1. Legislative finance staff begin budget review.
January	1. Appropriation bills prepared and introduced in legislature for governor's proposed budget. 2. Governor usually makes State of the Budget address to legislature. 3. Agency presentations made to legislature. 4. Supplemental requests and budget amendments are prepared for OMB's review and approval.	1. Legislative overview analysis and budget details published for use by legislative committees in reviewing the governor's proposals. 2. Legislative subcommittee hearings begin. 3. Veto overrides considered/taken up by the fifth day of the second legislative session for bills passes in the first session. Attempts to override a veto can also be made in the interim between the first and second sessions of the legislature. .
February	1. Supplemental requests introduced in legislature by the 15th legislative day of the session. 2. Budget amendments introduced by 30th legislative day.	1. Finance subcommittees develop recommendations for action by full finance committees for appropriation levels. 2. Full finance committee review begins.

The State Budget

MONTH	EXECUTIVE BRANCH ACTIVITY	LEGISLATIVE BRANCH ACTIVITY
March	1. Agencies lobby for proposed budget. 2. Agencies and OMB respond to legislative requests for information.	1. Legislative budget development continues. 2. Both House and Senate pass versions of the budget. 3. Conference committee appointed/meets.
April	1. Agencies continue lobbying for proposed budget.	1. Conference committee concludes work on budget and presents it to both bodies for concurrence. 2. All other appropriation measures (e.g., capital, supplementals, reappropriations) approved by legislature.
May	1. Review appropriation bills and recommend final action (veto/reduce/approve) by governor. 2. Governor takes final action on legislation.	1. Transmit passed budget bills to governor.
June	1. Establish necessary accounting entries to record new budget authorizations. 2. Conclude spending for current fiscal year. 3. Establish encumbrances for outstanding financial obligations.	
During Legislative Interim, May–December	1. The governor may call a special legislative session to deal with specific issues, including budget items.	1. The legislature may call a special session to consider overriding a governor's veto or vetoes, including budget items.

Source: Developed by the author from a publication of the Alaska Office of Mangement and Budget.

The State Budget

There is also the Legislative Budget and Audit Committee (LB&A), a permanent interim committee which monitors the budget during that time. It's composed of five members from each house.

8. STATE REVENUES

Not all the money in Alaska's budget is raised by the state itself. Some funds in both the operating and capital budget come from the federal government. Its contribution ranges from 15-25 percent. In fiscal year FY15, for example, of the total state budget of $13.8 billion, $3 billion, about 20 percent, came from the feds. These funds included operating expenditures, such as aid for disabled students, and capital expenditures, including those for roads and harbors.

Alaska's Unbalanced and Unpredictable Revenues

Virtually all states have balanced sources of revenue, the bulk of which comes from a combination of a state income tax on individuals and businesses, and/or a statewide sales tax. Their revenues are stable in most years, so they can plan with a high degree of certainty because they know the funds will be available.

The State's Major Source of Revenue Available for Spending

By contrast, Alaska has only two sources of revenue it raises by itself. These are from oil and gas taxes and royalties; and investment income that come mainly from the Permanent Fund. In recent years, investment income has been greater than oil revenues.

Other than investment earning used to pay the Permanent Fund Dividend (PFD), investment income is deposited in a special account, not into the state's general fund. It's not available for general spending as part of the state budget, unless the legislature decides to appropriate some of it to pay for state services, which it has in recent years.

As the only state with no individual income tax or statewide sales tax, and with investment income generally unavailable for spending, the bulk of state revenues come from oil and gas taxes and royalties. This has been the case since the Alaska pipeline came on tap in 1978. Depending on the year, between 80 and 90 percent (an average of about 85 percent) of revenue the state raises itself comes from oil and gas. Box 4.5 shows Alaska's state revenues compared to the fifty-state average.

Unpredictable Revenues

While Alaska has some control over the level of oil production in the state, it has no control over the price of oil, which is determined by world markets. The volatility of these markets has resulted in oil

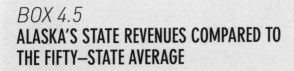

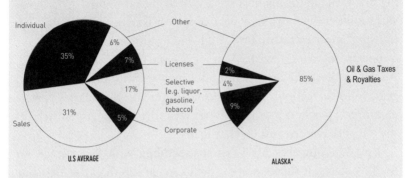

U.S AVERAGE

ALASKA*

* Does not include earnings from the Permanent Fund.
Source: Developed by the author from information provided by the Alaska Department of Revenue and the Council of State Governments.

The State Budget

prices fluctuating widely, and with them Alaska's revenues. In turn, this has resulted in periodic fluctuations, sometimes major ones, in the size of the state budget since the late 1970s.

Consequently, unlike other states, Alaska can't always be sure it'll have the money to pay for many of its programs and services. For instance, after the price of oil took a dive in mid-2014, for several years, the state had less revenue than it needed to cover its expenses. It had to draw money— $2 to $3 billion a year—from the Constitutional Budget Reserve (CBR) to make ends meet.

The state's failure to deal with the often financially debilitating relationship between oil prices and state revenues, means that the ups and downs in oil prices will, in some way or another, affect your lobbying effort.

Since Alaska became dependent on oil for over 80 percent of its revenues, the price has fluctuated from $15 in 1978, to an average of $60 in 2018, with a high of $148 in 2009, and a low of $11 in 1998.

9. STATE SPENDING

The three largest chunks of the budget go to education (K-12 and the university), social services (including financial aid for medical services—Medicaid—and various other types of aid to low income Alaskans); and transportation infrastructure (highways, harbors and airports). Together these account for over 60 percent of state outlays. Added to these are an array of additional expenditures, including: police and corrections; aid to local governments; the salaries of state employees; pension payments to retirees (the fourth largest item in the budget): and interest on state loans.

Box 4.6 compares Alaska's state spending with the average for the fifty states. It shows Alaska spends much less than the fifty state average on education and social services (the latter likely due to the conservative nature of the state); but much more on highways, due to higher costs and receiving more federal aid than any other state.

Alaska has been politically incapable of developing a stable revenue stream. Consequently, the state lurches from budget crisis to budget crisis.

10. STATE POLITICS AND BUDGET POLITICS

These, then, are the basics of the budget process and some of the factors that influence it. Like the overview of the formal organization of state government in the last chapter, this descriptive information provides a foundation for understanding how the policy process works.

As developing a budget is the most important function of state government, the budget process and the politics that surround it are the most important factors shaping

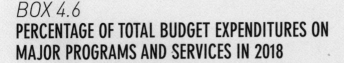

BOX 4.6
PERCENTAGE OF TOTAL BUDGET EXPENDITURES ON MAJOR PROGRAMS AND SERVICES IN 2018

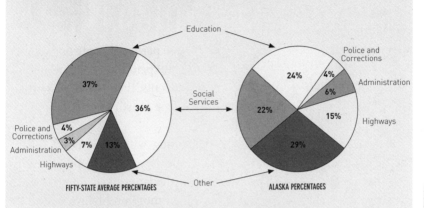

FIFTY-STATE AVERAGE PERCENTAGES   ALASKA PERCENTAGES

Source: Developed by the author from information provided by the Alaska Department of Revenue and the Council of State Governments.

Alaska politics and policy-making. For this reason, we refer to the politics surrounding the budget at several places in this book, and devote Chapter 8 to how it might affect your lobbying effort.

Despite constant calls to cut the budget, and some cuts in lean revenue years, spending almost always increases when revenues are high. Consequently, as in all states, the state budget has steadily increased over the years, and is likely to continue to do so.

The State Budget

THIS CHAPTER COVERS

1. Common Aspects of the Psychology of Public Officials

2. Legislators

3. Legislative Staff

4. The Governor

5. The Governor's Staff

6. Bureaucrats

7. Alaska's Congressional Delegation and Federal Employees

8. Lobbyists

9. The Implications for You

★ CHAPTER 5 ★

Delving into the Mindset
and Roles of Policy-Makers

*You've got to get inside the mind of politicians and bureaucrats
if you want to deal with them effectively.*

—Senator Johnny Ellis,
Member of the Alaska Legislature,
1987-2016

This chapter delves into the psychology of policy-makers, their roles, and operating styles. Even among public officials with similar jobs, such as legislators, there are different ways in which they approach their job. All this is important to know for your lobbying effort.

1. COMMON ASPECTS OF THE PSYCHOLOGY OF PUBLIC OFFICIALS

Elected and appointed officials and others involved in the policy process, vary in their motives, needs, and goals, depending on their job or the way they need to relate to other policy-makers. That said, there are common aspects of their mindset. These are:

- Motivation and policy focus.

- Problem solving.

- Loyalty.

- Job security.

- A shortage of time, power, and information.

Motivation and Policy Focus

Elected and appointed officials often claim to be in public office primarily for the betterment of the people and for the state. Certainly, this may be an important motive, and many are committed to the public good. But many seek public office because it gives them personal satisfaction, as well as the chance to work on issues they care about. Most of them also enjoy the recognition and status of being a governor, legislator, or department head, and in a position to wield some influence.

Elected state officials must deal with a broad range of concerns. Even for governors, with their large staff, and certainly for legislators, time does not permit them becoming conversant with all issues. This is even more the case for Alaska's congressional delegation.

Consequently, legislators tend to specialize in issues that interest them and affect their constituents. Some are interested in many policy issues. Others are more narrowly focused.

Still others are enamored with the competitiveness and wheeling-and-dealing of politics, relying on their staff, trusted fellow legislators, and sometimes lobbyists, for information and direction, and sometimes on how to vote.

State department officials are primarily interested in their department's area of policy, unless the governor directs them otherwise.

A Problem-Solving State of Mind

A large part of any public official's day is taken up with solving problems. Some of these involve dealing with major political conflicts between the legislative majorities and the governor, between the majority and minority, between legislators and senior administrators, among others. These often involve negotiation, clashes of power, and compromise.

But not all problems are major or political. Legislators and their staff deal with a myriad of constituent concerns and requests. For the governor, these problems include a host of challenges regarding the day-to-day operations of the state. For a commissioner it is the many challenges of administering a department.

Whether major or minor, problems are a constant in the professional lives of public officials. Consciously or subconsciously, they are continually in a problem-solving state of mind. They spend a lot of time trying to anticipate problems that may arise and how they might be solved.

Some are better at problem-solving than others, which, in part, is why some are better politicians than others. Understanding the problem-solving aspect of the mindset of public officials, tells a lot about how they may approach a situation, and how they may react when you seek their help.

Loyalty

The maneuvering, transactions, and ultimately compromise involves keeping political cards close to the chest. Consequently, loyalty (trustworthiness), is a prized commodity to public officials.

Legislators, governors, and senior appointed officials, couldn't advance many of their goals if their staff and others they deal with in the rough-and-tumble of the process were not loyal. In the case of staffers, this means always putting the interests of their boss first and protecting his or her interests. This requires tight lips and wariness of those trying to pry information to use for their own advantage. To be disloyal by betraying trust, is one of the worst sins a staffer or other person involved in a political maneuver can commit. If they do it often, it will likely destroy their reputation.

To ensure those working for them will be loyal, public officials hire staff they know and trust. Unless they have assurance from a trusted colleague or other confidant, that someone they don't know

The Policy-Makers

is trustworthy, there's too great a risk in hiring them. Most policy-makers prize loyalty over intelligence or knowledge of the issues of the policy process.

As Alex Miller, a prominent Alaska lobbyist in the years after statehood, told Governor Bill Sheffield after a few of his appointees had let him down: "Sheffield, there's a lot of smart people, but just hire the loyal ones—you can make 'em smart once they're working for you."

Job Security

Job security is a major concern to most policy-makers. For legislators this means getting re-elected, unless they're retiring. If he or she is in their first term, this is also likely a major concern of a governor. Legislative and governors' staff, who serve at the will of their bosses, are interested in keeping their positions too. Job security is also a major concern of senior

> **Job security is the major goal that motivates almost all elected and appointed officials.**

appointed personnel in the executive branch who can be fired at will, including commissioners, deputy commissioners, division directors, special assistants, and legislative liaisons.

Campaign Contributions

An important part of elected officials keeping their jobs is raising funds and finding volunteers to help get them elected or re-elected. Those who help often have the ear of that politician who will push their issues much more than those who stayed on the sidelines.

For fear of appearing mercenary and self-serving, very few politicians admit that financial contributions influence their actions. But they do. Anyone who's been around politics for a while knows this for a fact. It's only natural that those who support them will influence their actions in some way. To ignore their contributors would likely put their re-election in jeopardy.

A Shortage of Time, Power, and Information

The ever-present shortage of time, power, and information shapes the thinking of policy-makers. Even governors have a serious shortage of time. Plus, no public official has all the power they need, and the information they have, both factual and political, is always incomplete.

These three shortages force public officials to make decisions on how they operate. They can focus on certain issues and less on others; prioritize their time in meeting with people—with whom to meet and for how long. Still another choice is to use their power sparingly. For a public official, power is like money in the bank—every time they use some they have less to use.

To get more complete information than their staff can provide on an issue, legislators seek it from other reliable sources. These includes: other public officials; the legislature's research services; lobbyists; constituents; and various written sources, as well as social media.

2. LEGISLATORS

In addition to the general points on the mindset of public officials in general, what makes legislators tick politically?

Legislators as Individuals: A Microcosm of Human Nature

The public tends to think of legislators generically as "legislators," as if they all have a common mindset—cut from the same cloth in doing their job as representatives. On the contrary, like all of us, each has their own personal characteristics and approach to their job.

Personality and Style

Generally, legislators are affable and approachable people. Yet, they run the gamut from the hardworking to the lazy, the self-effacing and honest, to the down-home glad-hander, to the aloof, self-important,

> *However different legislators are in personal and professional style, even though most deny it, they have one thing in common—big egos. Some wear their egos on their forehead, with others it's not so obvious.*

and arrogant. And with everyone trying to get a piece of their time, and often paying them deference, it's not surprising some legislators have big egos.

It takes a particular type of person to run for public office—less than one percent of Americans ever do. Very few of us are willing to campaign and expose ourselves to public scrutiny every two or four years and, in effect, ask, "Hey, am I popular?" Legislators are in a political fish bowl for their time in office, also something most of us wouldn't want.

In terms of style and ambition, many legislators are low profile, and serve their constituents well. They have no ambitions except to rise through the ranks only as far as necessary to serve their districts. Others seek legislative leadership positions as stepping-stones to higher state or federal office.

Political Perspectives

Legislators' political perspectives or ideology often play an important role in their mindset, and shape their approach to issues, and those who have influence over them. These perspectives fall into three main categories:

- Conservative legislators want to create a positive environment for business, cut the budget, reduce the cost of government, and make government smaller, because they perceive it as wasteful. Unless, of course, spending money benefits their constituents and, consequently, their re-election.

- Liberals see government as a valuable means for aiding the less fortunate and promoting the "public interest."

The Policy-Makers

- Centrists and moderates combine parts of the conservative and liberal perspective, and are generally more pragmatic and transactional in their approach to political issues. They are often the facilitators of compromise.

But a common feature of the Alaska legislature is bipartisanship. To some extent this reflects the low level of partisanship among the electorate. Political ideology is not as important among many legislators in Alaska as in other states, particularly those from rural-bush areas.

Their Job Description

Legislators have one of the broadest of all job descriptions: to "represent" their constituents, the "public interest," and "the interests of the state." But what is and what is not representation, in the public interest, and the interests of the state, are subject to wide interpretation. Consequently, legislators have jobs with few boundaries. All see their jobs as primarily representing their constituents. But legislators have various approaches on how best to represent those who elected them.

One group sees representing constituents as paramount—subordinating it to all other considerations all the time. These are, more or less, ciphers of their constituents, invariably voting to reflect the majority will in their districts, which means the most vocal constituents.

By contrast, others see themselves as more informed than their constituents on most issues. These legislators make judgments based on the information available and, where possible, try to balance the interests of their districts with those of the state.

Given these different and justifiable approaches, who is and who is not a "good legislator" is largely in the eye of the beholder.

3. LEGISLATIVE STAFF

In effect, the job description and major goal of legislative staff, often called staffers or aides, is "to make their boss look good"; but in doing so, not to undermine their boss's principles. It involves helping their boss to be successful in all they do. This is important because aides can be fired at will. Staffers have various reasons for working in the legislature. Box 5.1 sets out the most prominent ones.

Staff personalities vary widely. Some are low-key, hard-working people who want to get the job done, are pleasant and easy to deal with. Others have big egos. Some see themselves as surrogate legislators and like to wield the power they have (or like to think they have). Some legislators give more leeway to their staff than others. This, in turn, may affect how staffers act and deal with people, which will affect the way the office operates and the tone it conveys.

BOX 5.1
WHY LEGISLATIVE STAFF ARE STAFFERS

One group is young people just out of college interested in politics. They want experience to figure out what to do next in life. They often work on campaigns to get their legislators elected, and their job is a "reward" for this work.

A second group is "career staffers" who may be political junkies and often strong Republicans or Democrats; though they may also be doing it for the good pay. These are frequently older staffers who've been around the legislature for years, and have worked for the same legislator, or just two or three of the same political party.

The third group is "career political operatives." These are also older and have been around state government for years. They may be a staffer because of an interest in politics, or see it as a phase in their careers.

Being paid a high salary, due to seniority, is likely their most important consideration—it's a way of making a living. A few don't display partisan loyalties and are willing to work for Republicans or Democrats. Some career staffers move between the executive and the legislature as administrations change. Many have held high positions in the governor's office, for a department or agency, as well as having been a chief of staff for one or more legislators.

4. THE GOVERNOR

Several specific factors shape a governor's thinking and approach to the job. The four most important, which are interrelated, are:

- Partisanship, political values, and pragmatism.

- Promoting statewide policy goals.

- Policy goals and rewarding campaign contributors.

- Personal and professional background.

Partisanship, Political Values, and Pragmatism

Other than Bill Walker (an independent), all Alaska's governors have been Republicans or Democrats. However, because of the minor role parties play in policy-making, for most governors, parties and their platforms have limited significance as part of their mindset and how they operate.

Political Perspectives and Pragmatism

More important are their political values; though some of their policies may reflect party positions, as with Governors Murkowski and Parnell. Politically, it's most accurate to see governors on a spectrum from conservative to liberal, rather than Republicans or Democrats. They are rarely at one end or the other, but usually left or right of center. This was true of Governors Egan, Hammond, Cowper, and Walker and, to a large extent, Governors Sheffield, Knowles, and even Governor Hickel. But less so with governors Murkowski and Parnell, both very conservative, and Governor Dunleavy, a strong conservative, with libertarian tendencies.

Like most legislators, of political necessity, most governors aren't die-hard Republican or Democrats, but in the political center. They emphasize pragmatism over ideology.

The Policy-Makers

What draws most governors to the center is the need to compromise with legislators and others involved in policy making. As with all elected officials, a major, if not the major, aspect of a governor's political mindset is the need to be pragmatic and conclude political transactions to get at least some of what they want.

Promoting Statewide Policy Goals

A statewide responsibility is part of the governor's political mindset. In some circumstances, they must also balance statewide with regional and local interests. This ever-present statewide perspective leads governors to ask those lobbying them: "How will this benefit the state?"

Many legislators also have a perspective on what's best for the state, but they frequently subordinate this to the interests of their districts (in some cases also their region), and what benefits their political futures. This statewide versus local perspective is often a source of conflict between the governor and legislators.

Policy Goals and Rewarding Campaign Contributors

Candidates for governor have a range of policies they promise to implement. If elected, these policy goals influence the actions they pursue in Juneau, much of which is reflected in their budget proposals each year. These goals are also a factor influencing who the governor hires as personal staff, to head state agencies, and to serve as members of boards and commissions.

Over the past thirty years, running for governor has cost $5-10 million. This means fundraising and assistance from volunteers is a major part of a campaign. Consequently, once in office, governors reward these people in a completely legal way. Rewards include: political appointments; pursuing the policies favored by his or her supporters, which are often the governor's own policies; and giving priority consideration to individuals and interest groups who endorsed them. Rewarding supporters is clearly an advantage if a governor is eligible and wants to be re-elected.

Personal and Professional Background

Personal experience and occupation influence how governors see the political world and, in part, shape their policy priorities.

Governor Sheffield, a very successful hotelier, wanted to run government like a business. Governor Hammond, a rural resident and fisherman, favored a balance between development and conservation. Governor Parnell, a lawyer who'd worked for the oil industry, advocated lowering oil company taxes to increase development. Governor Walker, also a lawyer, with a long-standing interest in a gas pipeline as a complement to the oil pipeline, made building a gas line a major policy focus of his administration.

They Are Who They Are

In combination, all four aspects of a governor's mindset, personal and professional background, shape who they are and how they approach their job. Like legislators, no two governors are alike. Understanding what makes a governor tick is essential in dealing with them.

5. THE GOVERNOR'S STAFF

The major role of the governor's staff is to aid in implementing his or her policy agenda. Like legislative staff, they need to make their boss look good, partly because they are also employees at will. These staff members likely have similar motives, needs, and goals as legislative staff. Many were campaign workers, are professional associates, or personal friends. In some cases, they are fiercely loyal to their boss and strongly committed to his or her agenda because they see it as the best way to make life better for all Alaskans.

Four members of the staff are particularly important to the governor. Their role and mindset are explained in Box 5.2 on the next page.

The Policy-Makers

BOX 5.2
FOUR KEY STAFF IN THE GOVERNOR'S OFFICE

The Chief of Staff

This is the governor's right-hand person. They have many roles: boss of the office staff; liaison to all cabinet members; policy executor: negotiator: arbiter: advisor: protector; and administrator. Each role changes constantly, depending on the day of the week, current events, and the chief's relationship with the governor. Typically, the governor delivers the good news to the public, legislators, and constituents; the chief handles everything else.

With all their responsibilities and major time constraints, the chief is not someone you should contact in the early stages of your campaign. If necessary and appropriate, he or she may get involved with your issue at a later stage.

The Legislative Director

For most governors, the legislative director is an important conduit, often a pivotal force, in the all-important relationship between the governor and the legislature. Because of their role, most directors have previous experience in the legislature and often in state agencies.

The director's main job is to deal with issues, policies, and legislation of concern to the governor and the legislature, to produce harmony between them. Therefore, the director is conversant with a wide range of issues and the governor's positions on them. With this knowledge, and depending on their availability, the director can be very useful to you.

Special Staff Assistants

The governor's special staff assistants deal with various policy areas, such as rural affairs, natural resources, and human services. They work on bills in their policy areas as they affect the governor's agenda. Usually, they work through the legislative director in relaying information to legislative offices. Special assistants also interact with departments and other state agencies, lobbyists, interest groups, and the public.

The number of special assistants varies from governor to governor. Some have several, covering most policy areas, as set out in Box 3.3 in Chapter 3. The drop in oil revenues in the summer of 2014 led incoming governor Bill Walker to hire fewer special assistants. Instead, he used general-purpose policy advisors, and department commissioners as sources of information, and facilitators with the legislature and state agencies.

Depending on the rules set by the governor as to who can talk to whom outside the office, special assistants can be a valuable source of information for you.

The Director of the Office of Management and Budget—OMB

The OMB director works with the governor's staff and agency personnel to develop the state budget from early July to December 15 when the governor presents the budget to the legislature. The director also monitors the budget as it proceeds through the legislature, frequently testifying to legislative committees. Once the legislature passes the budget, the director works with the governor to determine which proposed expenditures might be approved, reduced in amount, or vetoed.

OMB has a staff of specialists who deal with particular aspects of the budget. These, together with the director, can be a valuable source of information, and are often lobbied to include items in the budget. But in most cases, neither the director nor the staff has the authority to make budget decisions. These ultimately come from the governor.

6. BUREAUCRATS

Those working in various state departments, boards and commissions, and other agencies, are of two types: political appointees; and permanent employees.

The Policy-Makers

Appointed Officials

These include commissioners, deputy commissioners and some heads of boards and commissions, as well as division directors, deputy directors, and legislative liaisons. All are appointed by the governor and can be fired at will.

Commissioners and Deputy Commissioners

Technically, two department heads are exceptions to the rule that the governor appoint commissioners. These are the commissioners of the Department of Education and the Department of Fish and Game, who are appointed by boards. In practice, however, governors have a lot of say in hiring and firing these commissioners. The major reasons why governors chose the people they do as commissioners, deputy commissions, and other senior agency personnel, are set out in Box 5.3.

Not all those who fill these positions are from the same party as the governor. One thing they all have in common, however, is that their major task is to aid in implementing the governor's agenda.

Motives and Job Focus: Commissioners and deputy commissioners have a variety or a combination of reasons for accepting the governor's offer of a job. These range from the desire to have a positive impact on a public policy issue they care about, to the prestige of the

BOX 5.3
HOW SENIOR DEPARTMENT AND AGENCY PERSONNEL GET THEIR JOB

- They helped elect the governor. This could be having made, and perhaps encouraging others to make, major financial contributions; being a strong supporter in other ways, such as their endorsement as a prominent Alaskan; or having been a major campaign worker.

- They are loyal friends or long-time associates of the governor.

These first two types of appointees may or may not know much about the department, board, or commission they are selected to head.

- They are technical experts in their field. For example, a Commissioner of Corrections having experience in prison administration; a Commissioner of Public Safety with a background in law enforcement; a Commissioner of Labor with experience in union management or labor issues.

- They are prominent elected or appointed officials from state or local government, business, or Alaska Native corporations, who are known quantities to the governor, and likely to be loyal.

office, to using their appointment as a stepping stone to elected state or federal office, or a senior management position in business.

Most are hard-working and well informed about the range of activities, issues, and politics affecting their department or agency. Others are less interested in the big picture, leaving the details to the permanent staff, and focus on a few major issues. Over the years, some have proven lazy, uninvolved, uninformed, and often incompetent. Likely, these appointees lobbied the governor hard to get the job, mainly for its prestige.

Besides working to implement the governor's agenda, most top political appointees have major issues they want to deal with. This may shape the role and focus of their department or agency while they are in office.

A reality most political appointees face is that they are in office for a limited time: usually just the life of an administration. This could be less if they make a major mistake that gets bad press, or they get at odds with the governor in some other way.

A Major Challenge: Even commissioners with previous experience in the field, have a steep learning curve to get to know the functioning and politics of their department or agency. This means they must rely on the permanent staff, whose tenures transcend administrations, for information and aid in achieving the administration's goals.

This gives the permanent staff significant influence in advancing that agenda; or in some cases, if indirectly and subtlety, thwarting it. One of the major complaints of past and present administration political appointees is the difficulty of herding the permanent employees in the direction necessary to achieve the governor's agenda.

Division Directors

These, and deputy directors, fill key positions in the day-to-day operation of their departments. They are important decision-makers in the technical administration of their divisions and need to be politically savvy. Division directors are often the target of lobbyists, constituent groups, and others with an interest in their division's

Legislative liaisons, division directors, and deputy directors, are key people a lobbyist should get to know for dealing with state agencies.

jurisdiction and activities. This may include working to get funds into the division's budget for a specific project, or providing input into writing regulations. Division directors frequently deal with legislators and their staff, including presenting testimony to legislative committees.

Legislative Liaisons

As facilitators of information between their departments and the legislature, the governor's office, and other state agencies, department legislative liaisons must always be on top of virtually all issues affecting their agencies.

Much of a legislative liaison's job involves advocating for their department or agency. In effect, they are a type of lobbyist, though not officially considered as such. Their role in this regard is considered later in Box 5.4, which covers the four types of lobbyists.

Permanent Employees

These do the day-to-day work of the departments, boards, and commissions. They are nonpartisan and have specific job descriptions, which determine their role and how they go about doing their job.

Permanent employees include: some deputy and assistant division directors; specialists, such as scientists; and those in information technology, finance, and personnel. Most have specific qualifications, extensive training in their professional area, or managerial experience. Besides keeping their positions to make a living, they are primarily concerned with performing their job as professionals or semi-professionals.

The Policy-Makers

State Agencies and Your Lobbying Effort

As a lobbyist, you need to understand the role of an agency or agencies and the key personnel who can help or hinder you. It's particularly important to be aware of the politics that may exist between an agency, other agencies, the legislature, and the governor's office.

While division directors, deputy directors and legislative liaisons, can provide factual and political information, in some cases they may be less forthcoming. This is where a contact network, which includes those knowledgeable about the politics of the department, will be invaluable.

7. ALASKA'S CONGRESSIONAL DELEGATION AND FEDERAL EMPLOYEES

Likely you'll need to have little, if any, contact with Alaska's Congressional delegation. But if your issue directly involves federal agencies, or might at some point in Alaska or Washington, D.C., some knowledge of the delegation and federal employees is useful.

The Congressional Delegation

The motives and goals of Alaska's two U.S. Senators and sole Representative are likely similar to other politicians regarding public service and seeking re-election. They are often particularly mindful of the ambitions of state politicians and others who might have an eye on their seat.

Balancing State and National Issues

All three must balance the regional and general interests of the state with the national interest. But their primary goal is to get as much for Alaska as they can and protect the state's existing benefits. Consequently, their national perspective on many issues is colored by how they affect the state. The delegation has considerable influence

The Policy-
Makers

Since the early 1980, Alaska's Congressional delegation has been politically conservative, pro-development, less supportive of environmental and other liberal causes, and receive major campaign contributions from out of state.

on federal policies that affect the state. These include: land issues: federal funds: and regulation by federal agencies and other bodies, like the North Pacific Fishery Management Council (NPFMC).

The Influence of Campaign Funds

It costs a lot to get elected to Congress. So all three members are constantly fundraising for the next election. Senator Lisa Murkowski spent just under $10 million for her races in 2010 and 2016. In 2014, incumbent Mark Begich spent close to $30 million and lost. It even costs over $1 million to run for Alaska's single House seat.

Some campaign money comes from Alaska, but much from out of state. Out of state contributions come mainly from interests who see Alaska's delegation as furthering their cause as the delegation works to benefit their Alaska constituents. As predominantly Republican and conservative, a major goal of the delegation has been to promote development. As a result, most of their in-state and out-of-state financial contributions come from development interests.

Federal Employees

Career bureaucrats in federal departments and agencies have a professional mindset like Alaska's career bureaucrats. Foremost among these are job security and an approach to their job shaped by professional training and responsibilities within their organization.

Yet, even those based in Alaska have a national perspective as opposed to an Alaska-centric view, because their prime responsibility is to implement their agency's mission. Often, this involves federal

The Policy-Makers

employees working with Alaska agency personnel. This includes: aiding in complying with federal laws and regulations; and working on various joint federal-state responsibilities, such as aspects of air and water policy, fisheries, and land management.

Federal-State Personnel Antagonisms

Generally, however, federal employees, including senior agency officials, keep to themselves and rarely interact with state politicians. Most legislators have never had an Alaska-based federal bureaucrat contact them in their professional capacity.

Certainly not always, but some interactions between federal and state agency personnel are antagonistic. This often results when federal policy conflicts with state policy or goals, and federal agencies are heavy-handed in implementing regulations. These include joint responsibilities with the state, or a federal agency simply ignores the state in dealing with issues that affect Alaska—a sort of "Alaska be damned" attitude.

Justified or not on the part of Alaskans, this can lead to strained relations between the feds and the state. As a result, many public officials have a negative attitude to the operations of the federal government in Alaska.

8. LOBBYISTS

What all lobbyists have in common is advocating the cause of their group, organization, or client to try to influence government policy in their favor. The tools of their trade are: gathering and presenting information; building contacts and relationships with key public officials; establishing trust and credibility, which includes confidentiality; monitoring activities which affect their cause; and planning and adjusting their strategies and tactics.

Lobbyists vary in the types of organizations they represent, what they can offer policy-makers, and their potential power bases. There

The Policy-
Makers

are, in fact, four types of lobbyists. Box 5.4 identifies these, their backgrounds, and assets as political advocates.

Contract lobbyists, who get the most publicity usually regarding their high fees (though most make modest incomes), make up only about 25 percent of the lobbying community. In-house lobbyists and legislative liaisons both constitute larger percentages, and receive only a salary from the business or organization they represent.

Mindset

Three considerations are foremost in the minds of all lobbyists:

- They look at the policy process and actions by policy-makers through the lens of how it might affect their client, group, or organization's lobbying goals. A lobbyist's mind is geared to perusing and reacting to various developments in working to promote this major goal.

- As contacts are so important on a day-to-day basis, lobbyists work to maintain their contacts and take great pains not to alienate anyone in their network. They never know when they might need a contact.

- Consequently, lobbyists are constantly processing both factual and political information in implementing their strategies and tactics, and adjusting these as circumstances change. Mastery of the facts is an essential foundation for advocating for any cause. Lobbyists need to think politically in the most extensive way to deal with the range of circumstance and power points that affect their issue.

The Pros and Cons of Being a Lobbyist

Another perspective on the mindset of lobbyists is how they view the pros and cons of their job. These views provide insights into why they are lobbyists, what's important to them as political advocates, and how they see the political environment in which they work.

BOX 5.4
THE FOUR TYPES OF LOBBYISTS

Contract Lobbyists

These are hired on a contract (hence their name) for a fee specifically to lobby. Sometimes referred to as "hired guns," they often represent several clients: approximately 20 percent represent five or more. Many are former elected or appointed state officials, usually legislators, political appointees, or legislative staffers. Contract lobbyists constitute about 25 percent of all lobbyists (as defined and explained in Chapter 1, section 1).

Who Hires them and Why?

Contract lobbyists most often represent clients with major stakes in one or more aspects of public policy. Among these are: securing funding; shaping government regulations that can aid or harm their client's business or other operation; reducing taxes; and seeking approval to develop large projects, such as mines and oil and gas facilities.

Their clients include: big business, such as oil and seafood corporations; contractors; liquor and hospitality interests; healthcare interests; telecommunications and utilities; and various local governments. As political insiders, contract lobbyists are hired because:

- They know how the political system works and have close contacts with public officials. This enables them to be pathfinders through the legislative and executive labyrinth.

- They help their clients get what they want, keep them out of political trouble, and get them out of trouble.

- Some have specific knowledge of one or more areas of government operations, such as: the ins-and-outs of the budget; the operation of a department; or a specific aspect of federal policy.

Their Value to Public Officials

Contract lobbyists play four main roles for public officials. They:

- Provide information about their clients and their client's needs.

(continued . . .)

BOX 5.4 *CONTINUED*

- Facilitate meetings and other contacts with clients.

- Are good sources of political information.

- Often help raise election funds by recommending that their clients and others contribute to the campaigns of particular politicians. But there are major restrictions on what lobbyists themselves can contribute to election campaigns.

These four roles, combined with the fact that they usually represent major economic and other interests, is the basis of the influence of contract lobbyists.

In-House Lobbyists

These are employees of an association, organization, or business who act as lobbyists as part or all of their job. They represent one client only—their employer. Most have experience in the profession, business, trade, or other activity they represent, such as education, health care, or banking. They constitute about 30 percent of the lobbying community.

Role and Power Base

In general, they have a narrower political role than contract lobbyists. In-house lobbyists are often viewed by politicians as issue advocates, because they are concerned with only one policy area, such as senior citizens, mining, and commercial fishing. The in-house lobbyist's potential influence lies mainly in:

- Their unequaled knowledge in their policy area.

- The ability to mobilize their members or employees during a lobbying effort.

- Where allowed by a group or organization, by making election campaign contributions in cash and in kind.

Government Lobbyists and Legislative Liaisons

Most state agencies, large local governments, and federal agencies, have one or more legislative liaisons. These are not required to register as lobbyists so it's difficult to assess their numbers. Based on surveys, legislative liaisons likely comprise 20 to 25 percent of the lobbying community.

The Policy-
Makers

Role and Potential Influence

As conduits relaying information and advocating for their agencies or government and reporting back on the reaction to their efforts, the job of a legislative liaison involves:

- Monitoring political activities that may affect their agency or government.

- Dealing with the legislature, the governor's office, and other state agencies.

- In some cases, dealing with local governments, federal agencies, and the governor's office in Washington, D.C.

- Dealing with lobbyists and client groups who have an interest in their agency's area of authority.

State agency liaisons are political appointees, most often career bureaucrats with broad experience in government and in the agency or government they represent. But in contrast to contract and in-house lobbyists, government lobbyists have only one major political asset—information. Though they can, and sometimes do, utilize client groups or constituents to their political advantage.

Citizen, Cause, or Volunteer Lobbyists

These represent citizens' and community organizations or informal groups. Usually they lobby as needed, not regularly, and are unpaid. In most cases, they're not required to register as lobbyists. As is the case with legislature liaisons, it's difficult to determine their numbers. An estimate based on surveys is 10 to 20 percent of the lobbying community.

Lobbying Strengths and Weaknesses

Volunteer lobbyists rely mainly on moral suasion to sell their causes. This can strike a positive chord with a public official who may view them as deeply committed, not just representing their cause for a fee or as part of their job.

These lobbyists may also provide information not available elsewhere.

But cause lobbyists often represent shoestring operations lacking the resources needed for effective lobbying, do not have the status of political insiders, and generally cannot make major campaign contributions.

The Policy-Makers

These perspectives are valuable for anyone considering being a lobbyist, as they summarize the practical realities of what to expect.

A synthesis of the views of over 100 lobbyists is provided in Box 5.5. The ten pros and cons are listed randomly. All lobbyists expressed several of these views.

> *Even though they more or less perform the same functions, there is no typical lobbyist— every one of them has their own personal and professional style.*

Personalities and Styles

The personalities of lobbyists span the range of people in general, but most have some traits in common.

One is being outgoing and personable. Whether this takes the form of the glad-hander or the low-key lobbyist, they need to convey a cordial, approachable, likeable image. After all, it's hard to be nasty to someone who's pleasant and has a positive attitude.

BOX 5.5
TEN PROS AND TEN CONS OF BEING A LOBBYIST

The Pros

1. Being able to make a positive influence on public policy.

2. Helping navigate clients through the "rocks and shoals" of the policy process.

3. Being a political junkie—having an addiction to the rough-and-tumble of politics.

4. The challenge of putting all the parts of the lobbying puzzle together, and getting what you want (or some of it).

The Cons

1. Losing on an issue when you feel passionate about it.

2. Being a punching bag for legislators and some staff; and dealing with arrogant, self-important public officials (mainly the view of some contract lobbyists).

3. Issues do not always get decided on their merits—politics and personal benefit often win out over a needed policy for a group or the public.

The Pros *(continued)*

5. Helping legislators and other public officials deal with their problems, and receiving their gratitude.

6. Working to defeat causes and policies that are objectionable.

7. Being part of a sort of club of political insiders who understand how things work, and being seen as a valuable part of the club.

8. Educating our members and dealing with disagreements to come to a consensus

9. Doing pro bono work for a group, or helping those new to lobbying, to show them how things are done (mainly contract lobbyist said this).

10. The money and the summers off (mainly the view of some contract lobbyists).

The Cons *(continued)*

4. People going back on their word, not keeping confidences, using a lobbyist as a foil.

5. Dealing with the gridlock between the House and Senate is very frustrating, with all the posturing and meaningless political rhetoric.

6. That most people don't understand our job and often express negative attitudes, sometime insulting statements. Much of this is the result of negative press coverage.

7. The craziness of the end of the legislative session when it's hard to see people, to find out what's going on, when tempers often flair, and you wonder if you'll ever get close to what you want.

8. The constant struggle to develop, foster, and nurture relationships.

9. Filling out APOC reports and attending their ethics sessions.

10. Having no family life during the session.

The Policy-Makers

Source: Developed by the author based on interviews with over 150 lobbyists in Alaska, six U.S. states, and fifteen countries between 1972 and 2018.

Ideally, a lobbyist should also be a good communicator, be able to present arguments succinctly, have patience, not be easily riled in conflict situations, or when told "no" by a public official.

Style

Perhaps the most common image of a lobbyist is the backslapping, cigar-chomping, good ol' boy in a polyester suit, who does business in a smoke-filled room, and wines and dines elected officials. Today, the reality is much different.

Certainly, wining and dining is still a part of some lobbyists' way of doing business. Some are "fixers," (making arrangements for politicians and other political operatives, sometimes of a devious nature), and operate as politicos, using— trading in—political more than technical information. Their view of lobbying is: "It's not what you know, but who you know."

While all lobbyists depend on contacts and relationships, recent developments have changed the style of many lobbyists across the states, including in Alaska. These developments include: public disclosure laws; restrictions on campaign spending; and an increase in public officials' levels of education and professional experience.

Most of all, the change is due to the major increase in lobbyists' need for technical knowledge, because of the expansion of government's role over the past fifty years. This has produced a skilled professional, who combines a network of contacts with technical information—a very different breed from the old image of a lobbyist.

Political and Representational Roles

In Washington, D.C. and the more populated states, such as New York and Pennsylvania, the tradition of strong, disciplined Democratic and Republican parties, with one or the other in complete control of the policy agenda, many contract lobbyists openly associate with one of the parties.

The Policy-Makers

By contrast, even though some contract lobbyists help raise money for political parties and their candidates, aligning with a party is much less so in Alaska. Furthermore, many associations, such as the Alaska Municipal League (AML) and the Association of Alaska School Boards (AASB), are bound to political impartiality by their by-laws.

> *Not all lobbyists are equal in the eyes of public officials. Some have good reputations, others mixed ones. A few are seen as sleazy and untrustworthy; but continue to operate because they represent powerful clients or organizations.*

In part, the reason contract lobbyists tend not to openly associate with a political party, is that the power structure in the legislature is usually built around caucuses and not parties. Consequently, there are more minuses than pluses for a contract lobbyist to associate with a party. This gives them the flexibility to play both sides of the political fence in acquiring clients and dealing with elected officials.

Representation of Conservative versus Liberal Causes

Many contract lobbyists represent interests across the board from business groups to local government to non-profits. By contrast, some contract and in-house lobbyists represent particular types of interests.

One group works on Republican, conservative causes. They represent major economic interests, particularly big business. The other group tends to lobby on issues typically supported by Democrats. These include: social causes, such as environmental protection; trade union and labor causes; issues concerning the disabled; and various types of aid for the poor.

9. THE IMPLICATIONS FOR YOU

Becoming conversant with the mindset and role of elected and appointed officials and lobbyists, both in general and as individuals, has three major implications for your lobbying effort.

Understanding their Values, Goals, Needs and Constraints

Obviously, learning as much as you can about the psychology and personality of public officials, enables you to approach them in a way that indicates you've taken the time to understand them. Conversely, if you don't do your homework you could appear uninformed or uncaring, which will undermine your credibility.

As you become familiar with those involved in state politics, you'll get to spot the decent and honest ones, the unreliable ones, and some who are downright dishonest.

For instance, if you meet with a legislator about your desire to increase restrictions on the purchase of firearms, but don't know he or she is a hunter and a member of the National Rifle Association (NRA), you'll have committed a major faux pas. They'll likely tell you you're wrong, dismiss you for not doing your homework, and never meet with you again.

On the other hand, if you know this, you can approach them from a perspective that shows you've thought things through. Then they may consider your points, even if they don't change their mind.

Information on Particular Lobbyists

Knowing as much about a lobbyist as you can is also important. One good reason is they may be on the opposing side of your issue at some point. Another is, you'll want to vet them if you think they might be a good person to have in your contact network.

Helping Policy Makers with Their Needs

Anything you can do to help public officials with their needs, relieve some of their political pain, or at least not hinder them, will be welcome. This could include: respecting their limited time to meet with you; or helping them solve a problem, such as providing information they can't get anywhere else.

The Policy-Makers

Conversely, hindering or undermining these key elements of their job, and worse, threatening them, such as suggesting you or your organization will circulate negative information about them, will be met with opposition. Although their negative reaction may not always be obvious, they will likely cut you off and your relationship and ability to work with them, in both the short and long run, will be reduced, maybe to zero.

Where They Fit in the Policy Process

This involves knowing the styles of public officials, the issues most important to them and why, how they relate to their colleagues, the ones they work with most, and how much influence they have, if any. To know their personal styles, whether they're a detail person and a policy wonk, less directly involved and leave details to their staff, a wheeler-dealer, or impulsive and disorganized in their jobs, will help you deal with them, or not deal with them, as you see best. In some cases, it is more productive to deal with their staff.

Two Perspectives on Issues

Alaska Native legislators typically look at issues from a rural-bush viewpoint and, because there are few of them, they often take a bipartisan or nonpartisan approach to issues and dealing with legislative colleagues. While many are Democrats, to compensate for their small numbers, they often cross party lines and join the majority caucus in the House and Senate, which, since the mid-1990s, have been mainly majority Republican caucuses.

In contrast, a fiscally conservative legislator from the Matanuska-Susitna (Mat-Su) Valley, elected on the promise of cutting government spending, will likely oppose proposals to increase the budget (unless his or her district benefits), and work with other fiscally conservative legislators. They will be less likely to join a bipartisan coalition, or support increased funding for services in the bush.

1. The Dynamics of Power in Juneau

2. Personalities, Political Acumen, and Power

3. The Power Structure in the Legislature

4. Governors, Their Staff, and Senior Administrators

5. Information and Financial Responsibilities as Influence in the Departments

6. The Power Dynamics Between the Legislature and the Governor

7. Interest Groups and Lobbyists

8. The Intangibles of Relationships and Influence

9. Dealing with Changes in the Power Structure

10. Seven Lessons

★ CHAPTER 6 ★

Who's Got the Political Clout in Juneau?

Most of the time, those with 21 votes in the House and
11 in the Senate call the political shots, but not always.
Occasionally, other alliances and
close relationships carry the day.

—Tom Brice,
Former Alaska State Legislator
and Business Representative,
Alaska District Council of Laborers

Building on the mindset and role of policy makers, we turn to see how they fit into the power structure in Juneau.

The chapter identifies the various places in the legislature, the executive branch, including state agencies, and other forces that have the most influence on what gets done. Then, in the next two chapters, on the bill process and the budget, we apply this information to explain the realities of policy-making.

1. THE DYNAMICS OF POWER IN JUNEAU

A major challenge for lobbyists is to identity who's got the political juice to help achieve their goals, as well as those who have the power to thwart them. It's a challenge because, although we can identify a general power structure in state government, the specifics of where power lies depends largely on the factors set out in Box 6.1 on the next page.

BOX 6.1
WHAT SHAPES POLITICAL POWER IN MOST SITUATIONS?

- The political acumen (or lack thereof) of those in office.

- The nature of the issue: whether it is prominent in the legislative session, such as an item on the governor's agenda, which likely will involve prominent interest groups. Or if it's a low profile issue that, for instance, mainly involves a state agency.

- The relationship between the legislature and the governor in each legislative session. While power is dispersed across state government, on issues of major concern to the legislative leadership and the governor, power tends to be concentrated in these two places.

- Changing political circumstances, for example, changes in the make up of the party caucuses in the legislature.

- Factors beyond the control of policy-makers, such as a sharp fall in oil prices or a major shift in federal policy, can cause changes in the power structure.

- An unclear source of power. Sometimes there's an outcome—positive or negative for a group or organization—where it's hard to say how it happened and who had the juice to do it.

The problem is, you won't find the dynamics of these and other aspects of power written down anywhere. You need to use your observations as far as you can. But most of all, this is where a good network of contacts will pay major dividends.

Political Clout

2. PERSONALITY, POLITICAL ACUMEN, AND POWER

In their interactions with others—working to get the best deal they can—some politicians and bureaucrats are better at this than others. They are more adept at using what power they have, be it extensive or limited, regardless of if they're in prominent leadership positions or farther down the chain of authority. Whether due to their personalities, experience, innate ability, or a combination of these and other factors, some policy-makers have a greater ability to think and act politically.

There are four important implications of variation in political skill.

> *Many wheeler-dealer politicians have a file cabinet in their head with the names of those who owe them favors—chits they can cash in.*

- It can affect key relationships in state government, such as between the executive and the legislature.

- Some policy-makers are more adept at putting together alliances with others, sometimes including interest groups, and with colleagues across party lines.

- Expanding on the last point, just because a legislator is a member of the minority doesn't necessarily mean he or she lacks influence.

- In several instances, the contrast between a high level of political skill and a minimal level—or none at all—is sometimes easy to see. We give examples of this contrast below. In other instances, the contrast is not clear, but often as important regarding what gets done or not done.

3. THE POWER STRUCTURE IN THE LEGISLATURE

Not all legislators have equal power. For the most part, power lies with the majority caucuses, particularly the leadership, including key committee chairs. That said, the power structure has other elements to it. Box 6.2, on the next page, sets out these various elements.

Three points covered in Box 6.2 are worth emphasizing because they likely won't be clear to those new to lobbying.

ALASKA STATE CAPITOL

BOX 6.2
THE POWER STRUCTURE IN THE LEGISLATURE

Major Political Forces on Most Actions and Policies

House and Senate Majority Caucuses

These control the legislative calendar and determine what bills will and will not pass. In particular, they control the budget process in the legislature. Members of these caucus are expected to support the majority position on the budget (though more so for Republicans than Democrats), and in administrative matters, particularly rulings of the presiding officer in floor sessions.

Those who don't follow these rules may be expelled from the caucus. Republican Senator Mike Dunleavy was expelled from the Republican Senate majority in 2017; and Republican Representative Lora Reinbold from the House Republican majority in 2015. Both voted against the budget. The previous expulsions happened back in 2005.

Key Majority Leaders

Several leaders in the majority caucuses wield particular influence. These include: the Speaker of the House and President of the Senate; the majority leaders in both houses (who manage caucus business and enforce its agenda); and key committee chairpersons, particularly of the Finance Committees and the Rules Committees.

Important Forces in Certain Circumstances

House and Senate Minority Caucuses

The minority caucuses can be influential if the majority needs them. This includes: a vote requiring more than a simple 50 percent majority (such as, using funds from the CBR, and overriding a governor's veto); and if the minority's issue is not of major concern to the majority caucus.

Key Minority Leaders and Members

The minority leader in both houses wield influence in certain situations. Other minority members, usually because of their political acumen,

Political
Clout

personalities, or willingness to cross party lines (often the case with bush legislators), can have influence in certain situations.

Regional Alliances and Policy Issue Caucuses

The bush caucus (rural legislators from both parties) was very influential in the 1980s, but less so today. Regional cross-party caucuses, such as the Southeast and Interior caucuses, can exert influence on regional issues if the majority caucuses give tacit approval. Bipartisan caucuses, formed to deal with specific policy areas, such as the Children's Caucus and the Fish Caucus, can also be influential in certain circumstances.

Legislative Aides/Staff

Certain legislative staff, especially those with long service, are often important participants in policy making. Because many of them move between the executive and legislative branches as administrations change, they have long institutional memories that are valuable sources of information for policy-makers in both branches of government.

Don't Ignore Staff

Get to know legislative staff and build trust with them— it'll be well worth it!

Don't ignore legislative staff as you work to push your issue. In fact, start with them, as they exert some, in some cases considerable, influence in their offices. They can help you a lot, often more than their boss, regarding who else you should contact. Staff can also give suggestions on strategy.

Conversely, if you ignore them and rub them the wrong way, they can hinder your cause; though they are unlikely to tell you this directly.

Don't Dismiss the House and Senate Minorities

Legislators in the minority caucuses are not entirely powerless in the policy process. This applies to the caucus and to certain members, such as the late Senator Al Adams of Kotzebue. He was a master

Political Clout

at putting together alliances across party lines, and in the executive branch, to advance his goals. He was also adept at thwarting some actions of the majority.

Plus, the minority today may be the majority after the next election, or if there's a mid-session shuffle in the organization of the legislature. So, even though you may not be able to spend much time with minority members, don't ignore them.

Making Policy Requires Cooperation

Remember, the legislature doesn't make policy all by itself, even though that may be the impression we often get from the media. The legislature is part of a broader policy system in which the governor is, in effect, the "sixty-first legislator." He or she has considerable influence on the major issues the legislature considers. This is particularly true with the budget. In most cases, the governor has the say on its final form. We explain the basics of the power relationship between the legislature and the governor in section 6 below.

> There's a natural tension between the legislature and the governor; but to get anything done they've got to cooperate.

4. GOVERNORS, THEIR STAFF, AND SENIOR ADMINISTRATORS

Political Clout

The power relationship in the administration between the governor, his or her staff, and senior administrators, mainly commissioners and deputy commissioners, is shaped by the boss—the governor.

All governors have different experiences and political acumen. They vary in personality and management style: some are low-key; some controlling or proactive. They also differ in their political goals—the policies they want to push. The combination of these factors shape the power dynamic within the administration.

Governors who have no experience in elected office, like Bill Sheffield, often rely on their staff or commissioners for information and policy direction. After some notable achievements in his

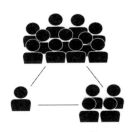

first two years in office, Governor Cowper announced he wouldn't seek a second term eighteen months before the next gubernatorial election. Sarah Palin also had major achievement during her first two years, but lost interest in being governor after the defeat of the McCain-Palin ticket for the presidency in 2008. She resigned the governorship in July 2009.

Generally, lack of experience and indifference gives senior administration officials greater influence over decision-making. In contrast, other governors, such as Tony Knowles and Frank Murkowski, are more proactive.

The Chief of Staff

The personality of the chief of staff and how he or she defines their role, can shape the power dynamic, not only in the governor's office, but across the administration. A dominant chief can control not only what gets to the governor, but may be directly involved in a range of policy issues.

A dominant chief may also be controlling of office staff, including the legislative director and special assistants, and how they operate. For instance, a controlling chief can set policy on which legislators, legislative staff, lobbyists, and members of the public, may deal directly with office staff and how they conduct those discussions. A more low-key chief may see his or her role as more administrative and less political.

The Influence of Commissioners

Besides the extent of the governor's political experience, three additional factors often influence his or her relationship with commissioners and deputy commissioners.

One situation is where the governor knew a senior administrator before being elected. This likely means the governor has a great deal

Political Clout

of confidence in them, resulting in these administrators having considerable influence with the governor.

A second circumstance is the extent a governor relies on commissioners and senior staff for political as well as factual and technical information. This depends largely on whether a governor decides to appoint several special assistants, each covering a specific policy area, or fewer assistants, each covering a wider range of policy areas. Most governors combine the two.

> *There are many power bases in the administration: from commissioners to division directors to various technical specialists, such as scientists and budget analysts. Some of them may be in conflict with each other or the governor's intended goals, and use their power to advance their own cause.*

Third are the policies that are most important to the governor. He or she will obviously have more contact with senior officials who are most important in advancing those goals and policies. Consequently, these likely have more sway over the governor's actions than other commissioners or deputy commissioners. Tony Knowles, for example, was particularly interested in social issues. Bill Walker's overwhelming issue was building a natural gas pipeline. Those who focus on cutting the budget, like Governor Dunleavy, tend to focus more on OMB.

A Unique Power Dynamic

All these factors and relationships make up the power structure in any administration—its unique power dynamic. To a large extent, this determines how lobbyists and others deal with senior administrators: the avenues of access, and who, when, and how they deal with each official.

Political Clout

5. INFORMATION AND FINANCIAL RESPONSIBILITIES AS INFLUENCE IN THE DEPARTMENTS

It is often said that information is power. Those who have information—mainly technical, but who also know the politics of their departments—is a good indication of who's got the ability to help those needing to deal with their agency.

Added to this, departments put together a budget each year. Their budget affects all the services they provide, which, in turn, affects constituent groups from teachers to local governments to small business owners. Departments also draw up fiscal notes to accompany bills, and write regulations for legislation after enactment. In combination, these factors give departments considerable political leverage.

The Management Style of Commissioners, and Dealing with Your Issue

The management style of the commissioner affects the extent of the flexibility that division directors, deputy directors, and the department's legislative liaison have in doing their job. That is, it determines how much power they'll have to help you. Even with a commissioner who has a hands-on style, there's still room for the division directors and the legislative liaison to help, if you deal with them first and not the commissioner's office or a legislator.

By contacting the division director or legislative liaison first, they have options in dealing with your issue. In contrast, their flexibility is reduced if you first go to a legislator or the commissioner and the director is given specific instructions on how to deal with the issue, and report back. In other words, starting at mid-level in a department often gives those able to affect your issue more influence than starting at the top. Then, if necessary, they can take your issue to the commissioner.

Remember, though, the power dynamics in each department are different. And the dynamics will change as administrations change, and even when a new commissioner replaces an existing one.

Political Clout

6. THE POWER RELATIONSHIP BETWEEN THE LEGISLATURE AND THE GOVERNOR

The relationship between the legislature and the governor is the most important one in state government. It largely determines what policies are enacted and those that fall by the wayside. Most important of all, this relationship is the major one in shaping the state budget. Box 6.3 lists the most important factors that shape these relations. Because of their significance, we briefly expand on three of them.

Conflict and Cooperation, Relationships and Alliances

To get what I wanted in my business, I didn't have to involve many people. But when I became governor, I had to involve a host of people and interests to get just some of what I wanted.

Political Clout

Despite some intense conflicts and political stand-offs between the legislature and the governor, the two must cooperate to get legislation enacted and other issues resolved. The majority caucuses have the strongest power bases to forge alliances with the governor and key administration personnel, such as the governor's chief of staff, the director of OMB, and commissioners. In addition, legislative committee chairs have a power base to build similar cooperative relationships that can be of mutual advantage.

In the hardball politics of working towards a final agreement, there may be threats by the governor to withhold benefits for key legislators, or use the veto, and lack of cooperation and stalling on the part of the legislature. The anticipation of these actions shape the strategy and tactics of both branches as they work to achieve their goals.

Different governors have different approaches to building alliances depending on their personal philosophies, style, and political necessity. For instance, when both houses are dominated by one

BOX 6.3

NINE MAJOR FACTORS SHAPING RELATIONS BETWEEN THE LEGISLATURE AND THE GOVERNOR

- There is no overall relationship between the governor and all 60 legislators because there's no single, united legislative voice. The governor has relationships with the majority and minority caucuses in both houses, other groups and factions, and individual legislators.

- The power dynamics are shaped by relationships, personality, and political acumen.

- Even with a group or individual in the legislature, the power relationship with the governor will differ on various issues.

- The governor's agenda may be similar to or at odds with the majority caucus in one or both houses.

- In situations of both conflict and cooperation, both in terms of constitutional authority and resources, the governor has a stronger political hand than the legislature.

- Even so, the legislature has considerable influence through its role in approving the budget, confirming the governor's appointment of top executive officials, oversight hearings, and holding the governor and departments accountable for their actions, including conducting investigations.

- Even when the governor and the House and Senate majorities are of the same party, parties are less important than the make up of the majority caucuses in the House and Senate.

- Because of changes in leadership and new members in the legislature after an election, in some cases a new governor, no two legislatures have the same legislative-executive power dynamic.

- External and/or unforeseen events, like a major economic downturn, a natural or man-made disaster, or a count decision, can have an effect on the power dynamic between the legislature and the governor.

Political Clout

party, and the governor is of the other party, he or she may enlist the support of minority members, and perhaps bring external pressure to bear, such as by generating public support to get things done.

Issues and Power Relationships

At any one time, a general assessment can be made about whether the relations between the governor and the legislature are good, bad, or middling. But in their day-to-day relations of developing cooperation, resolving conflicts, and finalizing policies, the general relationship is of little significance. In practice, the two branches relate on a series of issues. As a result, there are a host of power relationships between the governor and the administration and the legislature.

Reasons for Varying Relationships

First, neither the legislature nor the executive is a political monolith. As Box 6.3 points out, the legislature is an array of caucuses, groups, factions, and individuals, many in conflict with each other. And while the executive branch, headed by the governor, is more united, it also has many political factions and power bases.

Second, both the governor and various members of the administration will relate to various groups and individuals in the legislature differently. It depends on the issue, the importance of the issue to each involved, or any past relationships they may have, among other factors. The result is that the power relationship on each issue will likely be different, too. In fact, the governor and administration officials may agree with a group, faction, or individual on a specific issue, but disagree on others.

> *Political power is best understood issue by issue. Not all issues are of concern or of the same level of importance to the governor, the majority caucuses, or other policy makers. The power dynamic in each situation is different depending on whose concerned about the issue.*

Personality, Personal Relationships, and Political Acumen

In essence, the relationship between the governor and the legislature is largely shaped by three factors. These are the very root of politics and lobbying—personality, personal relationships, and political skill or lack of it.

Personality and personal relationships can come into play in several ways. Some legislative leaders and governors are easy going and mesh easily with one another. Others are more self-important, arrogant, or have prickly personalities that can cause problems in their relationship. Sometimes there are major conflicts with bad blood between a governor and a legislator. All these types of relationships lead to different power dynamics across a range of issues.

Then there is the extent of the political skill of those in the legislative leadership and the governor and his or her top staff. Some governors and legislators are good politicians, some are mediocre, and some are just not good at politics. But since legislative leaders typically must be around for some years before acquiring leadership positions, they typically have considerable skill. Governors, however, can get elected without political experience, as were Governors Bill Sheffield, or very little experience, as with Bill Walker.

Personal relationships and political acumen can sometimes trump the superior resources the governor has over the legislature. They can also aid a governor in overcoming a situation where they face major opposition in the legislature.

Political Clout

7. INTEREST GROUPS AND LOBBYISTS

The public views the influence of interest groups from two perspectives, even if these are not clearly distinguished in their mind.

One of these is the political power of individual lobbies, groups, and organizations, such as the business lobby or the University of Alaska. The other is the impact of the interest group system overall—all the groups and organizations in combination. The influence of individual interests is considered in Chapter 10, section 4. Here we look at the second aspect of group influence.

A common view of this overall impact is that, "special interests are running the state." This was true in Alaska before statehood, with mining and corporate fishing interests. But it's no longer the reality.

The Realities of Interest Group Operations in Juneau

Let's look at this in regard to both groups and lobbyists.

Groups Never Act in Concert

All the interest groups in the state never act together as one combined and united force to influence a policy. Quite the reverse: they are often in intense competition with their opponents, such as developers versus environmentalists, and often work to undermine their opponents to promote their own policy goals.

All Groups have a Specific Focus

No group or organization is concerned with all policy issues. They typically focus on their areas of policy only, such as K-12 education, local government, or domestic violence issues. Now and again, several groups band together to promote a general cause, such as the need for a long-range fiscal plan for Alaska. But this is rare and often goes nowhere politically. In reality, in the vast majority of cases, groups neither seek nor have influence outside of their policy areas.

Are Interest Groups Running the State?

The short answer is "no". No single group or interest is running Alaska politics to the extent that they can determine the outcome of any policy, as was the case in territorial days.

There are certainly some prominent interests, particularly the oil industry, including both individual companies like ExxonMobil and the oil industry's trade association, the Alaska Oil and Gas Association (AOGA). Their prominence is due to the state's dependence on oil for revenue. It's also because the industry is a major donor to the election campaigns of legislators, especially Republicans who push the industry's issues in Juneau. Yet, even the oil industry loses sometimes.

The Influence of Lobbyists

As a consequence of the last point, whatever influence a lobbyist has is largely confined to the group or interest they represent.

Even big-time lobbyists, like Kent Dawson, Wendy Chamberlain, and Bob Evans, who represent several clients, are not concerned with other policy areas, unless they come to affect their clients and their particular issues. So lobbyists also have no overall influence across the board on all policies being considered by state government.

8. THE INTANGIBLES OF RELATIONSHIPS AND INFLUENCE

Beyond the obvious power relationships between the legislature, the governor's office, and the departments, other, less evident forms of influence exist. These are intangible aspects of power. They involve relationships between friends or long-time associates, or meetings of the minds between public officials and lobbyists, or others working to push an issue.

Often in these cases, the major factors that generally determine influence and lobbying success may be less important. Lobbying is an industry based on relationships. It isn't always about who is the biggest, strongest, who gives the most campaign funds, among other factors. It's more about who knows who and how they get along.

Such intangible situations are another confirmation of the importance in the lobbying business of contacts and relationships to get things done. For the novice, and even for

Political Clout

some with experience in lobbying, this adds to the complexity and, in many ways, the challenge of figuring out the less obvious political operatives who have some political clout in Juneau.

9. DEALING WITH CHANGES IN THE POWER STRUCTURE

Who has the political clout, how much they have, and on what issues is not static. Recognizing changes, and how to deal with them, is one of the major but most challenging jobs of the lobbyist. Box 6.4 offers some guidance on these challenges.

10. SEVEN LESSONS

From what we've explained, there's no simple answer to the question: "Who's got the political clout in Juneau?" This is largely due to the nebulous nature of political power set out in Box 6.1. Nevertheless, the chapter reconfirms three key points that apply specifically to the major players in Alaska politics. It also explains three points only alluded to so far in the book. Most important of all is lesson number 7.

Reconfirming Three Points

Lesson 1: Although there are key players on many issues, particularly the legislature and the governor, power is not located in any one place. It's dispersed throughout state government.

Lesson 2: While the extent of a public official's authority is often an indication of their power, this is not always the case.

Lesson 3: Related to the first two points, relationships, combined with political skill, are important factors in exercising influence. In many cases, they are the key factors, whether it's a public official working to influence their colleagues, relationships between the legislature and the governor or a state agency, or a lobbyist working with a politician.

BOX 6.4
DEALING WITH CHANGES IN
THE POWER STRUCTURE

A Major Change in the Legislature's Relations with the Governor during a Legislative Session

Is there likely to be a significant change in their power relationship during the session? That is, a change such as control of the legislature or a new governor causing a fundamental adjustment in their relationship, that might affect your campaign. This is not very likely.

There have certainly been major changes over the years. Examples are the legislative coup of 1981 that changed who ran the House, and a new governor in 2009 when Sean Parnell took over from Sarah Palin when she resigned. Likely there will be some indication that a major change is about to occur.

Personnel Changes in the Administration, and in the Role of Individual Legislators

Much more likely are changes in the top personnel in the executive, and a shuffling of positions in the legislature.

There are staff changes in the governor's office from time to time. This is also true of departments regarding commissioners, deputy commissioners, legislative liaisons, and division directors.

Obviously, if these changes affect your issue, and you don't have personal knowledge of the new appointees, you need to get to know them and figure out how this might affect the dynamics in your situation, if at all. Someone among your contacts is likely the best source of information.

In the legislature changes sometimes occur following resignations, when members get kicked out of the majority caucus for voting against the budget, and occasionally when a member dies. Again, you need to be able to react to this if it affects your lobbying effort. Your contacts are likely to be your best source here too.

Changes after an Election

Obviously, an election is likely to bring the major change in the power structure in the legislature and, in a gubernatorial election year, perhaps a new governor. Even if there's no new governor, and no change in control in one or both houses in the legislature, there is often a change in

(continued . . .)

Political Clout

BOX 6.4 *CONTINUED*

leadership. Plus, there will be new members in both bodies. More extensive changes occur if the majority caucus shifts from one party to the other.

There are three major ways to deal with these changes in the legislature; but less specific ways in the case of a new governor.

Keep in Touch with Minority Members

Be sure to touch base with minority leaders as you go about lobbying. While you can't devote much time to these contacts, they will pay dividends in the future. Some minority members may join the majority after the next election, or even during a session (though this is rare). More importantly, if there's a change in control of the legislature you need to have access to the new majority caucuses in each house.

Contribute to Their Campaigns

Another type of political insurance is contributing to the campaigns of minority members and encouraging others to do so. Even if your group or organization prohibits such contributions, you can give as an individual citizen. Although they rarely admit it, campaign donations are one of the most important, if not the most important, things you can do to encourage a public official to help you.

Working on their Campaign

This is probably even better political insurance in your relationship with a minority member. Just putting up a few yard signs, answering the phone in the campaign office one or two evenings a week, or helping with e-mails and social media, will be much appreciated by the candidate.

A New Governor

Taking steps to prepare for a new governor and a major change in the power dynamics in state government, is a much more difficult task. Everyone in politics is trying to do this. The situation is made more difficult by the number of candidates running for the job.

Your best bets here are to contribute to as many candidates as you can; choose the most likely winner and do some work on their campaign. If you have minimal funds or time, wait until after the primary to help. This Johnny-come-lately approach will not be as appreciated as being on the campaign from the start, but it's better than nothing.

Political Clout

Three New Insights

Lesson 4: While there are major power players, influence is not exerted in a general form, as is conveyed when people talk of "the power of the governor" or "the power of the legislature." The exercise of power is always specifically focused—it is issue oriented.

Power relationships revolve around particular issues. Plus, even among the same players, the power relationship may be different on different issues. Just because two politicians have good relations and see eye-to-eye on one issue, may not be the case on all issues.

Lesson 5: Information can be an important power base, which is one reason why authority is not always identical to power. Those with information, such as a middle level manager in a state agency, may be able to influence a situation more than the top dog who lacks that information.

Lesson 6: The fluidity of the political environment means that power is dynamic and will change, sometimes in the short-run, but certainly in the long-term. A lobbyist must always keep this in mind, and, as far as possible, be able to adapt to it.

Lesson Number 7: Contacts and Relationships

The most important lesson in this chapter is the need for a contact network and develop good relations with those who might be helpful in your lobbying effort.

The location of power on a particular issue, how it might be brought to bear, and how it has changed or might change, among other aspects of political clout, cannot be found in any book or on the Internet. The only way to get it is through being part of a network with those in the know.

Political Clout

THIS CHAPTER COVERS

1. Distinguishing Between the Bill Process and Policy-Making

2. The Formal Bill Process

3. The Realities of Policy-Making

4. Interaction Between Legislative Majorities, the Governor, and State Agencies

5. The Role of the Minority

6. Interest Groups and Lobbyists

7. The Media and the Public

8. The Sources, Drafting, and Introduction of Bills—the First Reading

9. The Committee Process

10. The Rules Committee

11. The Second and Third Readings of Bills

12. Conference Committees

13. Consideration by the Governor

14. After the Bill Becomes Law: Writing Regulations

15. Completing the Policy Cycle

★ CHAPTER 7 ★

Realities of the Policy Process: The Politics of Making Laws

If you like laws and sausages, you should never watch either being made.

—Attributed to Otto von Bismarck,
German Chancellor,
late 19th. Century

This and the next chapter cover the fundamentals of the policy process. This chapter explains the realities of public policy-making and how they affect the way laws are made. Law-making includes the most important aspect of the legislative process—putting together and approving the budget. The budget is covered in the next chapter.

At the end of that chapter, we bring together the general law-making process and budget politics to provide a holistic view of the realities of policy-making.

1. DISTINGUISHING BETWEEN THE BILL PROCESS AND POLICY-MAKING

Earlier, we defined the policy process as: *How conflicts over political issues are resolved or, in some cases, not resolved so that the status quo remains.*

Settling disagreements is the norm in policy-making, but not all policies are the result of resolving conflict. Sometimes there's agreement on a course of action, such as on stricter laws against drunk driving, or naming a state building after a famous Alaskan.

Although they largely involve the same activities, there is a difference between the policy process and the bill process. The policy process includes all activities that need some form of action by government to turn them into a policy—a course of action. This could include: the legislature approving the appointment of commissioners by the governor; a special commission set up to investigate an issue, such as revising the guidelines for prison sentences; or the governor declaring a state of disaster for a part of the state badly damaged by a storm. But it is the bill process—enacting or repealing legislation—that forms the lion's share of policy-making activity.

2. THE FORMAL BILL PROCESS

Box 7.1 shows the formal bill process as required by the Alaska Constitution. The process is set out in various sections of Article II, dealing with the legislature. These include Section 14, which states:

> *The legislature shall establish the procedure for enactment of bills into law. No bill may become law unless it has passed three readings in each house on three separate days, except that any bill may be advanced from second to third reading on the same day by concurrence of three-fourths of the house considering it. No bill may become law without an affirmative vote of a majority of the membership of each house. The yeas and nays on final passage shall be entered in the journal.*

Once a bill is passed by the legislature, it goes to the governor, whose constitutional authority is set out in Article II, Sections 16 and 17. The various options open to the governor in dealing with a bill are set out in Box 7.6 in section 13 below.

Now let's move to see how all this works in practice.

Legislative
Politics

BOX 7.1
STEPS IN THE PASSAGE OF A HOUSE BILL

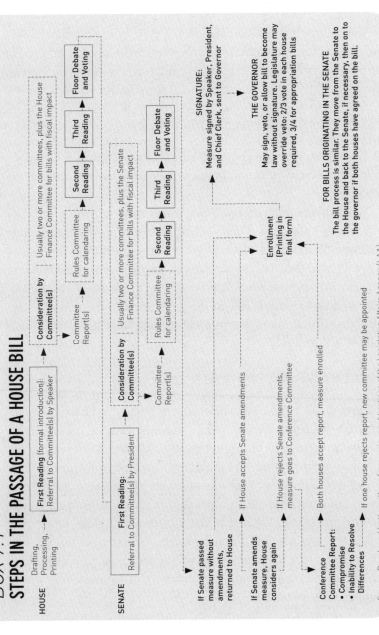

HOUSE

Drafting, Processing, Printing → **First Reading** (formal introduction): Referral to Committee(s) by Speaker → **Consideration by Committee(s)**

Usually two or more committees, plus the House Finance Committee for bills with fiscal impact

Committee Report(s) → Rules Committee for calendaring → Second Reading → Third Reading → Floor Debate and Voting

SENATE

First Reading: Referral to Committee(s) by President → **Consideration by Committee(s)**

Usually two or more committees, plus the Senate Finance Committee for bills with fiscal impact

Committee Report(s) → Rules Committee for calendaring → Second Reading → Third Reading → Floor Debate and Voting

Enrollment (Printing in final form)

SIGNATURE: Measure signed by Speaker, President, and Chief Clerk, sent to Governor

THE GOVERNOR
May sign, veto, or allow bill to become law without signature. Legislature may override veto: 2/3 vote in each house required, 3/4 for appropriation bills

If Senate passed measure without amendments, returned to House

If Senate amends measure, House considers again

If House accepts Senate amendments

If House rejects Senate amendments, measure goes to Conference Committee

Conference Committee Report:
• **Compromise** — Both houses accept report, measure enrolled
• **Inability to Resolve Differences** — If one house rejects report, new committee may be appointed

FOR BILLS ORIGINATING IN THE SENATE
The bill process is similar. They move from the Senate to the House and back to the Senate, if necessary, then on to the governor if both houses have agreed on the bill.

Source: Developed by the authors from various publications of the Legislative Affairs Agency (LAA).

Legislative Politics

3. THE REALITIES OF POLICY MAKING

The policy process is best viewed as a cycle of six stages with overlap between some of them. This cycle is set out in Box 7.2. All parts of the political system—including the legislature, the executive, interest groups, and the public—are usually involved in this process.

Political Complexity and Influential Policy-Makers

The number of players involved and their various interactions make the policy process complex and adds uncertainty to the outcomes.

What drives this process is not what's right or wrong, good or bad, fair or unfair, but power—whether explicitly wielded or subtly exercised. Plus, certain players have major influence on most policy proposals and their fate, particularly in stages 1 (getting government to deal with a proposal) and 2 (considering the proposal) of the process. Besides the major role of the governor and the majority caucuses on virtually all issues, this will include administrative officials and interest groups.

Stages 1 and 2: The Key Parts of the Process

Since stages 1 and 2 are particularly important in enacting or killing proposed legislation, as well as repealing existing laws. As these will likely be the parts of the process that will most affect your lobbying effort, we devote most of the chapter to these two stages.

Control of these two stages by the majority caucuses, and to some extent the governor, mean proposals that make it to stage 1 and go forward to stage 2, are mostly those on their agendas. Other proposals are considered in the bill process, but often do not get very far. These include many proposals widely seen as good policy and in the interest of the state (however defined), or supported by a large segment of Alaskans.

Legislative Politics

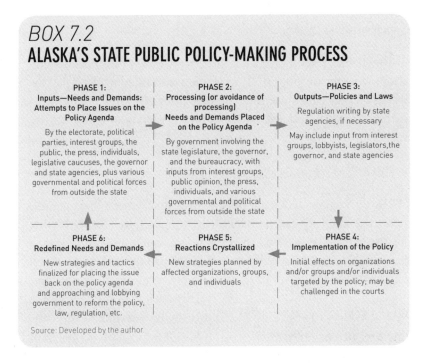

BOX 7.2
ALASKA'S STATE PUBLIC POLICY-MAKING PROCESS

PHASE 1:
Inputs—Needs and Demands: Attempts to Place Issues on the Policy Agenda

By the electorate, political parties, interest groups, the public, the press, individuals, legislative caucuses, the governor and state agencies, plus various governmental and political forces from outside the state

PHASE 2:
Processing (or avoidance of processing) Needs and Demands Placed on the Policy Agenda

By government involving the state legislature, the governor, and the bureaucracy, with inputs from interest groups, public opinion, the press, individuals, and various governmental and political forces from outside the state

PHASE 3:
Outputs—Policies and Laws

Regulation writing by state agencies, if necessary

May include input from interest groups, lobbyists, legislators, the governor, and state agencies

PHASE 6:
Redefined Needs and Demands

New strategies and tactics finalized for placing the issue back on the policy agenda and approaching and lobbying government to reform the policy, law, regulation, etc.

PHASE 5:
Reactions Crystallized

New strategies planned by affected organizations, groups, and individuals

PHASE 4:
Implementation of the Policy

Initial effects on organizations and/or groups and/or individuals targeted by the policy; may be challenged in the courts

Source: Developed by the author.

4. INTERACTION BETWEEN THE LEGISLATIVE MAJORITIES, THE GOVERNOR, AND STATE AGENCIES

Of the various dynamics involved in the often prickly relationship between the governor and the legislature over bills, three are fundamental:

- The adjournment package and other legislation.

- The political struggle between the two branches.

- The need for cooperation.

These are in addition to the governor's advantages in information and other resources.

Legislative Politics

The Adjournment Package

The majority legislative caucuses always have positions on legislation, whether in support or opposition: bills they work to pass or defeat, among which are their highest priorities. This is known as the adjournment package. In effect, it's the agenda of each majority caucus for the two-year legislature.

Putting the Package Together and the "Must-Haves"

The package includes the bills, budget items, and other requirements the majority caucuses insist they "must have" before closing out the legislative session. The emphasis is on "must." If they can't secure these "must haves," the session will go until they get them, whether this is for its full 120 days, or in one or more special sessions.

During the session, particularly in the last two or three hectic weeks the adjournment package drives the relationship between the legislature and the governor.

The specifics of the package are not usually determined until the middle of the legislative session or later. But the majorities start discussing their packages, in broad terms, right after an election as they put together the leadership and organizational structure before the legislative session. As part of organizing the majorities in both houses, members advocate for including their requirements in the package. The way committee chairs and committee members are chosen reflect parts of this package. It evolves as the legislative sessions progress, with additional bills included at the request of powerful members of the majority.

Adjournment packages are not published. Nevertheless, a caucus's behavior during the session provides clues about their content.

The Governor's "Must Haves:" Agenda and Relations with the Legislature

The governor also has an agenda, which may be similar to the legislative majorities to some extent. But sometimes there are major

Legislative Politics

differences in their respective "must haves." This is particularly the case when the governor is of a different party than one or both houses of the legislature. Usually, there are also differences in the adjournment packages when both houses are controlled by the same party; and particularly when the majority caucuses of different parties control the two chambers. This often adds another political complication to closing out the legislative session.

The mix of these circumstances is the major focus and driving force of the relations between the governor and the legislature during the session, particularly regarding the budget.

Other Legislation

What's included in the adjournment package are not the only bills proposed by the legislature or the governor.

While the governor and various state agencies have an interest in most legislation proposed by the legislature, unlike the budget, some legislation is of little concern to the administration. These are usually non-controversial bills or those with little impact on the budget. There may be groups and individuals for and against some of these issues, but the governor will likely let the interested parties settle their differences themselves.

The Political Struggle Between the Two Branches

Whether over their respective "must haves" or other issues, conflict is a prominent part of relations between the legislative leadership and the governor. Sometimes, and particularly when legislation is being finalized, key legislators meet with the governor. More often, this interaction involves the governor's legislative director, the director of OMB, sometimes the governor's chief of staff, and various senior agency people, including commissioners, deputy commissioners, legislative liaisons, division directors, and deputy directors.

Messages and proposals come from both sides, as they maneuver to get what they want on legislation. This can involve some hardball politics and fierce disagreements, often shaped by personality and style.

Legislative
Politics

Determining Each Others' Intentions Throughout the Session

Always in the minds of legislators and the governor, though rarely openly expressed, is the governor's authority to veto all bills and line item veto parts of budget bills. For this and other reasons, legislators are constantly seeking information on what the governor thinks about various pieces of legislation, particularly budget bills.

The governor and agency officials are concerned about how the legislative leadership will react to the various stances of the administration. The legislature can make life tough for governors by refusing to consider their proposals, or amending them significantly, among other actions. The legislature also has leverage because it reviews budget requests for the governor's office itself.

In many ways, the relationship between the legislature and the governor, when they disagree on legislation, is a game of political chicken. The question is: who is likely to blink first, on what issues, to what extent, and what might be the consequences for their relationship as to what legislation emerges from the legislative session.

The Need for Cooperation

Despite conflict, as in all aspects of the legislature-governor relationship, their major mode of interaction is cooperation. This is essential to get anything done. It is particularly so with finalizing the budget so state government can continue to function and provide services to Alaskans.

Overall, the relationship between the two branches is transactional, involving forthright negotiations, compromise, and trusting the commitments on both sides.

5. THE ROLE OF THE MINORITY

Both the House and the Senate minorities are often vocal in reacting to majority caucus decisions. But their high profile is not an indication of their influence. Other than in a few circumstances, the minorities have little effect on policy-making, particularly in the budget process. They'll never admit this, however, and claim they have considerable influence. To admit otherwise in a process driven by power would, in effect, acknowledge their impotence in affecting decisions that impact the state in a major way.

Minority bills rarely go anywhere unless they have a majority co-sponsor, or the bill's not controversial.

Minority bills rarely get enacted because the majority thwarts them, particularly in committee hearings, even when the minority position is supported by facts or public testimony. This often causes frustration among minority members that sometimes spills over into heated debate in committees, and in floor sessions.

When the Minority May Have Some Influence

In some circumstances the minority can exert influence. Individual members can get bills passed by recruiting a majority member as co-sponsor, better still several majority co-sponsors, to boost their chances of getting their bill enacted. In some cases, they can get a committee to sponsor their bill. If a minority bill is not of importance to the majority, they'll give it consideration. Otherwise it'll be killed. Sometimes, a governor needs the minority to achieve a political goal, particularly if the majority caucus is of a different party to the governor.

The minority has leverage when the majority needs them for a supermajority vote (two thirds—40—or three-fourths—45—of 60). A supermajority is required to draw money from the Constitutional Budget Reserve (CBR) to cover the cost of state government, and to override a governor's veto.

Legislative Politics

6. INTEREST GROUPS AND LOBBYISTS

Interest groups and their lobbyists comprise a sort of fourth branch of government. Large, influential groups are constantly involved in the thick of legislation, particularly the budget process. Every public official will tell you that these and many other advocacy organizations are political forces to be reckoned with.

Many major interest groups hire contract lobbyists or use their in-house lobbyists throughout the legislative session. As seasoned political operatives, they are involved in all stages of the legislative process, from helping draft legislation through consideration of it by the legislature and implementing new policies.

The influence of any particular group on legislation depends a lot on the political circumstances at the time. It also depends on their resources and the political skill of their leaders, and to what extent they have other issues to push with government that will shape their strategy and tactics. Most of all, it depends on the leverage a group has on politicians and officials in state agencies. Nevertheless, even the big players do not always get their way on budget or other matters.

> *When a lobbyist and a legislator have a policy or budget goal, they work to achieve alignment of interests to get smooth sailing to secure it.*

7. THE MEDIA AND THE PUBLIC

Assessing the impact of the media, including blogs and social media, and the public on public policy, is difficult. That said, in certain circumstances all of them can influence public policy and bills.

This is largely because politicians are very concerned about what's covered by the media and how the public feels about certain issues, particularly those that are high profiles, like the PFD and education. So in certain circumstances, how politicians see media and public attitudes could affect your issue.

Legislative Politics

The Traditional Media

The media can influence legislative action by pursuing major developments, such as the opioid epidemic, and problems with crime. They can have a significant impact through investigative reporting or pursuing a current event, such as a corruption scandal, that may lead to legislative action, hamper, or even topple political leaders.

Many interest groups use the media to push their issue. There are, however, pitfalls in doing so. These are explained in Chapter 12, section 6.

Blogs and Social Media

Blogs and social media can be bias, often unreliable sources, but many public officials consult them regularly. So they can be important in conveying information to politicians, particularly social media.

For this reason, social media is used increasingly by interest groups. While its impact is also hard to assess in general, social media posts do influence individual public officials on particular issues, especially when these affect their constituents. As with using the traditional media, interest groups also run risks in using social media, which are covered in Chapter 12, section 7.

The Public and Public Opinion

As with the media, there are circumstances when the public can impact public policy. Some are general impacts; others are more specific. The first can influence the political environment in which you operate; the second includes options to consider using in your lobbying campaign.

General Impacts

The electorate (in effect the public) can shape the public policy making environment by electing candidates who are conservative,

Legislative Politics

liberal, or middle of the road. Voters may also have an import on public policy when there's a major issue in an election, such as a proposal to enact a personal income tax, or stricter gun laws.

But most of the time, elections send a mixed and often contradictory public message. This means public officials can interpret the results in a way to suit their agenda, and provides an excuse to oppose your issue.

The public can also have an impact through opinion surveys, such as what to do about rising crime. While these can also act as a political barometer for politicians, their message is also often mixed, unless there's overwhelming support for or opposition to an issue. Even then, politicians can drag their feet on following up on the public's opinion or ignore it completely.

Two other forms of public input that are more focused are advisory votes and direct democracy.

An advisory vote is where the legislature seeks direction from the public on an issue. For example, in 2007 there was an advisory vote on whether to amend the state constitution to allow same sex marriage in the state (which failed, but was made moot by a U.S. Supreme court decision in 2013 allowing it). Again, however, advisory votes are just that—advisory. The legislature has no legal obligation to follow them; though they may calculate that there are political consequences for not doing so.

An example of a referendum question is whether to increase the minimum wage; and an example of an initiative, a vote on whether to overturn a law givng a tax break to the oil industry. If the referendum or initiative pass they automatically become law and directly affect public policy. Though even a successful initiative can be overturned by the legislature within two years of its passage, and they can amend it at any time.

Specific Types of Public Input

These include: e-mails; letters; phone calls; public opinion messages (POMs) sent from one of 23 Legislative Information Offices

(LIOs) across the state; and, as mentioned above; various forms of social media. Petitions may be presented to public officials in the form of documents full of signatures, or by social media. Public rallies and protests can also send a strong message. But most public demonstrations will have little impact if they are against the views of those in power.

A more direct form of public input is through public testimony. This is taken at meetings of state boards and commissions, legislative committee hearings at the Capitol and around the state, special meetings held by elected officials in their districts, and at open forums by the governor. Public testimony, however, including that on budget issues, is perfunctory if it goes against the House and Senate majority positions. Some minority members and bureaucrats will also have their mind made up on an issue before a public hearing.

Most public officials see contacting them individually as the most likely way to influence their decisions. On high-profile issues of wide public concern, direct contact may have a significant impact.

8. THE SOURCES, WRITING, AND INTRODUCTION OF BILLS— THE FIRST READING

This is stage 1 in Figure 7.2 above. The idea for a bill (proposed legislation) can come from a legislator, a legislative committee, a group of legislators, a state agency, a business, association, an individual citizen, a lobbyist, or the governor, among other sources. For bills originating in the legislature, an outline of the proposal is sent to the Legislative Affairs Agency's Legal Services Division for drafting.

Once the bill's sponsor accepts its form and draft language, the bill is passed to the House Clerk or Senate Secretary (the administrative officers of both houses), to be put in official form and scheduled for introduction on the floor of the House or Seante. This is also when the bill is assigned a number, for example, Senate Bill 239 (SB 239), or House Bill 63 (HB 63).

Legislative Politics

The Politics of Bill Numbering

If a bill is important to a legislator, a measure with which he or she wants to be associated for political or other reasons, they "pre-files" it. That is, they have it drafed and filed with the House Clerk or Senate Secretary before the session begins. This way, the bill gets a low number, such as HB 3 or SB 4.

In many cases, this ensures that, if bills filed later on a similar subject are combined with the original bill into a committee substitute (with the designation CS), the substitute will likely have the number of the original bill, and the legislator who filed it will remain as the sponsor. But this is not always the case.

If the sponsor is a minority member and a member of the majority sponsors a similar measure, the majority may take the idea and give all the credit to their caucus. This is yet another example of the power of the majority and the weakness of the minority.

The First Reading of a Bill

All bills must be introduced by a legislator, several legislators, a legislative committee, or the governor. The governor's bills are introduced "'by request" through the Rules Committee. The first reading involves the bill being read for the first time; though the bill is not actually read in full. The Clerk or Secretary reads only the title and name of the legislator who sponsored it. Then, the presiding officer (House Speaker or President of the Senate) refers the bill to at least one committee, most often two or three committees. Box 7.3 provides an example of the first page of a House bill. From the top of the page, the information includes:

- The number of the legislature (in this case, the Thirtieth) and the session in which it was introduced (for this bill, the second session).

- The sponsor or sponsors.

- Date introduced.

BOX 7.3
FIRST PAGE OF A HOUSE BILL

HOUSE BILL NO. 151

IN THE LEGISLATURE OF THE STATE OF ALASKA

THIRTIETH LEGISLATURE - SECOND SESSION

BY REPRESENTATIVES GARA, Spohnholz, Drummond, Parish, Fansler, Tuck, Grenn, Ortiz, Millett, Kawasaki, Josephson, LeDoux, Kopp

Introduced: 3/1/17
Referred: Health and Social Services, Finance

A BILL

FOR AN ACT ENTITLED

1   "An Act relating to the duties of the Department of Health and Social Services; relating

2   to training and workload standards for employees of the Department of Health and

3   Social Services; relating to foster care licensing; relating to placement of a child in need

4   of aid; relating to the rights and responsibilities of foster parents; relating to subsidies

5   for adoption or guardianship of a child in need of aid; requiring the Department of

6   Health and Social Services to provide information to a child or person released from the

7   department's custody; and providing for an effective date."

8   **BE IT ENACTED BY THE LEGISLATURE OF THE STATE OF ALASKA:**

. . . . first page continued of 12 pages of the bill . . . . . .

- Committee referrals.

- The title and an overview of the content of the bill.

- Beginning with the title, the lines are numbered for ease of reference, citing parts of the bill, and for amending it.

- The enactment clause: BE IT ENACTED BY THE LEGISLATURE OF THE STATE OF ALASKA:

- The text of the bill.

Legislative Politics

The Politics of Stage 1

Getting government to take up an issue can be difficult. It's often less to do with the urgency or necessity of the issue, than the political influence of those behind it. Novices at lobbying often think of proposing bills just before or during the legislative session. Such belated efforts face an uphill climb and usually go nowhere.

How Seasoned Politicos Lay the Groundwork for the Success of a Bill

Majority and minority members, the governor, major organizations, and lobbyists, develop their legislation long before the session begins. This is usually done behind closed doors.

Anyone who wants to promote a bill, change or stop legislation, should do so before there's any public attention paid to it.

To increase the chances of their issues being considered, businesses and organizations that can afford to, hire contract lobbyists or use in-house lobbyists who work year-round with key policy makers. Seasoned lobbyists line up support for a bill even before it's drafted and anticipate its likely opposition. A good lobbyist knows how to accomplish their client's or organization's wishes and placate detractors, often by helping draft the bill to accommodate everyone's concerns. Shutting off opposition, in private ahead of time, is virtually always preferable to battling through disagreements before a legislative committee, even if you're victorious.

Skilled advocates not only advance their client's or organization's goals, but advise legislators on the best courses of action—how to align all the interests concerned, including the governor—to increase the chances of the bill's passage. Because of the political skill and influence these insiders wield, they have a good chance of getting their bill passed; though there are no guarantees. Virtually all bills are amended or go through other changes.

Legislative Politics

The Challenges Facing those with Little Political Clout

In contrast, those with less influence face more hurdles. They often have difficulty in getting government to consider their issues. When they do find a sympathetic legislator to introduce their bill, that individual may be a new or minority member with little influence on the legislative leadership. The majority caucuses discuss every bill before first reading. For bills they don't like, they often recommend the presiding officers refer them to three or more committees. Getting a bill through three committees, and scheduling it for a second reading, is difficult and often fatal.

Aside from securing legislative support, like all lobbyists, the novice must work with the governor to avoid a veto. It's necessary to ascertain in advance whether he or she supports the bill, opposes it, or is neutral. If the governor strongly opposes a bill and cannot be convinced otherwise, there's not much point—it's a waste of time—to try to push it.

9. THE COMMITTEE PROCESS

The information about the lawmaking process published by the legislature explains that the committee stage involves the following. It's where a bill is examined in depth. Its pros and cons are discussed through committee hearings involving legislators, the affected interest groups, government agencies, the public, and other interested parties. Then, if necessary, the bill is amended (and similar bills are often combined) and then voted on. This is certainly an accurate description of committee procedure; but it tells nothing about the politics involved—how the committee process really works.

Legislative Politics

Factors Shaping Committee Action

The committee stage is the most crucial. If a bill gets through this stage it has a good chance of being enacted. But most bill don't make it through committee. The major factors determining committee action are explained in Box 7.4.

The Reality of the Committee Process

The reality is that, for the most part, committee action is driven by the chair and the majority's agenda. With their political influence, if the majority wants a bill, even if 30 people testify against it and only two in favor, it will pass. Politics often determines the outcome and not the merits of a proposal (however merits may be defined). What this boils down to is the committee process is often perfunctory—going through the motions in considering a bill.

Furthermore, some legislators introduce a bill on behalf of a constituent but put little, if any, juice behind it. Even if they do push it, if a bill makes it through the first committee, it likely has one or two more committee referrals—two more hurdles to clear. The highest hurdle of all is the finance committee.

Committee chairs want their fingerprints on key legislation that passes out of their committee.

But if the bill is one of the 10-15 percent or so that clears the committee process, it still has more hurdles before it's enacted into law. The first hurdle is the Rules Committee.

10. THE RULES COMMITTEE AND LEGISLATIVE POLITICS

The Rules Committee in the House and Senate (often referred to simply as Rules) has three functions. First, from time to time, it interprets the uniform rules that govern legislative operations. Second, it deals with the internal administration of its respective bodies, including allocating office space and equipment. The Committee—in

BOX 7.4
FACTORS SHAPING COMMITTEE ACTION ON A BILL

The Chair and Majority Bills

Committees have a majority of majority caucus members, who determine the fate of bills. But it's the committee chair who has by far the major influence over the fate of a bill.

The chair can usher through a bill the majority supports, one that he or she wants, or stop bills they or the majority oppose. The chair decides the calendar for hearing bills. They will not schedule a bill if they don't want to, which means it will likely die.

However, if the bill is important to the majority caucus but the chair won't schedule it, the leadership will work with the chair to give it serious consideration. If this doesn't work, the caucus will likely take a vote to have it scheduled or pull it from the committee. This so-called "rolling the chair," is an unusual measure of last resort. This is a situation a chair wants to avoid. Most are politically savvy enough not to let things go this far.

The Governor's Bills

When a bill before a committee is a governor's bill or one from the administration, the chair and committee members must be very mindful. Working to stall or amend a governor's bill may have consequences, including the governor not supporting bills of committee members, and the threat of a veto.

Nevertheless, there's often hardball politics between a committee and the governor on administration bills, and those the governor opposes. In the end, however, there must be cooperation and compromise.

The Bills of Individual Legislators

Many bills are neither majority bills nor ones of concern to the governor. Several factors determine if these get a hearing; if so, how they'll fair.

If it's a majority member's bill it will likely get a hearing, but may or may not get serious consideration unless the member is in the leadership.

As mentioned earlier, while most minority bills go nowhere, if they're not controversial, with several sponsors, most importantly one or more majority members, they may be reported out of committee. Again, however, assessing the governor's position on the bill is essential.

Whether it's a majorty or minority member's bill, in many cases, unless it has an influential player behind it, the major factor in determining if it gets out of committee, is how much it will cost to implement. A bill with a high fiscal note will have an uphill battle.

Legislative Politics

practice, the Rules chair—hires or authorizes all staff in the legislature, which gives them considerable influence with individual legislators.

Third, most important for our purposes, Rules schedules bills for their second readings by the full body of the House or Senate. This is usually referred to as consideration "on the floor" and the process of decision-making as "floor action."

The Committee Chair and Political Circumstances

It seems a simple mechanical task to schedule bills for floor action. In most cases, this is exactly what it involves, with little or no controversy. In some instances, however, scheduling certain bills can become very political and contentious. In this case, the committee can become a bottleneck or even a roadblock. Any politics involved in the committee's decisions is most often due to actions by the chair. Box 7.5 explains the circumstances in which action by the chair may become political.

The Risks

All these actions involve political risks for the chair. For this reason, it's important for them to have the support of the presiding officer and majority leader. As with other committee chairs, if they don't have this support, or alienate members of their caucus, they may be pressured to schedule the bill or even "rolled" if they refuse.

11. THE SECOND AND THIRD READINGS OF BILLS

At the second reading the bill is read again, it is debated, and any amendments approved. Amendments can only be made during this reading. When amendments are complete, the bill advances to third reading and it's voted on by the full body. If the bill passes, it is sent to

Legislative Politics

BOX 7.5
POLITICAL DECISIONS BY THE CHAIR OF THE RULES COMMITTEE

Four circumstances, two or more often related, are likely to embroil the committee's actions in politics.

One is if the chair is highly ideological with issues that are paramount to them, such as opposing a bill to increase public funds for abortions; or designating an area as a state park, thus closing it to development by the private sector. In such cases, the chair may simply not schedule these for consideration for a second reading.

A second circumstance is a pragmatic one. This could be where the chair didn't get what he or she wanted in the bill, or the parts they disapproved of taken out. In this situation, they may use their influence to try to get promises to change it in the floor session.

Third, and a similar circumstance, the chair holds a bill hostage to get a future benefit from the sponsor—garner a chit to put in their power bank. Or, where the chair's bills are not moving, he or she sits on other bills as a negotiating tool to get action on their bills.

Fourth, the chair may be pressured by an interest group or other outside influence that has supported them. For example, such pressure can be exerted when a major donor or supporter want to kill a bill.

the other house. Again, all this is certainly the case, but it says nothing about the reality of what happens.

Majority Caucus Control

In most cases, the members of each house do not weigh the pros and cons of a piece of legislation and then vote based on the strength of the arguments—far from it. As in other aspects of the policy process, the majority caucuses control these two stages of law-making. So despite all the debate that may take place, like the committee process, these two stages are most often perfunctory.

With majority control of floor sessions, how ever much the minority objects to a bill, and how ever many amendments they offer, the bill will pass virtually unchanged.

As a result, virtually all majority bills scheduled for a second and third reading are assured of passage. If there's any doubt, the leadership won't bring a bill to the floor until this is assured.

Minimal Politics—More a Mechanical Process

Although there may be some politics involved in these two stages, this is minimal (though, as we'll see in the next chapter, this may not be the case with budget bills). For the most part, the politics involves the minority offering amendments, all of which are invariably defeated.

There may also be some politics if a member gives notice of reconsideration of his or her vote on a bill (cancels their vote and request a second vote be held). This will be politically significant only if they are a majority member, the majority caucus has a slim majority, and the vote was very close.

Most often a bill that has been read a second time is advanced to third reading for final passage on the same day. This requires a three-fourths vote of the members in each house (30 in the House, 15 in the Senate).

Then the bill is sent to the other house and goes through the same three readings. In some cases, particularly when the majority sees a bill as urgent, it will be introduced in both houses at the same time. The chances are, however, that the version of the bill that comes out of each house will be different.

12. CONFERENCE COMMITTEES

When the second body passes the first body's bill with additional amendments, the first body considers the changes and either concurs with or rejects them in a formal vote. In the former case, the bill advances to the governor's office for action. In the latter, a conference committee is appointed to reconcile the differences.

Legislative
Politics

The Committee's Charge and Membership

Conference committees are charged with specific tasks and disbanded after their work is done. Presiding officers grant a level of power to each committee, from free to limited.

Free conference committees may negotiate any aspect of the bill; limited conference committees work on only those parts specified by the presiding officers.

There are six members on each committee: two from the majority caucus in the Senate, and two from the majority in the House, each appointed by their respective presiding officers. The two minority members are also appointed by the presiding officers, one from the Senate, one from the House. Each presiding officer usually consults with the leaders of the minority in each house as to which minority members should be appointed to the committee.

However, politics is often involved in these appointments. The Speaker or President may appoint any minority member from their body, even one who has not been involved with the bill. The leadership tries to avoid assigning minority members who are highly adept politically, and might cause problems for the majority on the committee. So, as with virtually all parts of the legislature's role in law making, this stage is dominated by the majority caucuses.

The Politics of Conference Committees

How much politics is involved in the conference committee process is a function of the importance of the differences between each house. It is also determined by the political leverage that the majority and minority can exert to get as close as possible to their desired version of the bill.

In many cases, however, it's not so much a matter of political maneuvering, but of compromise and coming to a consensus, especially with budget bills. Conference committees are often more bipartisan than most stages of the bill process.

Legislative Politics

Nevertheless, where there's major conflict, the majority, of course, has the upper hand. This is especially so if it's a bill that the majority wants badly and to which the minority is strongly opposed. In this case, the committee will likely not debate the pros and cons of the differences to come up with a compromise. The majority will dominate the reconciling of the two bills and call for a vote. And, lo and behold, the majority win the vote.

After the Bills are Reconciled

Once the two bills are reconciled into a new version, it goes to the House and Senate for approval. If the houses cannot agree, a new conference committee is appointed and the process begins all over again. When the bill is finally agreed upon, it goes to the governor.

13. CONSIDERATION BY THE GOVERNOR

In considering bills, the state constitution gives the governor several options. These are set out in Box 7.6.

The Politics of Sending Bills to the Governor

In some cases, politics is involved in the speed at which the governor receives a bill and the number of bills they receive at once. As Box 7.6 shows, when the legislature is in session, the governor has 15 days to act on a bill, 20 days if the legislature has adjourned. These 15 or 20 days is the time from when the legislature forwards the bill. Exactly when they send it over is entirely their decision.

Swift Submission to the Governor

When the majority and the governor are of the same party, they often work in close coordination, and send the bill over quickly for his or her signature. They do so in an attempt to reduce the extent of the governor being lobbied by those who oppose all or part of the

BOX 7.6
THE GOVERNOR'S CHOICES IN CONSIDERING BILLS

The governor has 15 days, Sundays excluded, to act on a bill if the legislature is in session. If the legislature has adjourned, they have 20 days, excluding Sundays.

By constitutional mandate, the governor must sign a bill, veto it, or allow it to become law without his or her signature. If the governor vetoes a bill or, in the case of a budget bill, reduces or vetoes an appropriation (exercising the line item veto), it must be returned to the legislature, with a statement of the reasons for the veto, within the constitutional time limits.

When the governor allows a bill to become law without a signature, he or she advises the legislature by special message as required by the constitution.

If the legislature is in session, both houses can meet to override or sustain a veto. For this, the houses sit in joint session as a unicameral body. It requires a two-thirds vote, three-fourths for appropriation bills, of the sixty members to override a veto and have the bill become law.

If the legislature has adjourned, the vetoed bill must be taken up within five days after the convening of the legislature in its second regular session or any special session. If the governor vetoes a bill after the adjournment of a second regular session, the veto will not be addressed unless a special session is called before the next legislature convenes.

the legislation. This is also often the case with non-controversial and bipartisan bills. For publicity purposes, many legislators like to get a public signing by the governor. As there are far more such requests than the governor can handle, these legislators also want their bill sent quickly.

Stalling Tactics

On the other hand, the legislature can stall in sending a bill to the governor; or inundate them with a large batch at the same time. Such tactics are often used when the governor and majorities are of different parties, or the legislature is divided between the two parties. This may be for strategic purposes, or just to give the governor grief.

Legislative Politics

Budget Bills versus Other Bills

Despite the politics of submitting bills, by the time a bill reaches the governor's desk, most of its problems have been sorted out. This is particularly true of majority caucus bills and the governor's bills that are part of the "must haves" in their adjournment packages. It's also the case with most other bills.

While the governor's consideration of all bills is similar, there is a major difference in the way he or she can deal with budget bills (appropriations bills), versus all other bills. As mentioned earlier, while they have a line item veto on budget bills, this is not the case on other bills, which must be signed or vetoed, or become law without a signature.

The politics involved in the governor's consideration of budget bills is covered in the next chapter.

In the rest of this section, we focus on the other type of bills. Some of these will be majority members' bills and some those of minority members. While not usually as political as some fights over bills in many adjournment packages, politics is often involved in the governor's consideration of these bills. Sometimes the politics are intense.

Potential Political Considerations

Politics can develop over a bill for several reasons:

- An interest group opposes the bill but was unable to kill it in the legislature.

- It may have been passed over the opposition of a department.

- Its opponents see it as too costly.

- In its final form, the governor may see it as bad public policy.

- It may conflict with his or her agenda.

- Some of the governor's major supporters during his or her election may oppose it.

Lobbying the Governor

In these and other circumstances, the governor will be lobbied, sometimes intensely, by forces pro and con the bill. This will include: the affected interest groups and their lobbyists; legislators; commissioners; prominent individuals, including the governor's major donors; and, in some cases, the public.

On bills with a high public profile, like those involving reducing the amount of the PFD, increasing the salaries of public officials, or highly divisive issues, such as cutting state funds for abortions, there may be a spontaneous public barrage of comments. The governor's office will be inundated with phone calls, e-mails, petitions, and posts on social media. Lobbyists and interest group staff may organize a coordinated effort by their members or supporters to lobby the governor.

Input into the Governor's Decision

Usually, the lobbying on a bill is funneled through the governor's legislative director. Ultimately, of course, the governor must decide. This will likely be with the advice of the chief of staff, the legislative director, perhaps a special assistant, and the director of OMB.

The governor may also involve key players involved or who may have a major interest in this legislation. If the governor is going to support or veto a bill that goes against those they may need in the future, he or she will likely notify them so they're not taken by surprise.

Use of the Veto

Because of agreement on the final form of most bills between the majority in both houses and the governor, veto of a bill is unusual. When bills are vetoed, they are rarely overridden by the legislature. However, in cases where one or both houses are of different parties to the governor, and the governor vetoes a bill, the legislature is more likely to override the veto.

Legislative Politics

14. AFTER THE BILL BECOMES LAW: WRITING REGULATIONS

This is the major aspect of stage 3 of the policy process shown in Box 7.2 above. Laws take effect 90 days after the governor's approval, unless the legislature designates a different effective date. Some laws can be implemented without the need for regulations, but many require regulations before they can go into effect. This means the governor's signature is not the final step in the lawmaking process. The politics involved in the new law may be far from over.

> *Constant vigilance is needed. Be aware of what happens after a bill become law—your lobbying effort may be far from over.*

The Need for Regulations: An Example

After passage, new laws are turned over to the department under which their jurisdictions falls. Take, for instance, a law to aid the blind in navigating state government buildings, and accessing and reading public documents. This bill would likely go to the Department of Health and Social Services with aid from other affected departments. The legislation will require regulations, such as defining precisely what facilities and documents are to be included, and whether Braille and/or a voice system will be used in elevators to designate floors.

The Range of Stakeholders and Types of Input

The way the regulations are written can make or break the effectiveness of a law. For this reason, besides the department or departments concerned, other parties will be interested in how these regulations are written. Legislators, their staff, the governor's office, and especially lobbyists, monitor and sometimes get involved in the writing process. This is another reason lobbyists need to develop close ties with state agencies that affect their issues.

Legislative Politics

Different departments have different policies for receiving input into the writing process. Some prefer input via their websites; others allow direct personal contact. Some welcome input at the drafting stage; others try to keep affected parties at arm's length.

The Politics of Writing Regulations

Most regulation writing involves technical considerations and little politics. So, in general, departments receive little outside pressure in writing them. In cases where politics is involved, the department writing the regulations holds most of the marbles. Box 7.7, on the next page, explains the major circumstances that influence writing regulations.

Input After the Regulations are Issued

Although some departments seek input on regulations during the drafting process, they're not required to do so. However, once written, they are required to publish them for public comment. In most cases, they are published on the department's website for people to submit comments.

The department reviews these comments, but is not obliged to include any of them in the final version of the regulations. This is yet another example of the power state agencies can wield.

15. COMPLETING THE POLICY CYCLE

Looking back at Box 7.2, it shows that, after regulations have been written, there are three more stages to the policy cycle. These are the parts of the process where there's reaction to the law and plans made to revisit it.

Stages 4, 5, and 6 of the Cycle

Stage 4, the implementation phase of the law, may cause some initial reaction. At this stage there's likely no plans to deal with the

Legislative Politics

BOX 7.7
FACTORS INFLUENCING REGULATION WRITING BY A DEPARTMENT

A department can write regulations quickly, within the 90-days before the law is scheduled to take effect, or they may move slowly. When they exceed the 90-day limit, this may be for technical or political reasons.

Technical Reasons

- The department may be overloaded and the regulations must wait their turn to be written.

- The regulations may be complicated and take time to write.

- The department may seek public comment before publishing draft regulations.

- If the law is new to the state, the department may seek advice from other states with similar laws.

- Several departments may need to provide input.

- Writing the regulations may fall between the cracks because of a change of administration.

Political Reasons

- The department (and perhaps other affected agencies) opposed the law and are intentionally dragging their feet (in some instances, a department may never write the regulations, so the law will not be implemented).

- There may be conflicts between departments over the details of the regulations, and some form of compromise needs to be reached.

- A powerful interest group sees itself as adversely affected by the law, and works with the governor's office, legislators, and the commissioner to delay writing the regulations.

- The law may be challenged in court and the state prevented from writing the regulations until the suit has been decided.

Dealing with a Tardy Situation

In situations where there's little movement in writing the regulations, some or all of the stakeholders may try to bring pressure on the department.

- The legislator or legislators concerned can write to the commissioner to request the regulations be written post haste.

- Legislators may get involved when the effective date of the law is soon after passage, such as a law to aid in combating the opioid epidemic. In some cases, the lobbyist or other prominent person may contact the department. But generally, contract lobbyists don't get directly involved in pressuring a department.

- If low-key efforts do not work, the legislators involved and the affected constituency may put pressure on the governor to encourage the department to get moving. Pressure by a constituency is often organized by a legislator or a lobbyist. Using the governor to get things moving often works.

concerns. By contrast, stage 5 involves the forces, pro and con, formulating plans to change or protect the policy. These might

Today's laws are often the root of tomorrow's problems.

include a court challenge, or an effort to put the law before the public in a referendum. Then, in stage 6, those who want to see a policy changed or repealed, work to get it back on the policy agenda. If they are successful, the cycle begins over again.

Among the reason for revisiting a law are that some people may oppose it because they disagreed with it in principle, or because they see it as not effectively addressing the problem. Another reason is that the necessity to compromise means that policy-makers rarely get all they want, and so try to modify a policy. It could also be that the law has flaws not envisaged when it was written and needs reforming. Plus, over time, values change, and consequently people want to amend or repeal a particular policy. A good example is the debate over the death penalty since the 1960s.

Legislative Politics

★ CHAPTER 8 ★

The Particulars of Budget Politics

*Dealing with the budget,
particularly closing it out at the end of the session,
involved some of the most intense politics
and personal conflicts I experienced in
my 14 years in the legislature.*

—Senator Lyda Green,
Alaska Senate President,
2007-09

Even though dealing with the budget is similar to the passage of laws, there are important differences. Passage of budget bills, particularly the operating budget, is the most prominent part of the legislative process. As such, it's the most important function of the legislature and one of the most important functions of the executive branch. Given this, the politics involved in the budget provide extensive insights into the realities of policy-making and the exercise of power.

The insights in this chapter do not focus on a particular budget or legislative session. They are observations that generally apply to any Alaska state budget.

Chapter 4 covers how the state budget differs from a business or family budget, major budget terminology, and the budget calendar, among other things. It's a good idea to read that chapter before this one.

1. PUTTING BUDGET POLITICS IN PERSPECTIVE

Partly because most public exposure to the budget process takes place in the legislative session, it's easy to get the impression that the legislature has the most influence on the size of the budget. Because of this, it may appear to many Alaskans that all the state spends is subject to change each year. But things don't work quite this way.

The governor and executive branch, particularly the Office of Management and Budget (OMB), have the first and major say on what goes into the budget. This includes all mandated and other required expenditures, such as for education, social services, and prisons. So the legislature is in a reactive position in considering budget bills sent them by the governor. Plus, compared with the administration, the legislature has both limited time and support staff to consider the budget in-depth. This means the legislature can only review a few areas of expenditure in any session to challenge the governor's numbers, or the budget request of a state agency.

There are always additions and cuts in several programs, and some shifts in priorities, in the adjournment package of both the legislative leadership and the governor. Despite this, in most years, the final budget includes much of what

FY15 BUDGET $13.8 BILLION

the governor sent to the legislature the prior December. And the total budget is usually within a billion dollars of the original proposal.

As to individual legislators, while they likely have concerns about its overall size and content, most are primarily concerned with getting funds included in the budget to benefit their constituents. Their ability to bring home the bacon can make or break their political career. This is especially the case with rural-bush legislators. One of their major goals is to close the gap between their districts and urban areas regarding infrastructure, power costs, and medical and school facilities, among other needs. In lean budget years, however, most individual legislators will get few if any funds for their district.

2. DEVELOPING THE BUDGET

Putting the budget together between July and December involves some politics. Besides mandated and essential state services, much of what goes into the budget are items on the governor's agenda. And by implication, expenditures not included are items he or she sees as a low priority, or not necessary to run government.

There is often a to-and-fro between what a department requests and what OMB and the governor want to include. At this stage, legislators often work to get items in the budget by including them as part of an agency's requests, or by promoting their proposed expenditure with the governor or OMB.

> *The budget process is a continual and a major aspect of the work of all parts of state government.*

Requests by Interest Group and Lobbyists

This is also the stage when various interest groups and lobbyists work to get funding for their program or issue, or to maintain or increase funding they received the previous year. They know it's much easier to get funding for a program included in the governor's budget than try to get it added by the legislature.

The message for you is: If you have an issue involving an expenditure, this is the best time to meet with your legislator, the agency personnel concerned, or someone at OMB.

Revenue Forecasts

One major factor affecting the governor's budget and how the legislature reacts to it, is the Department of Revenue's state revenue forecast for the upcoming year.

The forecast consists of projecting production levels and the price of oil over that period, as oil taxes and royalties constitute over 80 percent of state revenues (excluding federal funds). These forecasts are one element shaping budget politics, and usually the character of the legislative session, particularly in low revenue years.

3. INTRODUCTION OF BUDGET BILLS, AND LEGISLATIVE REACTION

This is where the real politics surrounding the budget begin.

After the budget is released by the governor on December 15, the legislature responds with their initial reactions. While there are various responses among legislators, depending on what they like or dislike in the budget, the most important reaction is from the majority caucuses.

This reaction depends a lot on the extent to which the governor's budget reflects their adjournment package, as well as the relationship between the leadership and the governor. The two majorities may respond positively to many or only some parts of the budget, and negatively, in some cases very negatively, to others. In the latter case, the Senate or House majority, or both, may issue statements that some items in the budget are DOA (dead on arrival).

If the legislative majorities strongly disagree with major parts of the budget, such as the amount allocated to K–12 education or social services, or the funding for particular items, they may indicate they'll work to increase, reduce, or eliminate some items, or even write their own budget. These and other reactions set the scene for consideration of the budget by the legislature.

4. INTERNAL LEGISLATIVE BUDGET POLITICS

We could write a book on the politics of this aspect of budget politics. Not afforded that luxury, the main points are set out in Box 8.1.

To emphasize the last point in the box, although legislative budget politics do not formally include the governor, he or she is ever-present on the minds of legislators.

Overall, and in many specific situations, the governor is the major influence shaping budget politics in the legislature.

BOX 8.1
BUDGET POLITICS IN THE LEGISLATURE

- The legislature spends the bulk of its time on the operating budget. The capital budget is usually decided after the operating budget is finalized.

- Because of the short time the legislature has to consider the budget, and its minimal resources, some parts of the budget receive more attention than others.

- The leadership in both houses, particularly the chairs of the House and Senate Finance Committees, have the dominant influence on the budget. They determine which parts will receive the most scrutiny.

- Legislators and the finance committees often propose budget amendments.

- Many disagreements within the legislature, between the legislature and state agencies and the governor, are due to many budget items being based on projections of their cost (in some cases, based on guesswork). Often there's also disagreement on the size of fiscal notes (see section 8 below).

- Dissension often exists within both majorities over what should and should not be supported or cut, and invariably between the House and Senate majorities on the final version of the budget. Resolving the conflict between the two majorities is usually key to bringing the legislative session to a close. More on this in section 9 below.

- Members of the majority, particularly Republican majorities, are required to vote for the final version of the budget. Those who don't are either expelled from the caucus, or stripped of their committee assignments.

- The minority caucuses have very little influence over the budget. In some situations, however, particularly when a two-thirds vote is need on the budget, the majority has considerable influence (see section 9 below on finalizing the budget).

- Legislative budget politics are constantly influenced by the role and budget priorities of "the sixty-first legislator"—the governor.

5. THE DYNAMICS BETWEEN THE LEGISLATURE AND THE GOVERNOR

The interactions between the legislature and the governor on the budget are, on a day-to-day basis, like those on general legislation. There are, however, three important additional elements:

- Major conflicts between the legislature and the governor often revolve around budget politics. This is because of the high stakes involved on both sides, and the necessity to produce a budget at the end of each session. And that these are linked to other priorities of the legislative majorities and the governor.

- The significance of the budget to the administration means that there is more interaction between the governor's office and senior agency personnel with the legislature on various aspects of the budget than on other legislation. This involves regular administration contact with the finance committees in each house, including presenting testimony, particularly by the director of OMB.

- More so than with most legislation, the legislative majorities are always mindful of the governor's line item veto power. Often, when there's bipartisan support on an issue, part of the legislature's calculation is: Can we muster the votes to override the governor's veto? This takes three-fourths for appropriation bills—45 votes—and two-thirds—40 votes—for all other vetoed legislation.

The Legislature's Investigative Power

The legislature's investigatory function can give the administration political heartburn.

The legislature has a Legislative Budget and Audit Committee (LB&A); though much of it's work is housekeeping. It provides fiscal analyses, budget reviews, and audits and performance reviews of state agencies. The committee also monitors the lending and investment activities of the state. Two agencies provide technical assistance to the LB&A: the Division of Legislative Finance and the Division of Legislative Audit.

What influence the committee has on the budget depends on how proactive the chair sees his or his role. Plus, LB&A works closely with the House and Senate Finance committees, and makes decision on expenditure of budget items in the interim.

Audit Requests and Reports

Any legislator can request an audit of virtually any aspect of state government. A mediocre or poor evaluation can affect a department's budget allocations by the legislature. It gives the legislature leverage in dealing with the department and the governor. More comprehensive reports by Legislative Finance, such as on projected state revenues, and how these might affect future state budgets, can, as indicated earlier, shape discussions on the budget between the legislature and the administration.

All this adds to the mix of budget politics in a legislative session, or over the course of several sessions.

6. SUPPLEMENTALS AND REAPPROPRIATIONS

Politics also surrounds the legislature agreeing to supplemental expenditures and reappropriating funds.

As it's difficult to definitively predict the cost of a program, as unforeseen expenses often arise, the governor presents a

At times, requests for supplemental funds and reappropriations, can lead to major conflicts between the legislature, the governor and state agencies.

supplemental bill each year to cover these costs. In addition, in some cases, not all the funds needed for a program or project are spent. These are available to be reappropriated for another purpose.

The need for a particular supplemental and its amount often produce disagreements between the legislature, the governor, and the agencies concerned. The question legislators often ask is: Why can't the agency cover this out of its existing funds?

Reappropriating funds sometimes lead to disputes between a legislator or legislators from a district where these funds were not spent. The legislator usually wants the funds transferred to another project in their district. But the governor or agency affected may want them for another program outside the district.

7. STATE AGENCIES AND BUDGET POLITICS

All departments and other state agencies are routinely involved in aspects of budget politics. But with a few exceptions, such as the University's budget, their involvement is less obvious because the media focus more on high-profile activities of the legislature, the governor, and major interest groups. In many cases, state agencies get involved in budget politics in dealing with requests from the constituencies they serve, negotiating with the governor and OMB on their budget requests, requesting supplementals and reappropriations, among other circumstances.

Justifying their Budget

Politics is often involved in an agency defending its budget to the legislature, especially if requesting a funding increase. The commissioner, deputy commissioner, legislative liaison, and division directors, testify before committees, and work with legislators and their staffs, some sympathetic to their cause, others not so supportive to their request. In addition to keeping their level of funding, secure an increase, or justify a supplemental, agencies work to avoid additional responsibilities that are not funded—so-called unfunded mandates.

Departmental Scrutiny

Whether through an LB&A review or a legislative audit focusing on a department, one of its divisions, or other state agency, at some time or another, all parts of the administration are involved in politics, sometimes intense politics, as the result of scrutiny by the legislature. These politics may take the form of a major clash between the members of a committee and senior agency staff and the governor. Such conflict is particularly the case when Republicans are in power. They generally want to reduce government expenditures, and eliminate what they see as unnecessary services or programs, while state agencies wish to maintain their levels of services.

Sometimes influential legislators have a long-standing concern about a department and, in some cases, a personality conflict with one of its senior administrators. Justified or not, these conflicts can add to the political involvement of the department and most likely increase scrutiny of its budget, ramping up the department's interaction with the legislature.

Agency Budget Maneuvering

An agency may or may not be happy with what they get in the governor's budget. Nevertheless, they are required to support the budget as it affects them in dealing with the legislature. In addition to a department having objections to unfunded mandates, it may object to new responsibilities even if they are funded. In these cases, even though the political risks are high in working against the parts of the governor's budget they don't like, or a responsibility or expenditure imposed by the legislature, an agency can work to increase, stymie or stall budget items.

> *State agencies, particularly those with large budgets, such as Education, and Health and Social Services, are always in the think of budget politics.*

BOX 8.2
THE POLITICS OF FISCAL NOTES

Fiscal notes become political for a combination of reasons. The fundamental factor is that implementation of a piece of legislation depends on it being funded. This opens up the amount in the note to manipulation by those who support it, oppose it, think the estimate is too high or too low, or simply want to put the brakes on government spending of all types.

Political Maneuvering

Manipulating the size of a note can be used to both reduce, even kill a piece of legislation, and to increase its chances of passage. For instance, a department that doesn't like a bill, or amended bill proposed by a legislator, can purposely inflate the size of the note to reduce its chance of passage.

Conversely, for a piece of their legislation or that of a legislator who they support, a department can draw up a note with lower figures than needed to implement it. Then they come back for a supplemental to cover its actual cost. On occasion, a department will give a bill a zero fiscal note.

Sometimes, however, and for some of the reasons mentioned above, when a legislative committee opposes a bill, they will reduce a note to zero, and tell the department or agency to fund it out of their current budget. On other occasions, a bill can pick up an amendment that requires an additional fiscal note that will increase its cost. This action, often disguised as a "friendly amendment," is also a tactic to kill a bill.

Efforts to Impose Accuracy

Either explicitly or implicitly, every governor comes into office with the goal of producing fiscal notes that are as accurate as possible. They try to impose this on all the agencies under their control. And certainly, OMB keeps an eye on things to be sure fiscal notes are as accurate as possible.

But, as we can see, politically the administration has little control of the legislature in this regard outside of a threatened veto. Plus, now and again, an agency finds it advantageous to work around the governor's directive.

The agency can work skillfully with supportive legislators to eliminate a part of their budget they oppose or to increase the parts they need. They can use their constituent groups, such as the Department of Commerce, Community, and Economic Development working with business groups, to promote specific aspects of their budget. In other situations, a department can advise the governor to veto an expenditure included in the final budget; or the agency can stall in writing regulations for a bill or policy and its expenditure.

8. FISCAL NOTES

All legislation requiring expenditures must have a fiscal note attached to the bill estimating its cost of implementation over time. Typically, writing these is assigned to the department(s) affected by the specific piece of legislation. Each fiscal note is signed by the person who drafted it, and/or who authorized the numbers in the note. This is usually a commissioner, deputy commissioner, or a division director.

Fiscal notes should be realistic projections of the cost of legislation, so putting them together shouldn't involve politics. Most do not, but others do. Many public officials will deny this; but observation confirms that this claim is political subterfuge. Box 8.2 explains why.

There's often no faster way to kill a bill than to hang a big price tag on it.

9. FINALIZING THE BUDGET: THE POLITICAL STAKES AND NEGOTIATIONS

As Senator Green notes at the beginning of this chapter, finalizing the budget involves some of the most intense politics and, often, major personal conflicts. Box 8.3, on the next page, summarizes reasons for the level of intensity and its political significance. Building on these general points, let's look at the specifics of what happens in the two branches of government.

BOX 8.3
REASONS FOR THE INTENSITY IN CLOSING OUT THE BUDGET

- Because the budget must be finalized for state government to continue to function, there is a sense of political urgency not present in most other legislation.

- In contrast to other legislation, all legislators, the governor, and state agencies, have a direct interest in the budget bills. Many more interests are at stake.

- The extent to which the legislative leadership and the governor can secure their "must haves" in their respective adjournment packages, largely revolves around what will be in the budget. Consequently, the extent of conflict in resolving their respective "must haves," is usually the major factor that shapes the political intensity in bringing the session to a close.

- As a result, of the first three factors, in finalizing the budget, lobbying involves more interests and interest groups than on any other legislation. They exert pressure on legislative leaders, the governor, and various parts of the administration, to get or protect their appropriations.

- The fact that the governor has a line-item veto factors into the wheeling-and-dealing in a major way.

- The wheeling-and-dealing tends to be more intense when state revenues are low. When they are high, the budget can be decided before the 90-day session limit. When revenues are low, the session may drag on, as all concerned jockey to get some piece of the budget. As a result, there may be one or more special sessions.

Finalizing the Budget in the Legislature

The budget bills that emerge from the House and the Senate are invariably different in what they include and exclude. A conference committee is set up to iron out these differences. If the differences are major, or the conflict between each house is intense, it may take several conference committees to come up with a final operating and capital budget.

Added to these efforts is the involvement of the governor and his or her principal staff. The major staff involved are the legislative director, the chief of staff, special assistants, the director of OMB, and perhaps some OMB staff assistants.

Budget Conference Committees

While budget conference committee meetings are held in public, most negotiations are conducted behind closed doors.

Over the years, major players in this process have been key staffers of the chairs of the House and Senate Finance Committees and other leadership staff. They move

Despite the often high drama of conflict that surrounds finalizing the budget, both in the legislature and between the governor and the legislature, in the end they all have to work it out—cooperate and compromise to keep government ticking.

between the various parties involved and check off differences as they are resolved. With the differences settled, conference committee meetings are mostly perfunctory. They often convene for only a few minutes with no discussion before the budgets are approved and sent back to their respective houses for approval.

Capital Budgets

When state revenues are high, the unwritten rule is that all legislators get some funds for their district. This includes minority members; though they get less than majority members. In lean years, with most capital funds needed for federal matches, there's often little discussion on the capital budget. Instead, with no capital budget handouts, but legislator still looking for some funds for their district and priority programs, there may be major fights between the majority and the minority over what is and is not in the operating budget. The minority often offers dozens of amendments to the operating budget bill, all of which are invariably voted down.

When there's a Need to Draw Funds from the CBR

One circumstance in which the minority may have a fair amount of influence on the final budget, is when there's a need to draw money from the Constitutional Budget Reserve (CBR). This produces a different political dynamic because it takes an affirmative vote of three-fourths of each house to appropriate money from the CBR. Getting this number requires wooing the minority for support.

According to the state constitution, the CBR is only to be used for budget shortfalls. But the majority-minority negotiations often subordinate this to political goals. The minorities use the promise of their vote to get commitments of appropriations for such programs as education and social services for the Democrats, and aid to business and development projects for the Republicans. So the political reality is that the use of the CBR for purposes other than revenue shortfalls has become another dimension of budget politics, one most likely here to stay.

> **When there's a need to draw money from the CBR to supplement the budget, is one of the few occasions when the minority caucuses can exert influence on parts of the budget.**

In the Hands of the Governor

The governor's review of budget bills is a major task as these are much more extensive than all other bills. Some of what goes on at this stage involves similar activity to other legislation, as explained in section 13 of Chapter 7. The major difference is that the governor can scrutinize every appropriation and use the line item veto to reduce or eliminate any appropriation. But the governor may not add funds to a budget bill.

The governor's line-item veto power means that potentially he or she, and others in the administration, could be lobbied on every appropriation, either pro or con, regarding its inclusion in the budget. But governors carefully consider use of the veto on budget bills for several reasons.

Legal Requirement and Negotiated Appropriations

As noted at the beginning of this chapter, constitutional, statutory, and various other requirements, mean that over 60 percent of the operating budget is spoken for. Although the governor may line-item parts of these appropriations, that he or she feels aren't necessary to comply with mandated requirements, not essential to the operation of state government, or need to be pared down in times of tight revenues, this is not done very often. This is largely because these expenditures have been agreed upon in the long negotiations with the legislature.

Of the amount of the operating budget left for negotiation, the legislature and the governor will also have agreed on allocation of most of these funds. This leaves only a very small portion of the operating budget open to the veto.

A similar situation is true with the governor dealing with the capital budget when the state is flush. In these years, as all legislators get some capital money agreed on internally in the legislature, the governor will be reluctant to veto any of these appropriations, particularly of majority members who he or she might need in the future.

Reasons for Using the Veto

Nevertheless, the governor does use the line-item veto on occasions. Some of the reasons may be similar to vetoing other bills. These include: that a state agency opposes the bill; it may not be supported by one or more of his or her major donors or supporters; or the governor may see it as bad public policy.

There are also reasons that may be specific to some unresolved conflicts on the budget. This could be: a fight over an expenditure that the legislature wants but of which the governor disapproves, especially in years where cuts are needed; or that the governor sees a program or service as too expensive. And human nature being what it is, on rare occasions, governors veto items meant

OPERATING BUDGET

State Ferry Maintenance $32,000,000

$8,500,000
Palmer Community Center $13,000,000

Knik Arm Bridge Access Ramps $53,000,000

> *Governors' vetoes of budget appropriations are rarely overridden by the legislature. So the governor's consideration of the budget is the make or break time for those with items in the budget, which results in the governor and their advisers being lobbied intensely.*

to benefit the district of a legislator or group they dislike for whatever reason.

With the advice of his or her senior staff and others the governor deems necessary for information or to consult for political purposes, all these decisions are made carefully after weighing the pros and cons. This is for a combination of reasons:

- To keep spending in line with his or her agenda.

- The need to balance the provision of services with using funds sparingly.

- Taking regional interests into consideration.

- In addition to members of the majority in both houses, alienating as few people as possible, particularly those they may need politically now and in the future.

- Reducing the likelihood of the legislature overriding any vetoes.

A Break with the Normalcy of Budget Politics

A major break with these general rules, and cooperation between the legislature and the governor over the budget, occurred under Governor Mike Dunleavy during the legislative session of 2019. A strong believer in major reductions in government spending, he was at odds with most legislators over his proposed massive cuts to the budget. He vetoed virtually every expenditure the legislature re-inserted in his original budget proposal. This was, in part, to have the funds to fulfill his campaign promise to pay each Alaskan a full PFD of around $3,000. Entrenched political warfare ensued.

In many ways, this changed the political dynamic of the budge process. The legislature was seen as not a co-equal in the process by the administration. And with his veto authority and the difficultly in over-riding the cuts, the governor made many of them stick (though he relented on some cuts due largely to intense public pressure). Many commentators called this government by veto.

After the Budget Becomes Law

Once the budget is signed, assuming there's no attempt to override some vetoes, the laws authorizing expenditures go to OMB for distribution to state agencies, local governments, and other organizations slated to receive funds. Although they have a pretty good idea, it still takes a while for state agencies to figure out what they've got and didn't get in the budget; and to adjust their responsibilities and provision of service accordingly, before the budget goes into effect on July 1.

Legislative Intent Language

Sometimes the legislature includes "intent language" in the budget bill. That is. it gives specific instructions on how appropriated funds are to be spent. In this case, the agency or other organizations receiving the funds more or less follow this intent.

In other cases, the legislature may express what it wants to happen with parts of the budget, but doesn't include funds for this purpose. In this case, intent language isn't worth much, even though lawmakers have taken a solid position.

Despite legislative intent, most agencies have leeway in spending funds, even in those areas where expenditures have been specified. The Department of Transportation is particularly known for its discretionary use of funds. In the case of the University, the legislature usually provides a lump sum and gives the Board of Regents and the President complete discretion to spend it. Though, again, this changed in a major way under Governor Dunleavy.

The Continual Budget Cycle

The end of one budget cycle marks the beginning of the next one. Beginning in July the governor, through OMB and state agencies starts to put together the budget for the next fiscal year. For all parts of state government, the legislature, the administration, the court system, and the University, as well as scores of interest groups, dealing with the budget is a never-ending process.

12. THE BIG PICTURE OF POLICY-MAKING, AND THE DECISIONS OF INDIVIDUAL POLITICIANS

Having considered the law-making process in the last chapter and the budget process in this one, by drawing on Box 8.4, we conclude by looking at how the policy process will affect your lobbying effort. The box sets out the big picture of the process and the factors that shape the decisions of all politicians, as covered in these two chapters.

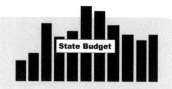

BOX 8.4
TEN REALITIES OF THE POLICY PROCESS

- You need a comprehensive perspective of the policy process. This requires focusing not only on the legislature but the governor, and state agencies if they will impact your issue, and they likely will. This perspective is necessary to integrate all parts of the policy process to stand a chance of success.

- The process is almost entirely political with power providing the juice to make it all work. The various policy-makers—legislators, the governor, top agency personnel, lobbyists—all jockey to get what they want. They all think and act politically. So to deal with them effectively, you've got to think that way too.

- The dominance of the process by politics, combined with the legislature and the governor acting as checks on each other and that vetting legislation is often drawn-out, means that the policy process is by design inefficient and messy.

- None of the players in the policy process operate in isolation. They are all politically interconnected—the decisions of one affects one or more of the others in various ways on various issues and policies.

- In most cases, the epicenter of power lies with the majority in each house, particularly the leadership, and with the governor. In addition, state agencies as well as some influential interests, particularly natural resource and development interests, also wield considerable influence in cases of concern to them. In most situations, the minority in each house has little influence.

- With no players having enough power to get all they want, the system is built around compromise: coming to a consensus after a process of negotiation involving wheeling and dealings and a series of transactions where everyone gets something.

- The budget and budget politics are central to the process. It affects every politician and all senior agency personnel. So, you need to keep abreast of what's happening with the budget and how it may affect you.

- Besides building relationships with colleagues and the governor, based on benefit to their constituents or their own interest, individual legislators, majority and minority members, build relationships and alliances with administrative personnel. These include everything from economic development to energy to combatting domestic violence.

- Rarely does the passage of a law or the finalizing of a policy put the issue to bed for all time. Some affected interests will disagree with the law or policy, a new administration may be elected vowing to change these decisions; values and other circumstances may change. In all these and other circumstances, there will be attempts to change or repeal the law or policy. Consequently, most issues are present in the policy process over time, even though many may not be part of the process in some years.

- You've got to figure out which public officials have the political influence on your issue and identify other power points that might affect you, such as your opponents, a federal agency, the media, and public sentiment. So you should spend little time dealing with those who have little influence and can't help you.

What Shapes the Decisions of Individual Politicians?

In the end, the big picture of policy-making boils down to decisions made by individual politicians, both those in leadership positions and others. Combining the big picture with what shapes the particular decisions of individual elected officials, provides a holistic view of the policy-making process.

Faced with an issue, such as funding K-12 education for the disabled, dealing with a state budget deficit, or public pressure to reinstate the death penalty, what influences a politician's actions? Box 8.5 sets out the various circumstances that influences these decisions. One point to note is that, even the most influential policy-makers have constraints on their actions.

11. FROM THE REALITIES OF ALASKA POLITICS TO THE SPECIFICS OF LOBBYING

This overview of the policy process concludes consideration of the realities of Alaska politics—the essential foundation for anyone who wants to lobby effectively. The rest of this handbook explains the specifics of organizing and implementing a lobbying campaign.

Using Information to Suit Your Needs

While we can't assure you of success, the next eight chapters offer a systematic way of approaching a lobbying effort covering the major aspects involved in a campaign. This includes: what's involved in managing a campaign; developing a lobbying plan; what to do, and not do, when meeting with public officials, and much more.

That said, this information and advice should not necessarily be followed to the letter. Select from it depending on your level of knowledge and experience, and the needs of your campaign. Some

BOX 8.5
FACTORS INFLUENCING DECISIONS BY
POLITICIANS ON POLICY ISSUES

There are three main factors shaping the approach of politicians in decision-making: (1) the unique position of the governor; (2) when there's a collective decision; and (3) when a politician is free to decide the course of action. There is overlap between these categories, but the distinctions are important.

1. The Unique Position of the Governor

As the head of the executive branch and with extensive formal constitutional authority, governors have the most flexibility of any policy-makers in what courses of action to follow. Nonetheless, they are constrained by the need to get legislative support, and that of certain interest groups for their budgets and high priority issues.

In addition, the governor's approach is shaped by the fact that they represent the entire state and have to take statewide interests into consideration when deciding on policy. This will often include balancing regional interests. By contrast, legislators first and foremost represent their constituents, and often put this above state interests (but will rarely admit it). Though their regional interests often come into play (Southeast, Southcentral, etc).

2. When there's a Collective Decision on Policy Action

Collective decisions include:

• Those made by the majority caucuses in the legislature, particularly supporting the budget.

• A regional caucus that has agreed on a course of action for obtaining funds and how these will be allocated among the members.

• Unity among the governor's staff and senior department personnel, regarding the governor's policy approaches.

In these circumstances, the policy-maker risks being castigated or fired if they don't go along with this collective decision.

(continued . . .)

BOX 8.5 CONTINUED

3. When Policy-Makers are Free to Decide on Specific Action

When not constrained to vote or act along caucus or other lines, the actions of politicians, including the governor, are shaped by one or a combination of:

- Their political perspective (in some cases an ideology).

- The forces of political necessity, particularly representing their constituents and, as far as possible, satisfying their needs.

- Deciding to benefit one or more of their donors or supporters.

- In various other ways, promoting their personal interests, such as the need to be re-elected, a desire for higher office, among others.

When and in what ways one or more of these factors shape a politician's decision, will depend on the nature of the issue.

When the Issue is High-Profile

On high-profile issues, such as K-12 funding, tax issues, and criminal justice reform, policy-makers need to take a position. This will be shaped by their philosophy, the views of their constituents, and the benefit to their district, and perhaps by interest groups, among other factors.

of the information you'll find useful, other parts may not be relevant to your situation. Still others may fly in the face of your experience. Even if you are a novice, you'll develop your own style and, as you do so, use the  information and advice most useful as you become conversant with lobbying.

When the Issue is Low-Profile but of Major Concern to a Politician

When a politician has a major stake in a policy outcome, but the issue is low-profile, their action is most likely determined by those who can help secure the goal or block one they oppose.

Even if they are an influential legislator or executive branch official, including the governor, this involves building alliances and coalitions with other public officials and interest groups. For many politicians it may involve trading future favors or votes.

When the Issue is of Minor, if any, Concern to a Public Official

In terms of their policy approach, this is likely the one where politicians are most open to persuasion. Governors and legislators often don't take a stance on issues of little or no concern to them.

Despite this, the governor and legislators may be required to pass judgment on the issue. In the governor's case by signing or vetoing a bill or letting it become law without a signature; in the case of legislators by voting.

In these situations, they often rely on their staff, interest groups, executive branch personnel, their constituents, and other sources for information. In the case of legislators, they may rely on trusted colleagues to make a decision. This is a course of action known as cueing—taking direction from others on how to vote. Some may even take advice from their staff on how to vote.

Having been a legislator, worked in the governor's office, in a state agency, and lobbied for a while, I've had an inside view of the intricacies of the policy process and those involved. There's the maneuvering, the changing alliances, the often rapid turn of events, and a positive outcome emerging from chaos. I've seen those with the best of intentions and skill who make the system work; the idealistic and the naïve get eaten up; those with big egos, the self-serving and the self-righteous. And I've seen the deceptive ones and some who are dishonest.

THIS CHAPTER COVERS

1. The Relationship of the Fundamentals and Specifics of Lobbying, and What it Means for You

2. The Range of Strategies and Tactics

3. Types of Groups and How they are Viewed

4. The Nature of the Issue or Issues

5. Promotional, Defensive, and Maintenance Campaigns

6. Available Resources

7. The Present Level of Access

8. The Political Climate—Past and Present

9. The Lessons for Your Campaign

★ CHAPTER 9 ★

What Will Shape Your Lobbying Campaign?

Whether it's the United States, the European Union, Brazil, Australia, or anywhere around the world, there are fundamentals of lobbying that shape all advocacy campaigns. The trick is to apply these to the place where you're lobbying.

—Stanley Crossick,
Legislative Consultant,
European Policy Institute,
Brussels, Belgium

The implication of Stanley Crossick's insightful comment is: All lobbyists and group leaders need to understand the universal elements underling all lobbying campaigns, and figure out how these determine the strategies and tactics in the political environment in which they operate. This chapter melds the fundaments with the specifics of the Alaska political scene as a first step in understanding the practicalities of approaching and implementing a lobbying campaign.

1. THE RELATIONSHIP OF THE FUNDAMENTALS AND SPECIFICS OF LOBBYING, AND WHAT IT MEANS FOR YOU

Six key universal factors that influence a lobbying campaign are:

- The type of group and how it's viewed.

- The nature of the issue or issues.

- Whether a group is pursuing a promotional, defensive, or maintenance campaign.

- Available resources.

- The present level of access.

- The political climate.

In addition, there are several aspects of the implementation of a campaign that are common across the world. The most important are: use of a lobbyist; the importance of contacts; trust between lobbyists and public officials; the need to plan; providing information in the most effective way; and, in most cases, the need to compromise.

These fundamentals affect all aspects of a group's organization and operation: from its strategies and tactics to its day-to-day operations to the extent of its influence. But the way these universals work to shape any particular campaign is determined by many factors. Among the most significant are: the type of government system (parliamentary, separation of powers, authoritarian regime, etc.); the specifics of politics currently and in the past; attitudes of the public and public officials to political advocacy; the tactics available to a particular group; among other specifics of a particular country, state, province, city, or other government jurisdiction.

The Implications

The fact that the universals of lobbying have to be adapted to local circumstances, has two important implications.

No Two Lobbying Campaigns are the Same

There is no blueprint for all lobbying campaigns. Each campaign requires a particular approach because it will be shaped by the way the fundamentals of lobbying play out in your situation. What this means is, like all lobbying efforts, in its specifics your campaign will be unique.

Be Skeptical of Those Who Know the "Right Way" to run a Campaign

An important lesson of this uniqueness is that, although you may have observed other lobbying efforts, and perhaps been given advice on how to run your campaign, only use this info if it fits your needs.

Don't try to mimic other lobbying efforts or follow advice to the letter, and feel that, if you don't, you're not doing things right.

You must start from scratch by applying your interpretation of how the fundamentals of lobbying affect your political advocacy situation.

Applying the Fundamentals to Alaska

The purpose of the rest of this chapter is to raise your awareness of how the fundaments will affect

Take advice from lobbyists and others, but don't mimic their approaches, because they'll likely not be suited to your needs. Develop your own combination of tactics.

the perception, planning and implementing your campaign. As we'll see, this presents both opportunities and constraints, requiring many decisions in adapting these universals to the Alaska lobbying environment.

2. THE RANGE OF TACTICS

Box 9.1, on the following pages, sets out the range of direct and indirect tactics available in planning the strategy for a lobbying campaign.

The use of **direct tactics** involve the lobbyist and other group members contacting public officials directly, one-on-one, or using the courts. By contrast, **indirect tactics** are intermediate methods, such as using the media, to get a message across to policy-makers. These two types of tactics are not mutually exclusive: both are increasingly used in combination, especially by insider groups.

BOX 9.1
THE RANGE OF LOBBYING OPTIONS: DIRECT AND INDIRECT TACTICS

DIRECT TACTICS

1. Using One or More Lobbyists

This is the most traditional and most essential of lobbying tactics.

2. Lobbying the Legislature and Executive Branches of Government, including Federal, State and Local Government Agencies

These have always been the primary targets of direct lobbying.

3. Grassroots Lobbying—Using Group Members

Here the group leaders encourage (and, ideally, coach) group members to contact policy makers directly to support the group's cause. Grassroots lobbying can be a very effective lobbying technique if properly managed. But it can seriously go awry if members deliver inconsistent messages, make threats, or tell untruths.

4. Lobbying through the Courts

Although the courts and judges cannot be lobbied directly, as can the legislature and executive, interest groups use the courts to seek or oppose policy decisions that affect them. For example, since 2010, gay marriage advocates have secured major victories through the courts, overturning state bans on gay marriage.

However, most groups do not have concerns needing court action. Plus, it's very expensive to mount a court campaign. So, this tactic is open only to interests and interest groups with major resources.

INDIRECT TACTICS

5. Financial Contributions to Help Elect Candidates

This is one of the most effective ways to gain access to elected officials. Few will admit they'll trade campaign contributions for access if they get elected or re-elected—but it's a fact of political life.

6. Non-Financial Contribution to Help Elect a Candidate

Volunteering on a campaign or doing other "in kind" work to get in the good graces of politicians, is on a par with giving money—it's one of the most effective ways to get their attention.

7. Use of the Media, Public Relations (PR), Advertising Campaigns, and Social Media

The goal behind these tactics is to create a perception that the public strongly supports or opposes the policy concerned. Such campaigns can be successful. But they can also fall short or go wrong and adversely affect a group's reputation and advocacy effort.

8. Joining a Coalition

One reason for doing this is that there is strength in numbers. As such, joining a coalition with the right groups can help compensate for a group's minimal access to policy-makers and political influence.

However, being part of a coalition can constrain a group in its use of tactics. This can reduce its freedom to adjust to changing political circumstances.

9. Protests, Boycotts, and Strikes

Protest, boycotts, and strikes are employed by many groups, but most often by outsider groups that have little or no access to the policy process, and want to attract the attention of public officials. Because these tactics are often confrontational, they can easily backfire; but on occasion they can be successful.

10. Staging Rallies

In contrast to protests, boycotts, and strikes, rallies are used to show support for a cause or law, particularly those politicians who worked to promote it. Groups staging rallies include some insider groups, like schoolteachers, and outsider interests, such as a group rallying in support of politicians who favor the death penalty.

(continued . . .)

Shaping a Campaign

BOX 9.1 CONTINUED

11. Affiliation with or Support of a Political Party

Very few of the tens of thousands of interest groups across the nation identify with a political party. But some major and high-profile interests do, or have strong leanings toward one of the two major parties. These include: labor; some businesses; many religious groups; and many minority groups.

Such connections can increase group access and influence when a group's party is in power, but prove detrimental when it is not. Very few interest groups in Alaska have formal affiliation with the Republicans or Democrats. However, many have leanings toward one or the other; for instance, business to the Republicans and labor to the Democrats.

12. Involvement in Direct Democracy Campaigns

As stressed in Chapter 3, these campaigns are enormously expensive and usually mounted by a coalition of groups. So this tactic is not an option for the vast majority of interest groups.

Insider groups and organizations are those with long-standing and close relationships with politicians and administrative officials, giving them extensive access. However, the increasing competition among groups for the ear of public officials, has led these groups to also use indirect tactics to reinforce their direct tactics.

In contrast, **outsider groups and interests** have little or no access to the policy process. For the most part, they are forced to use the indirect tactics that are available depending on their resources. Their goal is, by employing these tactics they'll gain the access needed to use direct tactics.

Determining the most appropriate combination of tactic, and adjusting these as political circumstances change, is a major job of group leaders and lobbyists.

Without using some direct tactics, an outsider group won't achieve its goal. To get government to consider their issue specifically, a group needs to move from using only outsider tactics to using some insider tactics—particularly directly lobbying public officials.

3. TYPES OF GROUPS AND HOW THEY ARE VIEWED

Not all groups and organizations are viewed in the same way by policy-makers. Even if subconsciously, they have different expectations of how some groups should lobby, and what are inappropriate ways for them to advocate their cause.

For instance, legislators find it quite acceptable that an oil company, a mining corporation, or cruise ship organization, hire contract lobbyists and pay them well. Plus, politicians see it as appropriate that, from time to time, these organizations run full-page ads in the *Anchorage Daily News,* or TV ads, to promote their causes with the public, in an effort to build political support for their issues. Public officials also accept that many professional groups, such as nurses and lawyers, may use similar tactics. Most politicians and bureaucrats also find it acceptable that many local governments hire contract lobbyists to push their issues.

By contrast, most politicians would find it inappropriate for a citizen group, such as one seeking funds for improving their local animal shelter, to hire a paid contract lobbyist (though acceptable if a lobbyist works for them pro bono—for free). Similarly, public officials would also see a student group or alumni association hiring a paid lobbyist as inappropriate. In these cases, and again likely subconsciously, politicians expect lobbying to be done by the head of the organization and group members. Doing otherwise threatens the group's political credibility.

> *Before you begin lobbying, find out how the key policy makers view your group and your issue—in a positive, negative, or neutral way. Understanding this will shape how you deal with them.*

4. THE NATURE OF THE ISSUE OR ISSUES

The issue or issues a group is promoting can shape its campaign in two important ways.

How the Issue is Viewed

To be taken seriously, the issue must be considered legitimate and reasonable for it to gain any political traction.

For instance, the Alaska chapter of the National Federation of Independent Business (NFIB) working to lower corporate taxes, or the Alaska Municipal League (AML), trying to prevent cuts in state aid, would both be considered serious policy goals.

In contrast, students lobbying for free university tuition, or a group seeking state funds to attract a major league baseball team to Anchorage, would likely not be taken seriously. Plus, the lobbyists promoting these issues would be seen as lacking political savvy.

The Specific Targets of Lobbying

If you need to change a regulation, for example, the state certification for accountants, or secure funds from a program, such as one for start-up businesses, your lobbying focus will be on state agencies. In contrast, to pass a new law, repeal an existing statute, or block a proposal, you'll need to lobby the legislature, the governor's office, and the affected state agencies.

5. PROMOTIONAL, DEFENSIVE, AND MAINTENANCE CAMPAIGNS

The distinction between these three types of campaigns is important for two reasons. First, it shapes the focus, strategies, and tactics of a lobbying effort. Second, in most cases, it also determines the resources needed for a campaign. Box 9.2 explains the three types of campaigns.

BOX 9.2
PROMOTIONAL, DEFENSIVE, AND
MAINTENANCE LOBBYING CAMPAIGNS

A Promotional Campaign

This is the toughest type of campaign to mount and win. It involves working to get a policy enacted or an existing one reformed. The difficulties lie in the policy process favoring the status quo, and that political power is dispersed.

This means working to convince all those whose support is essential. It also requires overcoming or neutralizing the opposition, because it takes only one strong force at any stage in the process to kill a proposal. As the political cards are stacked against the effort from the start, the campaign requires major resources and an extensive lobbying plan.

The many steps in the lobbying effort include:

- Getting the bill through one or more committees.

- Obtaining a majority vote in the House and the Senate.

- Getting the governor's support.

- Support of the affected agencies, or, at least, securing their neutrality.

- In many cases, getting the regulations written in a way to implement the law as intended.

- Throughout this arduous process, besides combating one or more interests, public and media attitudes to the proposal, both pro and con, also need to be considered.

A Defensive Campaign

A defensive campaign is generally easier to mount than a promotional one. To kill a bill or proposal requires stopping it at any point in the process. This could be by a sympathetic committee chair, bottling it up in the Rules Committee, or getting the governor to veto it.

But victory is by no means assured. It depends on the political forces that support or oppose the proposal.

If the forces against the proposal are the leaders of the majority in both houses, the governor, a state agency, as well as interest groups with influence, or widespread public support, achieving the goal

(continued . . .)

BOX 9.2 *CONTINUED*

will be difficult. In these circumstances, a defensive strategy requires a major lobbying effort on a par with a promotional campaign.

A Maintenance Campaign

This is one in where an organization has no immediate lobbying goals, but need to make provision for when they have an issue.

Generally, a maintenance campaign takes the least resources and a basic strategy. Nevertheless, it's still necessary to do careful planning and constantly reassess the situation as circumstances change.

A maintenance campaign requires staying in contact with officials who might affect your political goals. This involves continuing to give them a reason to want to help you when the time comes, such as making campaign contributions, or helping make contacts that they may need.

Because maintenance campaigns can turn into active lobbying on an issue, is why many interest groups and organizations, that can afford to, keep a contract lobbyist on retainer.

6. AVAILABLE RESOURCES

Obviously, the extent of the resources a group has will significantly shape the type and extent of its campaign. Resources include:

- Money.

- Full-time staff or people to help with the campaign.

- The political skill of the group's leaders.

- The level of access to policy makers.

- The group's contact network.

- Relations with other groups and organizations, and, perhaps, the option of developing a coalition with one of more of them.

Groups and organizations with the most extensive resources are generally the most effective. But this doesn't mean that those with few resources can't be influential. The key is to use the resources they do have in the most effective way, and try to compensate for the ones they lack. This is one reason why planning a campaign is so important. We provide pointers on how to gear a lobbying effort to available resources in Chapter 13.

> *It's a reality that if your resources are minimal, you may not be able to mount an effective campaign.*

Shaping a Campaign

7. THE PRESENT LEVEL OF ACCESS

Whether an insider or outsider group, or one with elements of both, its present level of access will shape how it goes about planning and implementing its campaign.

With the major access that an insider group has, it's able to plan a campaign primarily focusing on contacting public officials personally—using direct access. If necessary, a group can also use indirect tactics to enhance its lobbying effort. It can focus these indirect tactics on the public officials who are most crucial to their cause, such as contributing to their election campaigns, or singing their praises in a newsletter or on social media.

> *If you don't have good access, a lot of your time will be devoted to securing it.*

On the other hand, an outsider group, or one with little direct access, will need to plan for developing its avenues of access. This requires a more extensive campaign and more resources than most insider campaigns, resources that many outsider groups do not have.

Building Success as an Outsider Group—Developing Insider Status

If an outsider group comes to the legislature for the first time with one issue it hopes to deal with in that legislative session, it will have

> **To be effective over the long-run, all outsider groups have to engage in direct tactics, and, to some extent, become insider groups.**

a very slim chance of success. It won't have the crucial contacts it needs, and likely won't be able to establish them in one legislative session. It takes time to build a contact network of public officials and other political operatives.

But if a group has a long-term interest, say to improve help for autistic children in K-12, or to reduce recidivism by providing those released from prison with various forms of aid, it can work to develop insider status, or at least develop a contact network.

8. THE POLITICAL CLIMATE—PAST AND PRESENT

Lobbying doesn't take place in a political vacuum. All advocacy groups are affected by past and present political conditions. What will affect your campaign, directly or indirectly, are the past and present realities of Alaska politics.

Six Characteristics of Alaska Politics

> **It's a valuable asset to know the major developments in Alaska politics since the 1980, as these may have affected, and continue to affect, your issue or related issues.**

Appendix 4, which lists further information on Alaska politics and lobbying, includes several sources that explain in detail what forces have shaped the state's politics over the years, and continue to do so. We can, however, summarize these influences in six points, as set out in Box 9.3.

BOX 9.3
SIX MAJOR CHARACTERISTICS OF ALASKA POLITICS

1. Alaska's economy has always and will remain dependent on natural resources and government

Alaska's economy will never be diversified like those in Michigan, Ohio, and many other states. It will continue to be dependent on natural resource extraction and government employment. Besides income from the Permanent Fund, on which there are spending restrictions, oil is by far the most important source of unrestricted state revenues. These revenues fuel government jobs.

Many politicians and members of the public insist that, if only the right politics are pursued, the state can diversity and reduce dependence on oil and government. This is dreaming and flies in the face of economic reality. If this were possible, it would have been done long ago.

2. The state has chronic revenue problems

The state's dependence on oil for around 80-90 percent of its unrestricted revenue, oil prices fluctuating widely, and many factors constraining oil production, it's feast or famine with the state's income. Many efforts have been made to deal with this, including establishing the Permanent Fund, to provide a cushion against revenue problems, especially after oil runs out.

But Alaskans' reluctance to pay taxes, give up their annual PFD, and develop a sustainable long-term fiscal plan to match revenues and expenditures, means fluctuating revenues remain a major problem. It has long been the major issue shaping Alaska politics.

3. Political party affiliations are not the major divisions in Alaska politics

In most states, the difference between Republicans and Democrats is a major, in some cases the major, factor shaping politics. This is not so much the case in Alaska.

This is partly because the majority of Alaskans are not partisan and do not affiliate with either party. With Alaska's small population, there's a close relationship between voters and politicians. And so people often vote for the person and not the party. But most of all, the lesser significance of party is due to the following three characteristics of the state's politics.

(continued . . .)

BOX 9.3 CONTINUED

4. Regionalism and urban versus rural interests often leads to bipartisanship

Regional loyalties, such as those of Southeast, Southcentral, and Interior Alaska, often trump party affiliation as politicians from both parties work together to secure benefits for their region. In some cases, the rest of the state gangs up against Anchorage to prevent it increasing its already substantial influence in state politics, including opposition to moving the capital.

Probably the most important aspect in Alaska politics is the urban-rural split. As a numerical minority in both the House and Senate, rural-bush legislators often cross party lines to join the majority to secure benefits. Many urban legislators, particularly Republicans, oppose major resources going to the bush. This often develops into major issues and conflicts, not only in the legislature, but among Alaskans in general.

5. Conservatives versus liberals

From statehood in 1959 to the late 1970s and the 1980s, there were three Democrats and three Republican governors. The state's congressional delegation was also more or less evenly split between the two parties. But for most of these twenty years, the legislature was controlled by Democrats, and several liberal reforms were adopted.

Since the early 1990s, the Republicans have controlled the state House and, for most of that time, the state Senate; though there have been some bipartisan coalitions in these years. With one exception (Mark Begich in the Senate, 2009-15), Alaska's Congressional delegation has also been Republican.

As in the past, the major conflict between liberals and conservatives today revolves around the allocation of state resources. With the Republicans in control, the conservative agenda, expressed through the majority caucuses, dominates policy-making. This includes:

- Emphasis on economic development as opposed to the environment. This often includes challenging federal policies that restrict development in the state.

- Cutting the state budget and reducing the size of government

- Providing more aid to the private sector.

This conservative dominance has put most liberal causes, largely championed by Democrats, on the defensive. As a result, their major causes, including education, both K-12 and the university, and increases in social programs, including affordable health care, have not been adequately funded.

6. Political pragmatism

At bottom, what characterizes Alaska politics is pragmatism. Politicians will abandon their party, shelve their ideologies, quietly ignore their campaign promises, or abandon previous political alliances, if they see a course of action in the interests of the state, but more likely in the interests of their constituents or themselves. For example:

- Conservatives who rail against the federal government and too much state spending, eagerly hold out their hands for federal and state benefits.

- If it threatens their re-election, liberals will sidetrack dealing with issues that are a major part of their policy agenda. For example, many support putting the formula for calculating the PFD into the state constitution. This is even though it would reduce available revenue to deal with budget shortfalls, as well as undermining developing a fiscal plan to deal with the chronic problem of fluctuating state revenues.

- Some governors, in effect, abandon curbing state spending in the face of constant pressure to increase spending. Such pressure can be overwhelming in high revenue years.

Present Political Circumstances

All six characteristics affect contemporary state politics in some way or another. Exactly how depends on what the major issues are among Alaskans and before state government during any legislative session. For instance, a dive in oil prices will set off a scurry to find money to fill a budget gap, including which programs will receive reduced funding or be cut completely. This will likely produce a conflict over allocation of funds for urban versus rural areas. Lower oil prices may also temporarily empower the minorities in each house, if the majority needs them to take funds from the CBR to cover the funding gap.

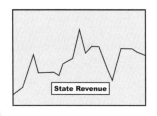

The state's continual, elusive search for economic diversity and development usually produces various proposals, such as lowering oil company taxes to encourage exploration, and building access roads for new mines.

Those legislators concerned about Alaska's chronic revenue problems introduce proposals to develop a long-range fiscal plan. This may include re-imposing a state personal income tax and drawing on Permanent Fund earnings. Conservatives may make proposals to privatize services, such as the ferry system, or to use private prisons to deal with Alaska's increasing inmate population.

Unforeseen Occurrences and Regular Events

Besides issues arising due to long-standing politics, unforeseen events and circumstances arise. In addition to spikes and dips in oil prices, there are major external economic changes nationwide or internationally, like the economic recession of 2008-10. Far-reaching events for Alaska include the Exxon Valdez oil spill in Prince William Sound in 1989; and the earthquakes in southcentral Alaska in 1965, and that one in the Anchorage area in 2018.

Less significant events can also shape political circumstances, such as when a major corruption scandal erupted in the legislature from 2006-08, which centered on the VECO oil service company. Such events could also be the result of federal legislation impacting the state. An example is passage by Congress of the Affordable Care Act (ACA), the implementation of parts of which is the responsibility of the states.

Regular events also shape the political climate, particularly with elections, especially when both a new legislature and a new governor take office. Announcement of projections of oil prices is another example.

How Will this Affect Your Lobbying Effort?

Whether the result of unforeseen circumstances, regular events, or long-standing characteristics of Alaska politics, these can shape your campaign. Depending on the circumstances and the event or combination of events, they offer opportunities or impose constraints. Two examples of each illustrate possible situations.

Opportunities

An example of an opportunity for a group is, over an extended period of low revenues, to suggest ways to reduce costs by implementing one or more of its proposals. Suggesting reducing costs or otherwise making savings is always a big hit with politicians of all stripes. For example, this could be providing compulsory counselling services to reduce the likelihood of those charged with domestic violence committing a second offence and be imprisoned with major costs to the state. Times of low revenues also allow conservative groups to push their agendas to reduce the size of government and privatize some of its services.

Upcoming elections also present opportunities for groups to place more emphasis on supporting candidates friendly to their causes. Using this tactic can increase access if their candidates get elected.

Constraints

One set of constraints often accompanies a conservative legislature. It will likely not be sympathetic to groups that want to increase spending on social programs, or to expand environmental protections. A conservative legislature is, however, likely to be friendly to business, support lower taxes, and oppose what they consider irksome regulations.

Another constraint, and perhaps the major one for most groups, is a fall in revenues. This will cause all sides in the legislature, Republicans and Democrats, majority and minority caucuses, and the governor, to consider decreased spending. So this is a difficult time for both insider and outsider groups to seek major funding for programs or projects.

The Necessity of Adapting to the Political Climate

Groups must adapt their strategies and tactics to the circumstances, and continue to adapt as circumstances change. If they don't, they'll likely find themselves in the political wilderness. So it's important to stay abreast of day-to-day political developments.

9. THE LESSONS FOR YOUR CAMPAIGN

What lessons can you take away from this review of the fundamental factors that shape a lobbying campaign to apply to your advocacy effort? Four are particularly instructive.

Each Campaign is Different

As we have shown, the specifics of every lobbying campaign are different and unique in their own way, as yours will be. Bear this in mind as you view the operation of other campaigns and are offered advice, even if it comes from a seasoned lobbyist.

Look at the Big Picture

Step back and look at the big picture of your campaign before starting to plan the specifics. You'll see the factors providing options and those limiting you. For example, be realistic about the way your group and your issue will likely be viewed, and how your current level of access will influence how you plan your lobbying effort.

Initial Insights on Influence

This information about the factors that influence all lobbying campaigns, should give you initial insights into what underlies the success or failure of a lobbying effort. Those trying to stop something—mounting a defensive campaign—start with a clear advantage.

Resources also count in a major way. The more resources a group has, the more opportunities it has to hire full-time staff, a lobbyist, and monitor critical developments affecting its campaign.

Dozens of Decisions to Make

Finally, the various ways the fundamentals affect your campaign should raise your awareness to the dozens of decisions you'll have to make in your lobbying effort. These include everything from the specifics of your lobbying plan to the most appropriate strategies and tactics to how to adjust to the changing political climate, and even when it might be necessary to suspend or terminate your campaign.

Again, lobbying is an art, not a science. There's no single blueprint for all lobbying campaigns.

Understanding all the factors that will influence your campaign, and the challenge of dealing with them, can be overwhelming at first. Approach each one separately, see how it may or may not affect your campaign, then it won't be as daunting.

Shaping a Campaign

THIS CHAPTER COVERS

1. General Perspectives on Interest Group Influence

2. Twelve Elements of Interest Group Power

3. The Realities of Interest Group Influence

4. Interest Group Power in Alaska

5. Three Qualifiers About Group Influence
   in Alaska and Elsewhere

★ CHAPTER 10 ★

The Factors Determining Interest Group Influence and their Lessons

The big special interests certainly get what they want most of the time. But in the over 20 years I covered state politics, I saw that sometimes a group of citizens or a few people with passion for a cause, could get a politician to make things happen, even in the face of opposition from the powerful lobbying outfits.

—Dave Donaldson,
Former political reporter,
Alaska Public Radio Network

It sounds obvious, but it's worth emphasizing: the most important aspect of the operation of an interest group is its ability to acquire, use, and maintain power to achieve its goals. This raises several questions:

- What determines the influences of an interest group?

- Why are some groups more successful at acquiring and using power than others?

- Can a group with little influence become powerful by pursuing a particular course of action?

Major interest groups tend to downplay their influence and overstate the power of their opponents.

- And specific to your lobbying effort, how can you increase the political influence of your group or organization?

None of these questions have definitive answers. But we can provide insights and the lessons they offer in organizing a lobbying campaign to maximize its influence.

1. GENERAL PERSPECTIVES ON INTEREST GROUP INFLUENCE

There are no simple explanations of the basis of group influence, such as the oft-heard explanation, "it's all about money."

Like the foundations and exercise of power in politics in general, interest group influence is a complex phenomenon. We can identify certain factors underlying the influence or the lack of influence of a group or organization, but there's no formula to guarantee the success of a group on all its issues of concern.

Political Management

One of the resources needed to develop an effective advocacy operation is certainly money. But success also depends on information, an effective organization, and good timing. None of these elements, alone or in combination, can form the basis of an organization's influence without skillful management, political savvy, and personal relationships to turn these resources into influence.

Promoting and Undermining Influence

Another aspect of power in the rough-and-tumble of interest group politics is that, a successful interest group is not only working to enhance its own influence. It's also trying to undermine the power of its opponents.

These are the two aspects of most lobbying campaigns whether promotional or defensive advocacy efforts.

Interest
Groups

Approaching the Challenges of Group Influence

Bear these general points in mind as you plan and implement your lobbying campaign, particularly in strategizing to overcome your lack of influence. Certainly, like all advocacy groups, you won't be able to overcome all your power deficiencies. But given the many factors that constitute group power, the ways to combine them, as well as the various avenues for exercising influence, provide a range of options to increase political power for pushing your issues.

2. THE TWELVE ELEMENTS OF INTEREST GROUP POWER

Let's remind ourselves of the definition of political power set out in Chapter 1:

The ability to direct and shape the political behavior of others or the course of political events. In essence, this involves making a policy maker or other political operative do something they'd not do otherwise.

Many factors determine the extent and ability of an interest group to exercise political power. The combination of factors will be different at different times, depending on a range of circumstances including: the political environment; the group's issue or issues; the support they can muster; and the opposition they face.

While it is difficult to identify all the factors at work in any lobbying situation, we can identify several that underlie the extent of group influence in general. Specifically, we identify the factors that shape the political influence of a group or organization over time. Box 10.1, on the following pages, sets out twelve of these factors.

Human Relationships and Group Power

Besides shaping a group's power over the long run, the list provides an indication of its likely influence on an issue at any one time. As the

Interest Groups

BOX 10.1
TWELVE FACTORS DETERMINING THE INFLUENCE OF INTEREST GROUPS, GROUP COALITIONS, AND LOBBYISTS

1. The degree to which public officials need the group, organization or coalition's services and resources

The more government needs a group, interest, organization, or coalition, the greater their political leverage. This could be providing factual or political information, delivering campaign funds and other support at elections, helping public officials solve problems, or supporting them on their major issues. For instance, government needs business to keep the economy functioning well. This is a major source of business's influence.

2. Lobbyist-policy-maker relations

A lobbyist's influence is a function of trust, information, and dependence.

In the uncertain world of politics, a public official must trust a lobbyist to deal honestly and straightforwardly, particularly providing reliable information. Together with trust, a skillful lobbyist can use information, both factual and political, to build a close relationship with a public official, making him or her receptive to the lobbyist's perspective, which lays the ground work for influence.

In addition to trust and information, if a public official needs an organization's assistance, the group's lobbyist has a particularly influential asset. The more skillful the lobbyist in creating a degree of dependence, the more successful the group is likely to be.

3. Whether the group's lobbying focus is primarily defensive or promotional

A group working to stop a piece of legislation has the so-called "advantage of the defense." It has only to stop the bill at one point in the process to achieve its goal. In contrast, to get a bill passed requires a group successfully clearing many hurdles, each a hurdle at which its bill can be killed.

The defensive political stance taken by many business groups is another reason for their influence. By contrast, environmentalists and other groups promoting reform, have a much tougher time achieving their goals.

Interest
Groups

4. The extent and strength of group opposition

Obviously, the stronger the opposition to a group and its cause, the more difficult it is to realize its goals. Some groups are natural political adversaries, such as environmentalists and developers, and, in many cases, business and labor. Other interests, like dentists and those advocating for stricter laws against child abuse, typically face little opposition.

5. The legitimacy of the group and its demands—how these are perceived by the public and public officials

A group must be seen as politically legitimate, but there are degrees of legitimacy and the acceptance of groups and their demands.

Some groups, such as senior citizen organizations and advocates against drunk driving, enjoy high levels of legitimacy. Others, such as labor unions, may be viewed as legitimate, but their demands may sometimes be viewed negatively.

Different policy makers view the extent of the legitimacy of various groups and their demands differently. This will depend on the public official's ideology and dependence on a group, among other factors. This, in turn, determines the extent of a group's influence with a particular official.

6. Group financial resources

Money by itself does not equate to political power. It must be used for lobbying purposes to influence policy-making. Therefore, groups need skillful management by their leaders and lobbyists.

At the same time, money is the most liquid of resources. It can be used to hire staff and lobbyists, make campaign contributions, mount media and public relations campaigns, and so on. Plentiful funds gives a group the flexibility to use the most effective strategies and tactics. If they have major resources, many groups create political action committees (PACs), organizations that make campaign contributions, hoping to influence those they support if they are elected.

7. The tenure, political, organizational, and managerial skill of group leaders, and the asset of institutional memory

Successful lobbying campaigns require leaders with organizational and managerial skill, knowledge of the political process, particularly the location of power, and a comprehensive understanding of the organization's or group's issues.

(continued . . .)

Interest
Groups

BOX 10.1 *CONTINUED*

In part, the potential influence of a group depends on whether the organization has a permanent, full-time staff, or can employ a contract lobbyist. Permanent staff enable a group or organization to spend considerable time on organizing and strategizing, and adjusting quickly to changing political circumstances.

Resources to employ a staff also enable group leaders and lobbyists to spend more time building long-term relationships with public officials, establish trust, and thus increase their access, as well as develop an extensive contact network.

All this establishes a track record for the organization and provides it with an institutional memory. Lobbyists can learn from past experiences, successes and failures, and don't need to reinvent the political wheel in each lobbying effort. Groups without permanent staffs often lack institutional memory and the advantages it brings.

8. Political cohesiveness of the membership

Group unity—presenting one voice and one voice only to policy-makers—is vital. The more united the group, the more likely it is to have its issues addressed. Public officials will not pursue a group's issue if it's divided. Ensuring group cohesiveness is an essential task of group leaders.

9. Size and geographical distribution of group membership

Generally, the larger and more geographically distributed its membership, the more pressure a group can exert on more public officials, especially elected officials.

However, much depends on several of the factors considered above. These include: how the group is perceived; the skill of its leaders and lobbyists; and its financial and other resources. Groups and organizations

list indicates, to some extent, organizational factors are important in determining group influence, such as the size of group membership and its ability to join a coalition.

In the end, however, group influence is determined by the human factors on the list. These include: how dependent public officials are on particular causes or interests, public official-lobbyist relations, the lacking these assets will find it difficult to turn their geographical reach into influence.

10. The potential to join a coalition

When a group can join forces with another group or groups, it can potentially overcome its deficiencies in one or more of the previous nine factors.

11. Extent of group autonomy in political strategizing

While the flexibility to join or leave a coalition can enhance a group's power, belonging to a coalition may mean less control over strategy and tactics.

If so, the group's potential to achieve its goals may be compromised, or its goals not addressed at all. Therefore, many businesses and local governments hire a contract lobbyist to advocate for their specific goals, while retaining membership in their trade or local government association.

12. Timing

Making judgments on timing is part of the necessary skill set of lobbyists and group leaders. Two particularly important aspects of timing increase the likelihood of success.

One is that the best time to first approach an elected official with an issue is during the legislative interim when they have much more time than during the session. Second, it is usually most appropriate to follow up on an initial contact with a public official when they have the issue forefront in their mind and are about to decide on it.

Source: Developed by the author from surveys and interviews conducted on all fifty states, between 1985 and 2018.

extent of group unity, and the ability of group leaders to turn group resources into influence. Here's yet another example of how important personal relationships and effective communications are in lobbying.

Interest Groups

3. THE REALITIES OF INTEREST GROUP INFLUENCE

Although not mentioned explicitly in Box 10.1, we can draw an implication from the elements that constitute group influence. This is: the fundamental right of citizens and groups to representation and participation in public policy-making is one thing, turning that right into power is quite another.

The Inevitability of Differences in Interest Group Influence

While a government like Alaska's can more or less ensure equality of representation, it cannot ensure equality of influence for all groups and interests. This is for the very reasons set out in Box 10.1: various types of economic and political resources are unevenly distributed, plus some people and organizations are better at using these than others. Not only that, as mentioned above, the competition between groups results in differences in power across a political system like Alaska's. Some groups are more adept at acquiring and maintaining power and undermining that of their opponents.

All this adds up to make some groups more powerful than others. Some are very influential; some have moderate influence; some little or no influence.

Lobby Regulation and Interest Group Influence

Some people see regulation of group activity as a means to even up the balance between powerful and less powerful interest groups. Is this the case? The short answer

> One thing I leaned after I got elected to the legislature, is how some lobbyists cultivate legislators, and sometime get together with them socially. It often appeared that this was less for social than political purposes on the part of the lobbyists.

is "no." Again, the reason is largely because some groups have more extensive economic and political resources than others.

This means that lobbying laws cannot turn hitherto powerless groups into powerful forces, nor reduce the political clout of long-time powerful groups. What regulation can do is publicize information about who's lobbying and how much they spend, restrict what lobbyists can give to a candidate or public official, and limit spending by interest groups in election campaigns.

These provisions have made it less likely that public officials and lobbyists will engage in underhanded and suspect activities. So, indirectly, lobbying regulation has likely reduced the influence of some powerful groups, but not enough to notice.

Interest
Groups

The Consequences—Some Groups are Always Influential

Adding all this up, we can answer one of the questions posed at the beginning of the chapter: Why are some groups more powerful than others? It's largely a result of possession of extensive resources and adroit deployment of political acumen.

As a result, some groups and interest are, more of less, continually influential. This includes: businesses and some professional groups, such as teachers and nurses; as well as organizations like public universitiess. By contrast, other groups have a much more difficult time securing their political goals, especially those run on a shoestring.

If all interest groups and organizations had the same level of power there would be political deadlock. Whether fair or unfair, it's a reality that differences in influence among interests make the political system work.

Those groups and organizations with a continual presence in Juneau with a contract or in-house lobbyist, are likely to be more successful over time than those who do not.

4. INTEREST GROUP POWER IN ALASKA

Identifying the groups and organizations that have lobbied in Juneau over the past 35-40 years illustrates that those with major resources, and the ability to bring them to bear effectively, have been the most influential.

Although not as all-powerful as they were before statehood, a major factor that determines how state policies are made, is the financial stakes of various influential interest groups.

What are the Most Influential Groups in Alaska?

Box 10.2 lists the most influential groups in Alaska in 2017-18 compared with those in the early 1980s. Groups listed as among the first rank of influence are the consistently influential interests and organizations, past and present. Those in the second rank have been present over the years or recently become active, but are not major influential forces; or had a one-time issue and then disappeared from the political scene. The longer list for 2017-18 reflects the increase in the number of groups and organizations lobbying in Alaska.

The oil industry, other natural resource industries, like mining, the Association of Alaska School Boards (AASB), and local governments, have been the most influential lobbies over the years. Some others, like the Alaska Municipal League (AML) and the University of Alaska, have moved between the two categories since the early 1980s. Not surprisingly, these influential interests have permanent organizations, substantial financial resources, skilled lobbyists, and easy access to public officials.

BOX 10.2
THE MOST INFLUENTIAL INTERESTS AND INTEREST GROUPS IN ALASKA IN THE EARLY 1980S COMPARED WITH 2017-18

2016-17	EARLY 1980s
FIRST RANK	
Oil industry (esp. Alaska Oil and Gas Association [AOGA], and individual oil companies, such as British Petroleum and ConocoPhillips Alaska	Oil industry
	AML and individual municipalities
	Education lobby (other than teachers/K-12 employees, particularly AASB)
Native groups (esp. Alaska Federation of Natives [AFN])	
Council of Alaska Producers (major metal mining industry)	State and local government employees (esp., ASEA and APEA)
Municipality of Anchorage	NEA-Alaska
Fairbanks North Star Borough	Electrical utility industry, including ARECA
Association of Alaska School Boards (AASB)	Environmentalists
Alaska Outdoor Council/Territorial Sportsmen the National Rifle Association (NRA)	
University of Alaska	
SECOND RANK	
National Education Association-Alaska (NEA-Alaska)	Alaska Native groups (esp. AFN)
Alaska Municipal League (AML)	Alascom
American Federation of Labor-Congress of Industrial Organizations (AFL-CIO), and traditional labor unions	Contractors (esp.AGC)
	University of Alaska
State and local government employees (esp. Alaska State Employees Association [ASEA], Alaska Public Employees Association [APEA])	AFL-CIO and traditional labor unions
	Trial lawyers
	Alaska State Medical Association
Environmentalists (esp. Alaska Environmental Lobby)	Insurance lobby (esp. medical underwriters)
Lawyers (trial lawyers, state bar)	General business (esp. ASCC)
Telecommunications lobby (esp. GCI, Alascom and Alaska Telephone Association)	Senior citizens
Liquor lobby (esp. CHARR—Cabaret Hotel and Restaurant Retailers Association)	
Contractors (esp. Associated General Contractors—AGC)	
Electric utilities (including rural co-ops, esp. the Alaska Rural Electric Cooperative Association—ARECA)	
Alaska State Medical Association	
Insurance lobby (esp. medical underwriters)	
Hospitals and nursing homes	
Alaska State Chamber of Commerce (ASCC)	
National Federation of Independent Business (NFIB)	
Commercial fishermen (esp. United Fisherman of Alaska—UFA)	
Pacific Seafood Processors Association	
Private prison lobby	
Northwest Cruise Ship Association	
Children's lobby	
Alaska Women's Lobby	

Interest Groups

Source: Developed by the author from surveys conducted between 1982 and 2018.

5. THREE QUALIFIERS ABOUT GROUP INFLUENCE IN ALASKA AND ELSEWHERE

First, the groups in Alaska listed as most powerful over time, and currently, do not always win. The oil industry doesn't always get what it wants; local governments have their funding cut by the state; and the University of Alaska often gets much less state funding than it asks for, and took major cuts under Governor Dunleavy. The table simply lists those groups that are generally the most effective, more so than many others.

Second, many groups that are influential in the state aren't on the list. This is because those in Box 10.2 are high-profile groups that lobby the legislature and governor's office regularly, and are well known by the public officials who, in the surveys conducted on group power, were asked to identify the most influential groups.

Many groups do not need to lobby the legislature or governor's office most of the time. Their issues can be dealt with by a department or other agency. These groups include chiropractors, realtors, and architects. Groups like these do lobby legislators, but are also interested in the regulations that affect them, rather than promoting or killing legislation.

The last thing many interest groups want is to be seen as powerful. It bring attention to them, may increase opposition to their goals, and generally cramps their political flexibility.

Third, just because a group or interest does not have many of the factors determining group power, does not mean it can't be successful in certain circumstances. The key is to use the resources they do have and focus them politically. As Dave Donaldson's points out at the beginning of the chapter, sometimes citizen and community groups, and those that run on a shoestring, are successful.

Sheer commitment to a cause, persistence, the help of sympathetic politicians, and perhaps taking advantage of wide support among the public, such as on combating domestic violence or child abuse, can make a difference and deliver a victory. In several of the chapters that follow, we make suggestions about how this might be done.

Interest Groups

THIS CHAPTER COVERS

★ CHAPTER 11 ★

Campaign Management

*Lobbying success doesn't happen overnight or by chance.
It takes a lot of groundwork and coordinating many elements.
You need to work on it all year-round, not just during
the session—the work never ends.*

—Norm Wooten,
Executive Director and Lobbyist,
Association of Alaska School Boards

Organizing and implementing a lobbying campaign involves extensive management—specifically political management. This chapter covers the basics of this and the initial decisions you'll need to make in organizing your campaign.

1. THE CHALLENGES OF CAMPAIGN MANAGEMENT

Most of those involved in management, such as running a supermarket, a law firm, or tennis club, can more or less accurately determine the resources they need, and have a lot of control in achieving the outcome they want. This is because of the stable conditions in which they operate. In contrast, lobbying campaign managers face the fluid and unpredictable environment of politics and the policy process.

This presents a range of challenges not faced by most managers. These include:

- Exactly what resources are needed, and how to organize them, given the uncertainties of what might be required.

- Acquiring and exerting political power, and working to compensate for a lack of power.

- Dealing with many people, in and out of government, and in their organization, who can influence the outcome.

- Anticipating and dealing with unforeseen circumstances, sometimes a rapidly changing situation, that can affect the success of a lobbying effort.

Five ways to attempt to deal with these challenges are to:

- Exert a degree of control over the lobbying effort.

- Choose a good campaign coordinator.

- Choose the right lobbyist.

- Build an extensive contact network.

- Gather and use information effectively.

2. CONTROL VERSUS FLEXIBILITY OF THE LOBBYING EFFORT

One obvious management technique to reduce uncertainty is to exert as much control as possible over the organization and its lobbying effort. To what extent can or should this be done?

Democracy, Representation, and Lobbying Campaign Management

Lobbying by individual citizens, and a multitude of interests and interest groups, is a foundation of democracy. The American governmental process is a political free-for-all with very few limitations placed on participation. This is in sharp contrast to a dictatorship. Ironically, the best way to run a lobbying effort is, in fact, to exert a degree of "dictatorship,"—top-down control over the lobbying organization and its operation.

The Need for Group Unity

A lobbying campaign is best run with strong, top-down control because of the need for group unity. The more people involved without direction, the more it's likely things will go wrong. If all those involved have different views on how the group's goal is best achieved and lobby accordingly, many mixed messages will be conveyed to public officials.

These officials will be very reluctant to act on behalf of such a divided organization. Control and coordination produce one clear message to give the lobbying effort the maximum chance of success.

The Desirability and Realities of Control

Ideally, then, interest groups should be run with the maximum control over the membership and the lobbying effort. In practice, this is not possible and often not desirable.

For a business involved in lobbying, such as Alaska Airlines or the Shell oil company, with their top-down organization, control is both easy and desirable. In contrast, imposing control is less possible and desirable in a membership organization, like the Alaska State Chamber of Commerce (ASCC) and the Alaska Environmental Lobby. Much of the strength of membership groups lies in participation by members in both its management and lobbying effort.

What this boils down to is: In most lobbying groups, there must be a tradeoff between control and direction by the group's leader and lobbyist, and participation by members. Striking this balance is a major part of the job of group leaders and lobbyists.

3. THE CAMPAIGN COORDINATOR

Every lobbying campaign needs a campaign coordinator. And the more people involved in organizing and implementing the campaign, the more important is the coordinator.

> *When everyone's in charge, no one's in charge. So it's essential to have only one person coordinating your lobbying campaign.*

The Coordinator's Job

As the title indicates, their job is to coordinate, to be a clearinghouse for the lobbying effort. This role is essential to ensure group unity. Without a coordinator the campaign will likely go awry. Many groups and organizations have learned this to their chagrin.

To this end, the coordinator is involved in all aspects of the campaign, from its organization to its implementation. All actions and developments are run through them to keep track of the status of the campaign at any one time, and what the next move might be.

Who Performs the Coordinator's Job?

In a shoestring operation the coordinator is also likely to be the lobbyist. Part of the reason some small organizations, that can afford to, hire a contract lobbyist is to perform this function.

On the other hand, almost all large organizations, such as those in the oil industry, large associations (such as state chambers of commerce and cruise ship operators), and the larger local governments, have someone who acts as a government affairs coordinator or legislative director. This is often the executive director in an association or a senior manager in a business. They will also likely be involved in lobbying as an in-house lobbyist, together with the organization's contract lobbyist, if one is hired.

Also, larger organizations often have a position, in some cases several positions, dedicated to government affairs, as does the University of Alaska. Many federal agencies and, of course, state government agencies have legislative liaisons.

Qualities of a Campaign Coordinator

Ideally, a lobbying coordinator should be a good communicator and diplomatic, especially when dealing with group members who want to go rogue and not follow the group's lobbying plan. Given all their responsibilities, the coordinator needs to be organized with a mind for detail, including being a good time-manager. Someone who's been involved in politics or, at least, can think politically, is a good choice.

4. CHOOSING A LOBBYIST

Here's the type of person you need whatever your type of group or organization. This includes choosing a contract lobbyist.

They should have the qualities of a campaign coordinator, with some important additional characteristics. A good way to start, as set out in Box 11.1 on the next page, is to identify the sort of person you don't want to lobby for you and, by deduction, those to seek out.

If you have members or volunteers involved in lobbying, they also need similar qualities as in Box 11.1. This is not always possible, of course, especially if it's important to involve members in lobbying. But you can do a crash course to make them aware of the basics of lobbying before they're let loose.

Choosing a Contract Lobbyist

If you are a group or organization, perhaps a business, that wants to hire a contract lobbyist, give it very careful consideration. As Box 11.2, on the next page, points out, you shouldn't rush into a decision. Take your time and choose the right lobbyist for your organization.

D A S *Political Advocacy Strategies*

When you hire a contract lobbyist, you're buying their contacts, relationships, experience, people skills, political acumen, and policy insights.

BOX 11.1
THE QUALITIES OF A GOOD LOBBYIST

If possible, avoid using those who are:

- Lacking in political smarts and judgment.

- Shy, inward people, who don't relate well to others, don't do well in conflict situations, or are easily offended.

- Self-important and self-righteous, big ego, know-it-alls.

- Gossips who are not discrete.

- Partying-types who want a free trip to Juneau to have a good time.

- Not able to handle details; not willing to do their homework before meeting with pubic officials.

- Of the opinion that public officials work for them, and overbearingly insistent that they must support your issue.

You need someone who's:

- A likeable, personable individual, with an even temperament.

- Understands the practical aspects and realities of how the policy process works.

- Very conversant with your group's issues and lobbying plan, or is willing to come up to speed on them quickly.

- Committed to your cause but not a zealot; someone who is open-minded and politically flexible.

- Not a fawning person, but has respect for public officials, their time limitations and problems, realizes they have the power, and not use threatening strong-arm tactics.

- Not easily offended, and willing to be treated as a punching-bag sometimes, when public officials rant and rave, or tell them "no." in response to a request.

- Trustworthy and can keep confidences.

BOX 11.2
CHOOSING THE RIGHT CONTRACT LOBBYIST

Be Cautious—Check them Out

When looking for a lobbyist, don't assume they're all able to represent your issue, are diligent, and will give you value for their fee. Many an organization has discovered too late that they hired the wrong person because they didn't check them out first.

There are many lobbyists who're honest, well respected by public officials, good political operatives, who will represent you well. But also those who are not so good, some who're charlatans, lazy and full of bluster.

Three Things to Keep in Mind

First, although many have experience in government, there are no professional qualifications to be a contract lobbyist. Figuratively speaking, all they need to do is hang out a shingle to advertise their services— "Lobbyist for Hire." Though, in practice, very few get their contracts from advertising; virtually all get clients through word of mouth and referrals.

Second, contract lobbyists are primarily sales people. They work to sell a cause to public officials, and use the same skills to get clients. Most likely they'll use all their sales techniques, including charm, promises, and past lobbying successes, on you.

Third, there's keen competition for clients among contract lobbyist in Juneau. This means that several poach clients from other lobbyists, which shows how good some of them are at making a sale.

Finding the Right Lobbyist

Step back, don't decide in a hurry—find the lobbyist who's right for your needs. A good source is public officials. The chances are you know someone in the legislature or a department, including your own representative and senator. No one knows the good lobbyists, and the not so good ones, better than legislators and their staff. Many contract lobbyists get their client through their recommendations.

Unless you are a rich group, organization, or business, you won't be able to hire one of the big-time lobbyists with their high fees—some over a million dollars a year. In any case, these may not be right for your cause.

Consider hiring a new lobbyist who's hungry. They'll be glad to get your contract, be diligent and much cheaper than many of the big-timers, and others who have been in the business for a while.

5. WHAT DO LOBBYISTS DO AND HOW DO THEY ALLOCATE THEIR TIME?

Both questions are not easy to answer because there's no typical lobbyist. Not only does it vary among types of lobbyists—contract, in-house, legislative liaison, or cause lobbyists—but also within each type.

That said, there are tasks most lobbyists perform at some time or another. Box 11.3 lists these and explains the similarities and variations in performing them and broad estimates of the time spent on each task. The information is based on interviews with lobbyists by the author over the past forty years.

Why is this Information Important to You?

There are three major lessons:

- Knowing what other lobbyist do and why, will help you understand where they're coming from when you deal with them, perhaps as part of your contact network.

- Lobbyists don't just deal with the legislature. Most also deal with the governor 's office and state agencies.

- A large percentage of a lobbyist's time is not spent lobbying public officials. It's spent in planning, dealing with clients and members, and other activities. They put many pieces of the lobbying puzzle together. This will be the case for you.

6. BUILDING A CONTACT NETWORK

Building a contact network is essential for any lobbyist, lobbying group, or organization. It's necessary to facilitate access to public officials, and as a source of political and factual information. You may

BOX 11.3
THE TASKS LOBBYISTS PERFORM: SIMILARITIES AND VARIATIONS

The Tasks Most Lobbyists Perform

1. Dealing with the legislature.
2. Lobbying the governor's office.
3. Dealing with state agencies.
4. Planning their campaign.
5. Keeping clients and members informed, and seeking their input.
6. In some cases, working with members to aid in lobbying.
7. Developing and maintaining their contact network.
8. Socializing with public officials and other political operatives.

These tasks are not usually performed separately. Most lobbyists are doing several simultaneously. But separating them is useful for our purposes.

Also, unlike contract lobbyists, in-house lobbyists and legislative liaisons have other tasks as part of their job. As far as could be determined, the information here is based on the part of their job devoted to lobbying.

A Similarity in Allocation of Time

The time lobbyists spend on tasks other than dealing with public officials directly—lobbying them—ranges from 50-70 percent of their job. The variation is due to several factors, some of which are explained below.

Variation in Time Spent on Various Tasks

Variations in the Use of Strategies and Tactics from Year-to-Year

Depending on the group and its issue or issues, over time, its lobbying effort will likely require a different combination of tactics. Thus, there will be variation in the amount of time targeting the legislature, the executive branch (particularly if a state agency regulates its activity), organizing grassroots or a public relations campaign, among other aspects of lobbying.

(continued . . .)

Campaign Management

BOX 11.3 CONTINUED

The Type of Lobbyist

Contract lobbyists who represent more than one client, spend different amounts of time on various tasks, depending on the particular needs and issues of each client. By contrast, the other three types or lobbyist—in house and volunteer lobbyists, and legislative liaisons—deal with a narrower range of issues depending on the major concerns of their organization, such as education, fisheries, or health issues. Consequently, the time these spend on each task is more predictable.

The Amount of Administrative Support Available

Much depends on the level of administrative support for such tasks as: gathering and preparing information; dealing with group members; and if there's more than one lobbyist working on an issue. Those with extensive administrative support can focus more time on lobbying. Those working for small, particularly volunteer organizations with little administrative support, perform a wider range of tasks.

Examples of Variations

- In many cases, lobbyists who represent groups with a large membership, especially those with governing boards and widespread participation in governance, tend to spend more time dealing with those they represent. This is in contrast to contract lobbyists, who have business and local government clients, with fewer people to deal with in the organization.

- Depending on how many clients they represent and how diverse their type of operation, contract lobbyists tend to spend a lot of time developing and maintaining their contact network. In contrast, as they have more focused issue areas, the other types of lobbyist need to spend less time at this.

- Some contract lobbyists do a lot of building relations with public officials through socializing, and over the dinner table. Most in-house, association and cause lobbyists, do less of this. They are more likely to use receptions and other functions to help build relationships. Legislative liaisons do virtually no professional socializing.

already have a network. If not, or want to increase your contacts, Box 11.4, on the next page, will help. From your contacts it's useful to develop a sort of "kitchen cabinet," a few close contacts you trust for regular reality checks on what you're doing, and if you're on the right track.

> *As a lobbyist, I find building and maintaining a contact network a tedious and time-consuming business. But I couldn't function without one.*

It takes time—months and months, even years—and lots of tedious work to develop a contact network. It's a never-ending operation, with changes in administrations, people coming and going in state government, and in lobbying groups. Once you established a network, it's important to keep in contact, even when you don't need help. Drop by to say a quick "hi," maybe take some cookies, so they'll keep you in mind.

All this can pay major, sometimes unexpected, dividends. Don't write off a contact. Circumstances change. You never know when someone you thought was an adversary can become an ally.

Campaign Management

7. WORKING WITH VOLUNTEERS

Here we're not referring to volunteers who are members of groups with major resources, such as the State Chamber, or a trade union,

with permanent staff who use their members to lobby as part of their coordinated lobbying effort. Our focus is on those willing to give their time for a small organization or citizen group with few resources.

> *Don't rush to take on volunteers, check them out first.*

The advantages of using volunteers are obvious. They provide free labor, are usually enthusiastic and committed to the cause, and, if your organization is not based in Juneau, they may

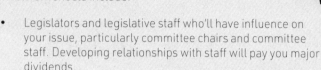

BOX 11.4
A CONTACT NETWORK AND HOW TO BUILD ONE

Your network should include:

- Legislators and legislative staff who'll have influence on your issue, particularly committee chairs and committee staff. Developing relationships with staff will pay you major dividends.

- Those in the governor's office who deal with your issue, particularly special assistants. You're not likely to get the governor, chief of staff, or the legislative director as close contacts, and it's best not to contact them initially. But the special assistant or a legislator will likely be able to facilitate this, if necessary.

- People in departments, boards and commissions, and other state agencies, who deal with your policy area. The legislative liaison, division director, and deputy director, are much more useful to contact initially than the commissioner or deputy commissioner.

- If your issue requires funding, those in OMB who deal with your part of the budget.

- If your issue has a federal element or directly involves local government, contacts in the relevant agency, borough, or city.

- The staff and lobbyists of groups and organizations that deal with issues in your policy area.

- Members of the capital press corps and others in the media. Plus, the majority and minority press person in each house. These issue press releases and know people in virtually all policy areas.

- Those who can provide factual information, including in state agencies in Alaska, other states, research institutes, and other experts, such as those at universities.

- People who've left government but can help you understand the politics of your issue or policy area, including its legislative history.

If you're starting from scratch to build a network, here's some ideas:

- Ask legislators and their staffs for leads on contacts.

- You likely know several people who've either been involved in politics in Juneau, or who can give you leads on good contacts.

- The capital press corps—they have the big picture of state government, and who's involved in what.

- The websites and social media pages of legislators and the governor.

- The websites of state agencies you'll need to contact. These list the legislative liaison, division directors, and deputy directors.

- APOC's list of lobbyists and organizations that lobby.

even be willing to pay their own way to lobby. Groups with minimal resources can't function without volunteers.

That said, volunteers don't come without costs. Even if you can't do everything yourself, don't welcome with open arms just anyone who walks through the door. Using the wrong person can undermine or even destroy your lobbying effort. Box 11.5, on the next page, sets out some suggestions for avoiding problems.

8. DEALING WITH ROGUE MEMBERS

At some time or another, most group leaders have had a problem member who we can call a political rogue. When it happens it can be a serious problem.

By a rogue member, we don't mean someone involved in a grass-roots lobbying effort, or who is part of a fly-in, who screws up by not being well-informed or

Ten Percent of my members cause me ninety percent of my problems.

BOX 11.5
THE DOWNSIDE OF VOLUNTEERS AND HOW TO DEAL WITH PROBLEMS

Downsides may include:

- Lack of knowledge of what you do, what you need, lack of political savvy and how to lobby.

- Too much enthusiasm, with all good intentions they'll go off and do things that may mess up your campaign.

- You get a know-it-all who wants to take over the campaign.

- They let you down at a crucial time.

- A volunteer may be good for one aspect of your effort, like research, but not another, such as lobbying—though they may not realize it.

Some tips to deal with potential problems:

- If you don't know them, vet them carefully: with their permission, of course. Weed out the potential problem ones; learn to say, "thanks but no thanks."

- Try to figure out where they'll best fit into your lobbying effort.

- Provide a basic orientation about your organization, its needs, and where they might fit.

- Give them some basic material about interest groups and their operation, including lobbying. Some chapters in this book are useful. Appendix 4 lists practical guides on lobbying.

- If possible, pair volunteers so if one can't do something at the last minute, they can hand it off to their "double." Then you don't get left in the lurch, especially at crucial times.

doesn't quite know how to deal with public officials. These people are usually open-minded, welcome an honest critique, and take advice on how to do things better next time.

We are referring to the difficult person who has one or more of the following traits:

- Think they know how to lobby best on your issue.

- Not open to advice, often disdainful of it.

- Sometimes arrogant.

- May make unwarranted promises to public officials.

- May use threats in meeting with officials.

For instance, they may not like the lobbying strategy and tactics you've decided upon. If rogues are board members, they may express strong opposition and cause a major conflict. An organization can be paralyzed by an individual or faction not willing to compromise.

If they have some acquaintance with top officials, rogues may start at the top of an organization. They might contact the governor, a commissioner, the President of the Senate or Speaker of the House, rather than deal with a staffer, special assistant, or division director more able to help them. Or they may express concern with group strategy when meeting with legislators or staffers. This behavior can undermine a group's ability to present a unified voice.

Dealing with the Rogue or Rogues

There's no easy answer or formula to do this, because there are all sorts of reasons why rogues act the way they do. Each case must be tackled in the best way possible. Box 11.6, on the next page, provides some suggestions.

9. INFORMATION YOU NEED AND WHERE TO GET IT

The foundation of every lobbying campaign is gathering and using information. You need seven types of information. Two of these relate to the political environment in which you'll operate:

- Current politics.

- The operation of state government.

BOX 11.6
DEALING WITH ROGUE MEMBERS: SOME SUGGESTIONS

- See if you can accommodate them in the meeting at which you approve your lobbying plan and upcoming lobbying effort. This may require giving them a particular task. It could include asking them to meet with someone they see as important. Or try to limit them to dealing with as few legislators as possible to reduce likely damage.

- Beyond some members trying to convince them in a meeting that their approach is not the best, don't get into a major discussion if they are insistent about their way of doing things. It'll make them dig their heels in further.

- Get a legislator or other public official that you know to talk to them.

- Try to accompany them to a meeting or other contact they have with public officials. But be careful not to offend them if they know other members are meeting or contacting officials on their own.

- Failing all this, you'll have to do some major cleaning up after they've met with legislators or others. This may mean skillfully explaining that your rogue is "enthusiastic but doesn't always get things right." In other words, try to isolate them from your lobbying effort.

The other five relate to your issue:

- Information on legislation.

- The public officials who'll affect your issue.

- Information for presenting your issue.

- Political developments that directly affect your issue.

- Potential long-term allies and opponents.

Campaign Management

The Current Political Scene

Directly or indirectly, your issue will be affected by the current political situation and developments that occur day-to-day. You need to keep up, not only because they'll affect your issue, but because if those you lobby see you're not up to speed on what's going on, your credibility and likely your effectiveness will suffer.

Follow the ups and downs of oil prices; the state of major pieces of legislation, particularly the budget; the tone of the relationship between the governor and the legislative majorities; and between the minority and majority caucuses. If it's an election year, who's retiring, running again, who might be positioning themselves for governor, or a run for Congress, now or in the future. It's also useful to know about the major developments in state politics over the past thirty years or so.

For information on current politics, besides the media, another source is political blogs; but these come and go. Gossip is a large part of the blog world, though scuttlebutt is often useful. The better blogs do, however, provide accurate information.

A long-standing subscription newsletter, *Bradners' Legislative Digest,* includes up-to-date information on what's happening in the legislature, including the status of bills. It also covers current state issues in occasional special issues.

Appendix 4 has suggestions on where to find current and historical background information.

The Operation of State Government

Be aware of the organization, operation, and procedures of state government. Basic information on how state government is organized is in Chapter 3. Supplement this by going on-line to the excellent websites the legislature and the administration maintain.

Among other useful information, the legislature's website provides details on: the deadline for filing bills; the procedure and protocol when giving committee testimony; and the function of legislative support agencies, like the Legislative Information Office (LIO). Information from the Legislative Finance Division and Legislative Research is very useful; but these services are only available to legislators and their staff. Nevertheless, a sympathetic legislator or staffer may get the information you need from one of these services, especially if your issue is a major part of their agenda.

BASIS is your most valuable tool for tracking current bills and researching past legislation.

Tracking legislation: A Gold Mine of Information

Knowing how to track legislation will provide a lot of what you need for presenting, monitoring, and pushing your issue. Box 11.7 explains several ways to do this.

The Public Officials who'll affect Your Issue

Obviously, you need information on the politicians and agency personnel who'll affect your issue, so you can deal with them in the most effective way. Find out about:

- Their professional and, if possible, their personal background (family, personal interests, and so on).

- How did their last election go—tough race, landslide, or what?

- Their experience as public officials.

- What issues are most important to them and why?

- Their committee assignments?

- Do they rely a lot on their staff to make many decisions, or want to be in on everything themselves?

BOX 11.7
HOW TO TRACK LEGISLATION

Reading the House and Senate Daily Journals

You can pick these up from the documents room on the ground floor of the Capitol, or access them on the Internet. Every lobbyist serious about their job, scans the Journals every day, for much of what happened the day before, including:

- What bills were introduced and their committee referrals.

- The bills considered by which committees, if a bill was given final consideration, moved from the committee or tabled, and how each committee member voted.

- How members voted on a bill on the floor of the House or Senate, and what amendments, if any, were made.

- Committee calendars for the next week, so you'll know when a bill you're tracking is up for a hearing.

What the Journals don't include is who testified, the discussion that occurred, and the politics involved.

Using BASIS—the Bill Action and Status Inquiry System

BASIS is the legislature's Internet site providing an extensive database for researching bills. You can download a pdf that explains how to use BASIS from: https://akleg.gov/docs/pdf/basis.pdf

Once you're familiar with this system, tracking bills is a snap. Among many features, BASIS enables you to:

- Access (and download) House and Senate Journals and committee calendars.

- See the text of individual bills.

- View the status of bills.

- Research the history of a bill.

- Search legislation by subject or sponsor.

(continued . . .)

Campaign Management

BOX 11.7 CONTINUED

BASIS is updated every 15 minutes or so, but at the end of the session when things get hectic, updates can take considerably longer. You may have to rely on your contact network to find out what happened at committee hearings, and other activities in the legislature. to be up-to-the-minute on bill status.

The following two resources in BASIS are particularly useful.

The Bill Tracking Management Facility—BTMF

This allows you to track the status of bills as they progress through the legislative process. It's free to use, but requires setting up an account. On the legislature's home page, select the "Bills and Laws" tab. Under "Tools," click on "Bill Tracking and Management Facility." With your account you can order e-mail updates on bills you are tracking, and the service will automatically notify you of changes in their status as they occur.

The Status Information Retrieval System—SIRS

This enables you to search existing Alaska statutes affected by bills or resolutions. Go to: http://www.akleg.gov/basis/Statutes/Sirs/31, enter a bill or resolution number to see the statutes affected. Or enter an Alaska Statute number to see a list of bills modifying that law.

Using your Contact Network and Talking to Public Officials and Staff

This is yet another reason to develop and maintain a contact network. You can use it to find out about the politics that may be involved as bills progress (or don't progress) through the legislative process.

To supplement this, legislators and administration personnel, particularly staff, will often be willing to give you information on the politics involved as you track a particular bill.

Attending Committee Hearings and Floor Sessions

You can attend committees to monitor your bill or those that may affect your issue. If you are fortunate enough to have your bill reach the floor, it's most likely to pass, though maybe with an amendment or two. So attending floor sessions is more for observation than gathering information.

Watch Gavel Alaska (formerly Gavel-to-Gavel)

Juneau's public television station, KTOO-TV, provides live coverage of selected committee meetings and daily House and Senate floor action on its Gavel Alaska program. This coverage is invaluable not only in tracking bills if you can't attend a committee or floor session, but in getting to know legislators and other legislative personnel. The schedule of what will be televised is usually determined 24 hours in advance.

The program can be viewed on screens throughout the Capitol, and is available on cable stations throughout the state on the 360 North public television channel. You can also stream it on your computer, iPad, and smart phone at: https://www.360north.org/.

If you are unable to watch a particular committee or floor session, or want to see coverage from the past, Gavel Alaska maintains an extensive, searchable archive of all broadcasts that you can access. The drawback is you may be tracking a bill that wasn't covered.

Watching Legislative TV

While less extensive than Gavel Alaska, the Legislative Affairs Agency provides AlaskaLegisature.tv (https://vimeo.com/akltv). This streams all legislative committee meetings live to the Internet. The site is also a repository for recordings of other selected meetings.

Lunch and Learn Sessions

Lunch and learn sessions are opportunities for a legislator to present details on an issue of importance to them to get the word out to other legislators and the public, and answer questions. As the name indicates, these are held at lunchtimes in a committee room. To encourage legislators and others to attend, food is often provided, sometimes by a lobby group with an interest in the issue.

If this issue affects your lobbying effort, you'll obviously want to attend. Even if it doesn't, if you're dealing with a legislator who's having a lunch and learn, it's worth attending. You'll likely learn something that can be helpful when you interact with that legislator. Plus, you may score points with them for attending.

Information for Presenting Your Issue

Gathering information, mainly factual but also political, for presenting your issue, is one of the most time-consuming parts of a lobbying campaign. But it's absolutely necessary you do your homework. If you don't, you won't be taken seriously. Box 11.8 sets out the types of information you need to present your case effectively.

Keeping Tabs on Current Developments Affecting Your Issue

From day-to-day, particularly in the legislative session, but also in the two or three months before, there are many political developments and maneuvering by various interest groups as they work to achieve their goals. Some developments will directly affect your issue, so monitor these activities vigilantly, and do it often, as things can change fast.

Depending on the group you represent, it may be important not only to monitor activity when you have a current issue or issues before government, but also to monitor things regularly. This is to be sure a public official or organization not friendly to your cause, isn't trying to undermine your gains and policy goals.

As you monitor what's going on, you'll come across new proposals for legislation, regulations, or policy initiatives. This being politics, things are not always what they seem. So, if you think a proposal may affect you in any way, take a closer look. Box 11.9, on the next page, provides a systematic way to get to the bottom of the proposal.

Potential Long-Term Allies and Opponents

Whatever your issue, there'll be groups and organizations with a direct or indirect interest in that issue area, including state agencies. As these are potential allies or opponents, if you plan to lobby over the long-term, find out about them. Research their:

- Positions on your issue and related issues.

- Involvement in lobbying in the past.

- Key personnel and lobbyists.

- Reputation by various policy makers, pro or con or neutral.

BOX 11.8
ESSENTIAL FACTUAL AND POLITICAL INFORMATION FOR PRESENTING YOUR ISSUE

- What specifically you are requesting to deal with your issue: a new law or regulation, repeal or reform of an existing provision, or block a proposal.

- Details on any existing legislation or regulations on your issue. Most of this you can get from BASIS.

- If any, past attempts to enact similar provisions in the state, and why they were not successful. Again, you can get some of this info from BASIS.

- How your proposal will deal with the problems or issue.

- An estimate, if you can get it, of the start-up and long-term costs of implementing your proposal.

- Who in which state agency deals with issues like yours.

- Examples of how your proposal has been tried in other places—other states or local governments, maybe in other countries.

- An assessment of the level of success where it's been tried and why?

- The problems encountered where it's been tried and how to deal with them.

- Who's for and against your issue.

- Based on the information above: What strategy do you propose to deal with your issue or problem, including dealing with your opponents?

One use of this information is to put together a written overview for your first contact with a public official. This overview we refer to as a first contact sheet or FCS. Chapter 13, section 8, explains how to use this information to develop an FCS.

BOX 11.9
"WHAT'S REALLY BEHIND IT?" GETTING TO THE BOTTOM OF THE POLITICS OF A PROPOSAL, POLICY, OR BILL

Ask five questions to help determine *What's Really Behind It?*

1. What's its Origin and Who Supports and Opposes It?

- Who submitted and sponsored the bill or proposal and why?

- At whose request and why?

- Which legislators favor it? Oppose it? Why?

- What's the administration's stance and why?

- What groups and individuals support it? Oppose it? Why?

2. Who and What will the Bill or Proposal Affect?

- Does it apply to the state in general?

- Is it directed to a geographical area?

- Is it directed to a specific group?

- What will be its effects on other groups and organizations?

- Will one or more state agencies be impacted?

- Will it require lobbying at the federal and/or local levels?

3. Pros and Cons of the Substance of the Bill or Proposal

- Is the idea new?

- Are there precedents? In Alaska? In other states? At the national level? Internationally?

- What are its strengths, weaknesses, and drawbacks? Given these, is it likely to accomplish its intended purpose?

4. The Cost and Administration of the Measure

- How much will it cost?

- Can it be funded?

- Will there be politics involved? For example, is the fiscal note accurate?

- Who will administer it? Do they support it? Do they have the funds to implement it?

5. The Chances of Success

- What are the chances of passage? Is it essential to an adjournment package?

- Who holds the key votes?

- What groups or organizations need to be involved to assure its passage?

- What groups or organizations need to be neutralized to prevent it being killed?

- How can the bill or proposal be stopped?

Campaign
Management

For example, if you have issues in education, you'll want to know specifics about the Department of Education and Early Development, about NEA-Alaska (the K-12 employees association), AASB (the school boards association), ASCA (the Alaska Council of School Administrators), and major school districts.

If you're in the environmental arena, there are several groups in Alaska, some Alaska-grown, others national or international with offices in the state. Your opponents will likely be some parts of the business community, particularly developers, even groups in the tourist industry. Learn about their operations, personnel, and lobbyists.

Gathering Versus Presenting Information

Gathering information is one thing, presenting it is quite another. You may be the best researcher in the world and want to give a public official all the information you've gathered—perhaps volumes of it. This is almost always a big mistake.

The way you present information can affect the success of your campaign. Delivering information is an art, and one measure of the quality of a lobbyist. We go into detail on how to present information in Chapter 13, sections 7, 8 and 9.

10. DEALING WITH THE FEDERAL AND LOCAL GOVERNMENTS

The federal government has a major impact on Alaska politics, policy, and the delivery of many services, particularly transportation, environmental protection, education, and social services. And, because local governments perform many essential services and receive considerable state funds, the state-local government connection is also significant.

Interests that lobby at more than one level of government include: mining; K-12 education; commercial fisheries; and tourism interests, especially the cruise ship industry. Specific interests include: the University of Alaska; the Alaska Federation of Natives (AFN); and individual Native corporations.

It's unlikely that you'll have to deal with any government other than the state. But if your group or issue is, or might be, impacted by any of these governments, here's some things to know.

Federal Impacts

Operating in Washington, D.C. is way different from lobbying in Juneau. There are close to 15,000 registered lobbyists (likely 20,000 or more, counting those who don't have to register); and an estimated 10,000 interest groups. Plus, there are 535 members of Congress, as well as scores more agencies and hundreds of thousands more government employees than in Alaska.

This complexity is why major Alaska organizations employ lobbyists in D.C. familiar with the federal policy process. Only large and well-financed groups and organizations can afford to have a major federal presence.

Chances are, you'll just need some information on how federal law or regulations affect your issue; or need to get information on fed-

> *If your issue will be impacted by the federal or local government, get to know the key people in these governments. As some federal bureaucrats are assigned to Alaska for only a short stint, monitor these changes and make the new contacts.*

eral policies that may be useful in planning your campaign. Box 11.10, on the next page, lists sources where you can find what you need.

Dealing with Local Governments

If you have an issue that affects a borough or city government, or you want to get their support, use the same approach in advocating your cause as in Juneau. If you don't know the elected officials or staff in the borough or city, but know someone who does, use them. Get them to introduce you and vouch for you and your organization. This is particularly important in Alaska Native communities.

11. LOBBYING AND ALASKA LAW

If you're an organization that has only occasional contact with public officials, you may not have to worry about registering as a lobbyist, or be concerned about legal restrictions on your lobbying activities. On the other hand, if you plan to lobby regularly, have status as a non-profit, or intend to hire a contract lobbyist, you need to

BOX 11.10
GETTING INFORMATION ON FEDERAL AGENCIES AND ISSUES

- The Internet, particularly the websites of federal departments and agencies.

- Groups and organizations in Alaska that deal with your issue, or a related one, that lobby the federal or local government.

- Legislative staff and others able to provide information on your needs in dealing with federal or local governments.

- Contacting groups and organizations at the national level that deal with your issue.

- Many Alaska state agencies have a person whose job is to liaise with federal agencies on policy and regulations that affect their agency. These can be very useful contacts.

- Alaska's congressional delegation and their staff. Each of them has an office in Anchorage, Fairbanks, and Juneau.

- The state also has an office in D.C., but this is primarily to coordinate the administration's policy with the congressional delegation.

be familiar with lobbying regulations. These are administered by the Alaska Public Offices Commission (APOC).

The law requires only contract lobbyists and in-house lobbyists working for associations and businesses to register. It doesn't include legislative liaisons, federal, state, and local government personnel, or most volunteer lobbyists. It does require contract lobbyists hired by local governments to register, as well as the governments that hire them.

Box 11.11 provides an overview of these requirements. This is not intended to be a complete guide to APOC regulations. It should not be considered as official or legal advice.

Be sure to check to see if you need to register with APOC.

Campaign Management

BOX 11.11
APOC'S LOBBYIST REGISTRATION REQUIREMENTS

INSIGHT
Online Filing

As of 2019, those required to register as lobbyists by state law include anyone who:

- . . . . is employed and receives payments, or who contracts for economic consideration, including reimbursement for reasonable travel and living expenses, to communicate directly or through the person's agents with any public official for influencing legislation or administrative action for more than ten hours in any thirty-day period in one calendar year;

or

- . . . . represents oneself as engaging in the influencing of legislative or administrative action as a business, occupation, or profession.

Those who meet the definition of a lobbyist, together with their employers, must:

- Register with APOC before engaging in lobbying.

- File regular reports on their activities and expenditures with APOC. Lobbyists file monthly reports, employers of lobbyists quarterly reports. All this information is available to the public.

- Attend an annual ethics training session.

- Observe restrictions in giving gifts and buying food for public officials. Lobbyists may contribute to statewide and federal candidates, but only to state legislative candidates in the districts in which they live.

In addition, a legislator and some senior administration personnel, may not work as a lobbyist until one year after leaving the legislature or administration.

There are penalties for violation of these provisions.

Full details on these requirements are on APOC's website: (http://www. state.ak.us/apoc/) or call their Juneau or Anchorage office.

It's important to check the regulations frequently, as rules for registering change.

Campaign Management

1. Choices and Challenges in Using Specific Tactics

2. Grassroots Campaigns: Their Value and their Risks

3. Using Group Members and "Average Citizens"

4. The Fly-In

5. Public Hearings, Issue Forums, Brown Bags, and Recognition at Legislative Floor Sessions

6. Using the Traditional Media

7. The Use and Abuse of Social Media

8. The Feasibility of Using a Public Relations Campaign

9. Coalitions: To Join or not to Join?

10. Should You use Protests and Rallies?

11. Contributing to Election Campaigns

12. The Implications and the Dynamics of Tactics

★ CHAPTER 12 ★

The Pros and Cons of Using Specific Tactics

What's the best way to lobby?
There's no single answer, no blueprint.
Figure out what you want to accomplish—
then use the methods that fit your needs.

—Ron Clarke, special assistant to two
governors, former legislative aide, legislative press secretary, and departmental
legislative liaison

This chapter considers the pros and cons of various tactics available to those involved in lobbying. Considering them provides
important information for planning a campaign covered in the next
chapter.

Two tactics listed back in Box 9.1 are not covered here: the use of
the courts and direct democracy (the referendum and the initiative).
These are neither realistic options nor a necessary tactic for most
groups, especially those with few resources.

1. CHOICES AND CONSTRAINTS IN USING SPECIFIC TACTICS

One of the many choices facing a campaign manager and lobbyist
is what specific tactics to use and in what combination. The right
decisions can increase the chances of success; the wrong ones can
doom a campaign. Interest group leaders have some constraints on
their use of tactics, including the extent of group resources, how the
group is viewed by policy-makers, and the nature of their issue.

Three other considerations when planning tactics are:

- The more people involved in a campaign, the harder it is to maintain group unity, and the higher the risk of sending public officials a mixed message.

- Not to push an advocacy effort across the line to overkill.

- Some tactics come with high political risks, especially indirect tactics.

In the rest of the chapter we'll see how these and other factors that shape a campaign explained in Chapter 9, present both options and constraints. This requires making decisions about the appropriateness and value of various tactics.

2. GRASSROOTS CAMPAIGNS: THEIR VALUE AND THEIR RISKS

Grassroots campaigns are those that involve a large number of members in a lobbying effort. This can include: sending on-line petitions to public officials signed by many members, or delivering them by hand; sending mass e-mails or POMs; and staging rallies and protests. This tactic can be a way to influence policy-makers to support a group's issue, and perhaps get others to take notice who've been unresponsive to their previous lobbying effort.

The Risks

As it involves many people, a grassroots campaign can take on its own life if not properly managed. Some of your members may not follow the script you provided. This can cause problems.

Some won't take the trouble to get conversant with your issues, and may send a mixed or the wrong message. Others may be overzealous and go beyond what you need; or go completely off script because they think they know how to do things better.

Any of these circumstances can undermine your group's unity and its credibility. This will put you in a very tough spot. And you'll need to do a lot of cleaning up with those lobbied by your errant members.

Overkill

Some citizen lobbyists and group members unfamiliar with lobbying, think the more phone calls, e-mails, POMs, letters, messages on social media, and visits they make to legislators and other public officials the better. They believe every contact increases their chances of getting what they want. In most cases this is not true—quite the contrary.

> As a legislator, nothing annoys me more than having my phones melt down, and my e-mail inbox overloaded by a group sending messages in their boilerplate campaign.

This is seen as overkill and a major complaint often made by those being lobbied. It will likely annoy them, reduce their willingness to help you, and see you don't understand how to deal with them. It may even lose you a potential ally.

One of the worst things a group can do is send masses of e-mails, POMs, Twitter postings, letters, or jam up a public official's phone lines, with the same message, word-for-word. Online petitions or written ones delivered in person signed by hundreds, or maybe thousands of people, are often worthless.

It'll be very clear that those sending these messages were following instructions from an unseasoned lobbyist and put little, if any, thought and effort into sending or calling to convey the message. It only makes sense that busy legislators and other public officials will put about as much effort into responding to these barrages of messages as was put into sending them—very little, if any at all.

Choosing Tactics

Dealing with the Risks

If a group makes all these mistakes, the entire campaign may spin out of control. It may even get to the point where you need to abandon your effort. To try and avoid all these problems, there are several steps you can take to stay in control and maintain a united voice.

The first is to ask the question you should ask before using any tactic: *Is a grassroots campaign essential to achieve our goal?* If the answer is "yes," Box 12.1 sets out ideas on how to avoid the problems.

3. USING GROUP MEMBERS AND "AVERAGE CITIZENS"

Good lobbyists provide information in a succinct and appropriate way. While public officials appreciate this, they see lobbyists, particularly contract lobbyists, as just doing a job, as go-betweens, or perhaps not conveying how those directly affected by the issue see things.

For this reason, depending on the client or group and the issue, lobbyists work to supplement their efforts with those they represent. Whether it's a contractor, a business owner, or an average citizen with passion for a cause, a personal account of how a policy has affected or might affect their life, freedom, business, or cause for which they have passion, can present a vivid and compelling case on an issue.

In preparation for meeting with public officials or giving committee testimony during the session, lay the groundwork by arranging for group members to get to know the key officials beforehand. This is best done in the relaxed atmosphere of the interim when a legislator has more time than in the legislative session. Failing this, have clients or members meet with officials early in the session before things start to heat up.

A well-informed and prepared "average person" with a captivating story to tell, can be a more effective advocate than the most seasoned lobbyist, even more so if the story involves children.

Choosing Tactics

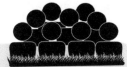

BOX 12.1
DEALING WITH GRASSROOTS LOBBYING PROBLEMS

- Always give your members guidance on approaching public officials, particularly what not to do. This can be done through newsletters, social media, an audio conference, or at an annual or other group meeting.

- Make a special effort to explain to your members the serious consequences of not following the group's planned strategy.

- If possible, limit your "grassroots campaign" to your board members or executive committee, or to those regularly involved in your lobbying effort.

- Or limit the campaign to a couple of dozen members at the most, and give them clear instructions on what you need. Choose those who will act responsibly and put effort into their contact with legislators and others.

- Choose members from across the state, if yours is a statewide organization. This makes members in all regions feel included, and enables you to cover as many key legislators as possible. It will avoid any criticism from members that their region is not represented, and reduce the likelihood they'll lobby on their own with all its risks.

There are, however, downsides to this tactic. Avoid overkill by too many members or clients dealing with politicians. There's also the possibility that a "real person" will convey a mixed message and mess things up, or they may have a poor grasp of the issue.

Again, one way to try to combat these problems is to provide an orientation or tutorial before their contact with public officials. Another is to attend meetings with them; though this is not always possible when many clients or members come to lobby.

4. THE FLY-IN

During the legislative session various groups, from school teachers to corrections officers to senior citizens to those seeking funds to subsidize day-care, bring members to Juneau for a so called "fly-in," to lobby legislators. In any one week, particularly at the beginning of the session, there may be as many as a dozen groups making the rounds in the Capitol.

Fly-ins take up a lot of time of all concerned and, if the organization pays expenses, a lot of money. The question is: are they worth it? Box 12.2 sets out the major pros and cons of fly-ins. Even if things go well in all the meetings, inevitably there'll be some concerns or questions raised in the minds of public officials. Again, usually the group's leader must do some clean-up after everyone's gone home.

Working to Minimize Potential Problems

These steps are similar to dealing with potential problems arising from grassroots and "average citizen" lobbying tactics. Bring in fewer members, ten or so, 15 at most. Provide an orientation before members lobby. To avoid overkill, have only one or two members meet with a legislator or their staff at a time, rather than overwhelm them with half a dozen or more who can't fit comfortably—or at all—in a legislative office.

You could also consider not having a fly-in. You'd avoid potential problems, but lose the advantages of the event, and may alienate some long-time members who expect their annual trip to Juneau.

Weighing the Pros and Cons

In the end, of course, it's a matter of striking a balance to advance the group's goals and keep the membership happy. The decision will vary from group to group, and may change over time due to factors internal to the group, or as political circumstances change.

BOX 12.2
THE PROS AND CONS OF FLY-INS

The Pros

- Legislators like to hear the views of those directly affected by an issue or situation, especially if they are constituents.

- Group members feel they are directly contributing to the political goals of the organization (because they genuinely are).

- It enables the group's leaders to show the membership what they do, and the importance of the group's political activities.

- When a member knows a legislator or other official who the group's leaders do not, but who may be useful in the future, the member can make the contact, preferably with the group leader or lobbyist attending the meeting.

The Cons

- The group risks overkill by inundating legislators with visits from too many people. This may annoy or even alienate some officials.

- Some of those lobbying may send mixed messages or, if not attuned to dealing with public officials, be too blunt or otherwise lacking in appropriate decorum.

- Members may stray from the agreed strategy and push their own agendas under the guise of the organization. This is often the case with rogue members who want to do their own thing when lobbying.

Choosing Tactics

Whatever the group or organization, as with any choice of tactics, the major question to ask is: *Is a fly-in a key—maybe an essential—tactic in our strategy to advance our political goals?*

5. PUBLIC HEARINGS, ISSUE FORUMS, BROWN BAGS, AND RECOGNITION AT LEGISLATIVE FLOOR SESSIONS

Public hearings, issue forums (sometimes called town halls), and brown bags, are opportunities for the public, and members of interest groups, to give input to politicians on proposed policies or needed action. Being recognized from the gallery during legislative House and Senate floor sessions can be useful to a get a group exposure.

Public Hearings

Legislators hold public hearings to get input on legislation or other proposals. They cover the gamut from the budget (on which hearings are held each year), to proposed changes in the PFD, to legislative proposals to reform the criminal justice system. People call in from all over the state, using the local LIO or other facility. Sometimes, a committee visits several communities in person to receive public comment.

A minimum of three days' notice must be given for a hearing. The chair of the committee has considerable control over organizing and running the meeting. He or she can decide the length of the meeting, whether members of the public or only invited guests may speak, how long people will have to testify, and the aspects of each topic to be considered.

Prior contact with the committee chair's staff is essential to find out what the committee wants and in what form.

The Value of Public Hearings

There are usually far more people who want to testify than time available. Even if they all testify, often these hearings are perfunctory—window dressing. Many legislators have already made up their mind. They are going through the motions to say they received public input on the issue.

Sometimes, though, the sessions can influence policy because legislators are genuinely interested in public input. Some legislators encourage their constituents to participate in hearings to show support for an issue, such as a proposed item in the budget. The more who testify, the more the legislator can argue the proposal is justified.

These sessions can also be a way for a group to get its issue in front of legislators. Members who give testimony can identify their group and press their issue. Generally, however, for an interest group, public hearings are hit or miss as far as conveying a specific and directed message. The message can easily be lost amid a myriad of wide-ranging comments from many witnesses.

Issue Forums

These are local events held by legislators to seek input from their constituents. Sometimes these include all legislators from one political party in an area, such as Anchorage. Less often, they involve legislators from both parties.

The public makes statements and asks questions. Issue forums are also opportunities for an interest group to get the word out on their issue. A group can show strength in numbers by having members stand up. In this way, these sessions get legislators familiar with a group, its issue, and its potential strength. Again, however, these sessions are hit or miss.

Governors sometimes hold town halls, occasionally in various regions of the state. But they generally don't want to walk into a contentious situation. For this reason, some of these sessions are orchestrated with invited guests and no question allowed, as in the case of some sessions held by Governor Dunleavy.

Opportunities in the Legislature

Two other ways to get your issue and campaign exposure to legislators who may not know your group and its goals, is to use opportunities provided in the Capitol building. These are brown bag events

Choosing Tactics

(also referred to as lunch and learn sessions) and having group members recognized at a House or Senate floor session. Box 12.3 explains what these involve and how to arrange them.

6. USING THE TRADITIONAL MEDIA

The traditional media refers to newspapers, magazines, television, and radio (as opposed to social media, covered in the next section).

An idea that often comes to a novice is to use the media to promote their cause. This is especially so if they're in love with their issue and can't believe anyone wouldn't support it.

In some circumstances, using the media can get a group major publicity, and policy-makers may take notice. It also has the advantage that it's free. Sometimes, however, media coverage goes awry.

Here are things to consider if you're thinking of dealing with the media.

Choosing
Tactics

The Realities of News Stories

The media in all its forms is under pressure to attract readers and audiences. Advertisers and sponsors look for high numbers when deciding where to buy ads or convey other messages, and how much they are willing to pay or controbute.

This pressure leads to compromises in both the quality and depth of reporting, including political reporting. People like to be informed and entertained and have their interest piqued when reading a headline or hearing the lead on a radio or TV story. For this reason, conflict or disagreement is often the essence of news, particularly reporting on political issues. Conflict makes stories more interesting than just reporting facts.

BOX 12.3
BROWN BAGS AND RECOGNITION
AT HOUSE AND SENATE FLOOR SESSIONS

Brown Bags

These are scheduled sessions in the Capitol, usually at lunchtime, where interest groups have an opportunity to present their issue as a group.

To hold a brown bag a group needs a legislator to sponsor them. The legislator then gets approval from the Chair of the Rules Committee in the house in which the sponsor is a member. A room, usually a committee room, is provided for the presentation to legislators, staff and others who might be interested. The group can distribute materials, use Power Point, and answer questions.

This is certainly an opportunity for a group to get exposure and present its issue. But it takes a lot of planning. Most important of all, you need to get the word out to all who might be interested, through social media or hand delivering flyers to offices. Providing food and stating this in your promotional info will likely increase attendance. Even after all this effort, often few legislators and staff turn up.

Recognition at Legislative Floor Sessions

With the permission of the presiding officer, legislators may recognize prominent people, constituents, local elected officials from a Member's home district, or group sitting in the public galleries. Introductions are part of the agenda at the beginning of floor sessions.

The Benefits

Such introductions provide name recognition for group members to legislators and the public. This is useful if you need to lobby a legislator who doesn't know your group and issue.

Recognition is particularly valuable to groups from out of town making brief visits. It lets legislators know they're in Juneau. And reminds them of the group's issue, even if indirectly, as those recognized are not allowed to make comments when introduced. Only former legislators can speak from the gallery during floor sessions.

(continued . . .)

Choosing Tactics

BOX 12.3 CONTINUED

If possible, group members should remain in the gallery after being introduced so interested legislators can approach them at the next "at ease" (break in the proceedings). Coach your members on how to skillfully advocate on your issue, as these informal contacts can be as valuable as appointments in a legislator's office.

Pre-Planning

Arranging to be recognized requires advance work. This includes: contacting the appropriate legislator; knowing the home districts and legislators of your members to be introduced; and providing brief bios on them; and why they're in Juneau.

The Strictures of Time and Space, and, Often, Disconnects Between Reporters and Editors

Reporters and editors have limited space in newspapers or time for broadcasting a story. They must make choices about which stories to present, and how extensive each should be. Inevitably, some things are covered extensively, some less so, others not at all.

Given these strictures, editors often make cuts to an interview or a press release sent in by an organization. Consequently, the story can be quite different than you'd hoped. This may include misquotes and distorted information due to cutting key words or phrases. Even if you get an apology, it'll likely be buried on page 9 or so of the paper, or on a radio or TV station's website. The damage is done and likely can't be undone.

Understand how the media works before dealing with them. Be well prepared and find out about the reporter and their media organization.

Alaska's Journalists are Generalists

Alaska's small market for news doesn't warrant media organizations hiring reporters in specialized, and certainly not in only one "beat" (subject they cover).

Virtually all Alaska reporters are generalists covering many beats. Some news organizations do have reporters in Juneau during the legislative session; but most of them cover a range of issues and events during the rest of the year.

As a result, these journalists are not experts in any one field. This is especially so with small newspapers around the state. So, while your issue is likely the most important one in the world to you, to many journalists it's just another story. After interviewing you, they may have to rush off to do a story on a missing commercial fishing vessel, construction of an arts center, or on an Alaska Native leader who's just passed away.

On Balance

Be cautious before rushing out to get media coverage. Once you talk to the media, you have little, if any, control over what's published. Media coverage may turn out fine—but it may not. Many a group thought they were getting a straight report on their issue, its importance, and a big boost for their cause, but it didn't work out that way. The story may even have been detrimental to their cause. This may also be the case in sending out a press release.

Dealing effectively with the media is a job for professional public relations people. This is why large organizations, and even medium-size ones, employ a person, often a former journalist, to work with the media. If you do need to deal with the media, or decide to do so, Box 12.4, on the next page, explains things to do before and during an interview.

7. THE USE AND ABUSE OF SOCIAL MEDIA

The use of social media, particularly Facebook, Twitter, Instagram, and Snapchat, are increasingly important aspect of lobbying for most interest groups. If you're already using social media, you likely have it tailored to your needs. If not, here's an overview of its value and some cautions.

Choosing Tactics

BOX 12.4
MEDIA INTERVIEW GUIDE

When a Reporter Calls:

- Get the name of the reporter and media organization.
- Understand the story and how you play a role.
- Allow enough time to prepare for the interview, even if it means calling the reporter back.
- Ask if the interview will be live or taped.
- Return the reporter's call before the deadline.

Before the interview:

- Set a goal: What do you want the public to know or learn?
- Prepare three key message points that include facts and statistics.
- Anticipate tough questions.

During the interview:

- Speak clearly and slowly and avoid jargon.
- Stick to your areas of expertise.
- Keep answers short.
- Offer solutions when asked about a problem.
- Correct misinformation.
- Stay positive.
- Be yourself.
- Ask for clarification if needed.
- Acknowledge if you don't know the answer, but promise to get the reporter the information and follow through.
- Tell the truth.

Source: National Council of State Legislatures (NCSC) 2018.
Printed with permission.

As an Information Tool

As covered in Chapter 11, section 6, social media is a very useful source of information for putting together several aspects of your campaign.

Use in Strategies and Tactics

Social media is useful to communicate with group members, and as an advocacy tool. Its beauty is it's a virtually free way to reach a lot of people in a very efficient way.

As a Communication Tool

It can be used to:

- Keep members informed (particularly through Facebook) about the organization's activities.

- Explain your political advocacy efforts and their status.

- Get feedback on your lobbying effort.

- Take the temperature of how your members feels about certain issues.

- Coordinate the participants in organizing a rally, protest, or other mass action.

As an Advocacy Tool

Particularly through Twitter, you and your members can send messages tailored to your issue, and get reactions from public officials, including how your issue is faring in the policy process. But this must be done with caution.

Social media can also provide immediate feedback on issues posted by public officials, particularly legislators and the governor. It's far more effective than e-mail; and miles better than a POM

(public opinion message) sent from an LIO that may take hours, days or even weeks to get a response, if any response at all.

If, for some reason, you can't have a face-to-face meeting with a public official, social media is useful to react immediately to a development on your issue. You can provide written material setting out a course of action that's more extensive than in an e-mail, a text, or a phone call.

Some Cautions

Besides being wary of some information on social media sites, there are three other things to be wary of in using this medium.

First, the ease of using social media brings the temptation to use it extensively and inappropriately. Don't overuse it in contacting public officials. Use it sparingly and in an organized way, so as not to blunt its effect by overwhelming a legislative or agency office, and maybe alienating the official concerned.

Second, ease of use means some of your members, especially those who know the legislative ropes (or think they do), may send Twitter messages that are not in line with your lobbying plan. Again, in the interest of unity, try hard to prevent this. An orientation for members that includes this warning can help.

Third, remember that social media is only one tactic in your strategy. There's no substitute for face-to-face contact or a phone call. Social media should be used to reinforce contact on your issue. Use it appropriately, which may mean using it a lot or a little, depending on your issue and as circumstances change.

8. THE FEASIBILITY OF USING A PUBLIC RELATIONS CAMPAIGN

As part of a lobbying effort, a public relations (PR) campaign is an effort by a group to gain public support to pressure policy-makers to deal with its issue and put political juice behind it. These campaigns can include one or more of the following: the traditional media; social media; getting the support of prominent people; and, in some cases, using rallies and protests.

PR campaigns range from those by big corporations that cost millions of dollars, like the Pebble Mine developers in southwest Alaska, to thousands of dollars spent on newspaper, TV, and radio ads by big oil to convince Alaskans that raising oil taxes is bad for the state, to efforts to increase penalties for drinking under age.

> **PR campaigns can easily backfire because you have little control over them once they're launched.**

The Pros and the Cons

A well-organized PR campaign can get your issue out there and draw the attention of the public and politicians with whom you need to deal. It can also help recruit members and perhaps raise funds through donations. That said, if you are a small organization, especially a shoestring operation, other than dealing with the media or perhaps staging a rally or protest, a major PR campaign is not something you want to embark upon. Box 12.5, on the next page, sets out the major reasons why.

9. COALITIONS: TO JOIN OR NOT TO JOIN?

Coalitions of groups are increasingly important, especially as competition for the ear of public officials increases. For example, the campaign in Alaska to deal with increasing health care costs brought together: business (mainly small business); the university; local governments; and social issue groups, particularly those dealing with poverty.

Joining a coalition can be advantageous, but also limit your lobbying options and potential influence. Box 12.6, on the following pages, lists four questions to ask before joining a coalition.

BOX 12.5
CAUTIONS IN USING A PR CAMPAIGN

- Like developing effective relations with the media, mounting an extensive PR campaign is a job for professionals. They know how to develop the appropriate materials and target their use. Professionals know how to weight the advantages and the downside, and develop a plan accordingly.

- To mount a serious PR campaign you'll need big bucks to hire a PR firm. To do it yourself requires lots of time, money, and labor.

- Whether your PR campaign involves only the traditional media or more extensive elements, such as a social media blitz, and public meetings, once it's launched you have little control over it.

- With little control, it's difficult to predict the impacts on the public and politicians. These may be positive; but there's a high risk they'll be negative and detrimental to your cause.

- After considering all these points, ask these three questions:

  ○ Is a PR campaign appropriate for our organization?

  ○ If so, is an extensive PR campaign essential to our lobbying effort, a wise one to use?

  ○ How will it be perceived by those we need to lobby?

Chances are you can achieve your goals by a combination of other tactics that are more direct and cost effective.

10. SHOULD YOU USE RALLIES AND PROTESTS?

During the legislative session you'll see people protesting particular policies and rallying in support of others on the steps of the Capitol, or in Anchorage and other places around the state, including outside legislators' offices. They protest about, or rally for, a range of issues from opposition to abortion to tightening gun control laws to more state funding for childcare.

Should you follow their example? The short answer: only if necessary.

BOX 12.6
FOUR QUESTIONS TO ASK BEFORE JOINING A COALITION

1. What do we have to gain by joining the proposed coalition? Will it:

- Get us better access to key policy makers and increase our political influence?

- Increase our ability to use tactics to promote our cause more than if we didn't join?

2. What might be the disadvantages?

- What will be our status in this coalition? Will we be a junior partner?

- Will our goals get less consideration than lobbying on our own?

- Will our identity with public officials be less, submerged in the broader coalition?

3. What are the Terms of the Coalition?

- Can we lobby on issues specific to our cause, while a member of the coalition?

- Will it disband after the goals are achieved?

- Is the expectation that it's long-term?

4. What would be the consequences of leaving the coalition?

- What would we lose?

- What might be the political repercussions if we do?

The Appropriateness of Protests and Rallies to Your Organization

Most groups do not use protests and rallies. Businesses and most professional groups virtually never use them (teachers being one exception). They see protests and rallies as inappropriate to the image they want to project, and not necessary, given their already extensive access and, in some cases, their influence.

By contrast, protests and rallies are a tactic quite acceptable when used by trade unions, many cause groups, environmentalists, and groups of citizens hopping mad about some action by the legislature. Some groups, such as peace activists and those who oppose racial profiling by the police, have no choice but to use protests.

Think long and hard before staging a protest. If you decide to, have a clear idea of what you want to achieve.

Box 12.7 sets out the major pros and cons of using rallies and protests. In general, the possible advantages are, at best, "maybes" for most groups. Their impact is far from certain, mainly because they are most often a political spray shot directed toward policy-makers in general and not focused on communicating with specific individuals.

For many groups, the downsides will outweigh the advantages and likely have negative effects on a campaign. Again, before you decide to use this tactic, ask yourself: *Is a protest a useful tactic that will advance our political goals?*

11. CONTRIBUTING TO ELECTION CAMPAIGNS

Contributing to a politician's election is probably the most effective tactic to use to promote your lobbying effort. They'll certainly remember you and you'll likely have easy access to them. The three major forms of help that small organizations can provide are:

- Giving money.

- Working on a campaign, which can include acting as an advisor on issues.

- Endorsing a candidate.

BOX 12.7
PROS AND CONS OF USING RALLIES AND PROTESTS

The Pros

- They can be effective for large membership groups, such as teachers, and spontaneous action, as with opposition to reducing the PFD. This is especially so if several protests are held simultaneously across the state. Media coverage can increase their impact and may spook politicians into taking notice of an issue.

- If you are an established but small organization, it might reinforce your position on pending legislation or other issues.

- Protests can be advantageous to outsider groups with minimal access to the decision-making process. They might get the attention of the politicians you need, but only if you follow up with direct contact soon afterwards.

The Cons

- Protests and rallies are hard to control and to focus their message because many people are involved. This tactic can take on a life of their own This may undermine the political unity of your organization.

- Disrupting the business of the legislature by blocking the entrance and filling the halls of the Capitol with protestors may annoy, even alienate, public officials and tarnish the image of your group.

- If you stage multiple rallies or protests in Juneau and around the state, it can easily appear as overkill. It may send a message to politicians that you don't understand how to target your lobbying efforts.

Choosing Tactics

Some groups also set up political action committees (PACs). These are organizations to channel money to candidates to aid their election. Sometimes PACs also give money to political parties.

You need to think long and hard, however, before making any type of campaign contribution.

There's no faster way to a politician's heart than helping them get elected or re-elected.

Financial Contributions—A Caution

Most large campaign contributions come from major economic interests, such as the oil and construction industries, and organized labor. This labels them as partisan, business with Republicans, labor with Democrats.

Some liberal cause groups, like environmentalists and pro-choice groups, typically associate with the Democrats. Conservative cause groups, such as those favoring privatization of state services, and anti-abortion groups, most often ally with the Republicans. If you are a cause group in one of these molds, you might want to throw your lot in with one of the political parties.

But remember, today's majority party can be tomorrow's minority opposition and you may be left out in the cold. If you want to keep your organization non-partisan, don't support candidates using the name of your organization. This doesn't stop your members from contributing, and making it clear to candidates the organization to which they belong.

Non-financial contributions

These include: going door to door to promote the candidate; putting up yard signs; organizing groups to wave candidate signs at prominent places around the district (busy intersections, malls, convention centers, etc); working in the campaign office answering phones or e-mails; posting campaign information on social media; and helping get out the vote. Some groups even recruit candidates, either from within their ranks or others who are sympathetic to their cause.

Check out the contribution limits with APOC before you give to an election campaign.

Serving in an advisory capacity during a campaign can be a way to educate the candidate on your issues and influence their positions.

Choosing
Tactics

It can help on issues where they have little experience, or clarify their thinking on
other issues. One important aspect of this
role can be helping draft responses to the
many questionnaires candidates receive.

However, the same caution applies in
appearing partisan. Though, again, this
does not exclude group members from
working on campaigns and pushing the cause of their group with
candidates.

Candidate Endorsements

Unlike giving money and working on a campaign, a candidate
endorsement by an individual (other than a prominent Alaskan) is
worth very little. Candidates want groups to endorse them, and the
bigger and more well-known the group, the better.

A questionnaire to a candidate is a useful tactic in considering an
endorsement. You can get a feel for what they support, if they're pro
or con your issue, the extent to which they may be persuaded, and if
they might be an ally or a foe. Their response, or lack thereof, will give
you the information you need to endorse them or not.

Once again, if a group endorses a candidate they are likely to be
considered partisan.

Political Action Committees—PACs

You're unlikely to want or be able to set up a PAC as a tactic, especially if you are a shoestring operation. All the same, it's important
for anyone involved in politics and lobbying to know about them.

Which Interest Groups Set Up PACs?

PACs are a major campaign tactic used by large economic interests, such as business and labor, but also some cause groups.

Examples of business PACs are: AMPAC, the Alaska Miners Association's PAC; the Alaska Hotel Lodging Association PAC; BP Alaska Employee PAC; and Alaska Business PAC.

Examples of cause group PACs are: the Alaska Conservation Voters for Clean Government PAC; Alaska Right to Life PAC; and Alaska First PAC, a nonpartisan PAC supporting candidates who place Alaska's interests above partisanship.

The PACs of large businesses make major contributions, mainly to Republicans. This accounts for much of their influence in Juneau.

Money is the mother's milk of interest group access and influence. No political interest knows this better than big business, which is why they set up PACs.

By contrast, cause groups make much smaller contributions, but this still improves their access to public officials sympathetic to their causes.

To keep a positive image, many of these groups deny the connection between their contributions and their influence; but reality shows otherwise. They don't give money just because they think someone is a nice person!

If you want to set up a PAC, contact APOC to find out the rules and regulations.

Choosing Tactics

12. THE IMPLICATIONS AND THE DYNAMICS OF TACTICS

This consideration of the range of specific tactics, confirms the points made at the beginning of the chapter: group leaders and lobbyists are faced with many choices and challenges in planning a campaign. The six most significant of these are listed in Box 12.8.

One other point to bear in mind is the combination of tactics you use today may not be the ones you'll need tomorrow. This is a consequence of something we've mentioned many times before—the fluid and often rapidly changing nature of politics and the policy process. The use of tactics is a dynamic process. A major development, such

BOX 12.8
A SUMMARY OF FACTORS TO CONSIDER WHEN CHOOSING PARTICULAR TACTICS

- The need to use the most appropriate tactics given the perception of the organization and available resources.

- To use as few tactics as necessary to achieve the group's goals in the most efficient way. The more tactics used, the greater the chances of something going wrong.

- Group leaders need to balance involving members in a lobbying campaign and maintaining group unity—sending only one position on their issue to policy makers.

- The risks of using some tactics may be too high, especially where the outcome can't be controlled, such as using the media or protests.

- Getting over a message effectively must be balanced against too much lobbying. Inundating public officials with e-mails, phone calls, or staging a pesky protest, may annoy the very people you need, and may even alienate them.

So putting all these factors together, the question to ask is: *Is the use of a particular tactic necessary to advance our cause?*

Choosing Tactics

as losing a key supporter or unforeseen opposition in a committee hearing, will most likely cause a rethinking of tactics. Reacting to these situations effectively is where a good lobbyist is indispensable.

THIS CHAPTER COVERS

1. The Need for a Specific Plan

2. Four Key Decisions Before You Begin

3. Your Feasibility Study

4. The Components of Your Lobbying Plan

5. Three Approaches to Developing Your Plan

6. The Do's and Don'ts of Developing and Presenting Written Materials

7. Developing a First Contact Sheet—FCS

8. Providing Additional Information

9. Planning a Lobbying Visit to Juneau

★ CHAPTER 13 ★

Your Feasibility Study, Lobbying Plan, and Written Materials

*The first time I went to lobby in Juneau,
I didn't think through what I needed to do,
set out the big picture, and avoid major screw-ups.
That time I didn't do too well.
I never made the same mistake again.*

—Carl E. Shepro,
Past President and Lobbyist,
United Academics

This chapter explains the fundamentals of a lobbying plan and tips on putting one together. It also covers what to consider before developing a plan; and the written materials you'll need.

1. THE NEED FOR A SPECIFIC PLAN

Take the advice of Carl Shepro in his quote above: Don't start lobbying until you've thought things through—consider what needs to be done to give you the best chance of success. This is because there are so many aspects to lobbying, including: dealing with the legislature; the governor's office; state agencies; perhaps involving your members in lobbying; and dealing with your opposition.

A lobbying campaign is an exercise in management, in this case political management, to help navigate the political shoals of the challenges you'll face. So you need a plan to see the big picture, put all these pieces together, and get them all in sync. Planning can be a tedious and time-consuming effort—but it'll pay you major dividends.

If you don't have a plan, your lobbying effort will lack focus, be uncoordinated, and you'll likely lose control of it, especially if a lot of people are involved. This increases the possibility that your campaign will fail. What's more, you don't want to be ill prepared and look inept to policy-makers, especially as you'll likely need them in the future. Remember, once you lose your good reputation, it's hard to get it back.

But before you develop a lobbying plan, ask yourself some questions.

2. FOUR KEY DECISIONS BEFORE YOU BEGIN

A common complaint from politicians about people who contact them seeking solutions to problems or issues, besides not having a plan, is that they've not considered the appropriateness and specifics of promoting their causes. So, before you embark upon a lobbying effort, ask yourself four questions.

1. Is a Political Solution the Best Way to Solve Your Issue?

Many people assume that they should go to the legislature to address their issue or concern, because they believe it can only be dealt with by a new law or by securing public funds. This may be true; but in many cases it may not.

Take, for instance, a group of citizens seeking funds to replace the roof on their local museum. Getting a grant from a foundation or raising funds from the public might be a challenge, but likely easier, with relatively less uncertainty, and requiring far fewer resources, than going to the legislature.

Another example is a group working to raise funds for a statewide publicity campaign to promote firearm safety, similar to the Firearms

Safely Coalition (FSC) referred to in Chapter 1. Rather than pursuing a political solution, they may be more successful using traditional and social media, pamphlets, and endorsements by prominent citizens, such as business people and former governors, to promote their cause. Again, this may not be easy, but more certain of success than trying to convince the state to fund it, particularly if the group has little experience dealing with state government and lobbying.

> *Do some serious soul-searching before launching a lobbying campaign. Is it the best way to deal with you issue?*

On the other hand, if your issue can only be dealt with by some government action, consider the following three questions.

2. What is the Best Way to Get Government to Deal with Your Issue?

Passing new laws or securing budget appropriations are extremely difficult and time-consuming endeavors, with no guarantees of success in the highly uncertain world of politics. Besides this, the need for compromise means you'll likely not get everything you want, even if you get a new law passed.

First, determine the course of least political resistance. It may be that your problem can be solved by a new regulation or amending an existing one. Or perhaps a department or other state agency has funds to help you with your issue. If appropriate to your needs, these and other avenues are well worth pursuing, enabling you to avoid the tortuous and uncertain legislative process.

3. Is the Time Right to Lobby on Your Issue?

The political climate must be right for promoting the solution to your issue. Obviously, you are more likely to secure funding in high revenue years than in austere times. You're more likely to get serious consideration if your issue is part of a wave of concern about an issue. For example, it could be the issue of domestic violence that's arisen due to the publicity of some serious incidents.

Planning a Campaign

But you may feel you can't wait for a more positive political atmosphere to advocate for your cause. In that case, you take your chances of appearing politically unaware and alienating policy-makers you may need in the future.

4. Defining Your Issue Specifically and Clearly: What Exactly do You Want?

Unless you define your goals specifically and clearly from the start, you can't accurately estimate the resources you'll need, the specific tactics to use and how, and to what extent to modify your plan when circumstances change.

Examples of Poorly Presented Requests

Going to a legislator with a proposal to raise the awareness of children to the problem of child abuse, and how to deal with it if they are victims, is too vague. You need to specify exactly what you want, such as: We propose that all social studies classes for grades 6-12 in public schools, include two hours of instruction on this issue annually.

Another example is the oft-heard need expressed to legislators by many Alaskans, and particularly conservative groups, that government needs to be made more efficient. The cost of the state's bureaucracy must be reduced by cutting waste and out-sourcing services to the private sector. The questions legislators will ask are, "Which services and programs specifically, and why?" and "How do you suggest it be done?" "What evidence do you have that it will save the state money?" When those questions come up, you need to be ready with specific, clear answers.

3. YOUR FEASIBILITY STUDY

If you've decided it's necessary to lobby to deal with your issue, and defined your goals succinctly and clearly, you're ready to move to the next stage. The feasibility study will help you see if you have the resources to launch your campaign. Box 13.1 sets out the basics of a feasibility study.

BOX 13.1
A LOBBYING FEASIBILITY STUDY

Step 1: State Your Goal and its Justification

State this in two or three short sentences.

Step 2: List What Resources You Need to Realize Your Goal or Goals

These will include:

- Time available for group leaders, members, and volunteers to monitor developments, coordinate the lobbying effort, lobby, etc.

- If you're not based in Juneau, financial resources for visits to the capital city to lobby.

- Informational materials for explaining and backing up your case.

- Necessary access for securing the support of public officials.

- The ability to recruit additional support from other groups, lobbyists, etc.

Step 3: List Your Available Resources

Catalog the resources you have and those you know you can acquire.

Step 4: Needs versus Available Resources

List, side-by-side, the resources you need and those you have available. The gap between them will either dictate the extent of your campaign, or indicate the necessity of fund-raising and other efforts to acquire more resources.

Step 5: Determining if the Campaign is Feasible or Needs Modifying

This is where you decide if the campaign is feasible given the goal or goals you have set. You have three choices:

- Go forward with the original plan.

- Modify your goal (if possible) to fit your available resources.

- Postpone the campaign or decide not to launch it at all.

Even if you don't conduct your feasibility study and develop your lobbying plan in the way suggested here, address all the point in some way. Otherwise, you'll have no logical way to approach your lobbying effort.

This is not a finely-tuned, detailed exercise as your lobbying plan will be. But it's an important step to see what you'll need to succeed and what it'll take versus what you have available.

Not all groups and organizations conduct feasibility studies in a systematic and deliberate way as suggested here. But, in effect, they all do so whether as a specific exercise or more informally. Without a review of some sort, a group barreling ahead with a campaign may realize halfway through that they don't have what's needed to complete their lobbying effort. Not only will they have wasted time and energy, but undermined their reputation, especially with those who used some of their political capital to support them.

After conducting this assessment, if you decide you have what's needed or can get it, you're ready to plan the details of your campaign.

4. THE COMPONENTS OF YOUR LOBBYING PLAN

Box 13.2 sets out details of what should be in your lobbying plan. Most of those who lobby, including major professional contract lobbyists and other seasoned political advocates, have likely not approached their lobbying efforts in this specific way, following all eight steps in this order. Or they may not see all these decisions as necessary before starting to lobby.

Similarly, you needn't follow this plan to the letter. Take some parts and leave others. But, at some time in your lobbying effort, you'll have to make decisions on all eight components. If you are a novice or someone who didn't do as well as you'd hoped last time you lobbied, it's a good idea to approach your campaign in the systematic way set out in the plan. This way you don't overlook any aspect of what you need to do this time.

BOX 13.2
THE LOBBYING PLAN

1. The Goal or Goals and Fallback Positions of the Campaign

Your Goal or Goals

This statement should be identical to the one in your feasibility study. Keep constantly focused on this goal or its modified version. Your goal or goals will shape all you do in the campaign.

Fall Back Position or Positions

See point 7 below.

A Point Where You May Decide to Abandon Your Campaign

See point 8 below.

2. Group Organizational Elements

Will include a list of who will perform tasks and their duties. Several or all tasks will likely be done by the same person in a small organization, several different people in a large one. Roles and tasks must be clearly defined, and include the following:

Campaign Coordinator/Clearinghouse Person

This is the main person running the campaign. In small organizations, this may also be the lobbyist. See Chapter 11, section 3, for details on the coordinator's responsibilities.

Lobbyist or Lobbyists

Besides dealing with public officials directly, the lobbyist's role will likely involve:

- Monitoring political developments that might affect the group.

- Advising on strategy and tactics

- Developing and coordinating the lobbying effort.

(continued . . .)

BOX 13.2 CONTINUED

If the organization has a lobbyist in addition to a campaign coordinator, the exact responsibilities of the lobbyist, particularly in relation to the coordinator or in conjunction with them, need to be spelled out to prevent confusion and ensure all tasks are on track.

Person Responsible for Monitoring Political Developments

If there are one or more people performing this task in addition to the campaign coordinator and/or lobbyist, their responsibilities need to be clearly defined, especially how and with whom information is shared within the organization.

Other Personnel

Depending on the size of the organization, the issue at hand, and the strategy employed, other roles may include: a volunteer coordinator; media liaison; and election support person.

3. General Strategy

This sets out the plan for how to execute your campaign. It includes:

- Which parts of the government are to be lobbied: legislature, governor, which agencies.

- Which (if any) groups to ally with.

- Indirect lobbying tactics to use (if any), such as the media, working on election campaigns, etc.

- Strategies to counter major opposition.

4. Specific Tactics

These include:

- Policy-makers to approach, who in your organization will do this, and the message to be conveyed, including materials to be presented.

- Specifics on how to execute indirect lobbying methods (if any) such as which outlets and people in the media, and who in the organization will do it.

- Details on working with coalition members (if any).

Planning a Campaign

- Specific ways to counter your opposition.

- The specific roles of your campaign coordinator and lobbyist(s) in each tactic.

- Specific directions to those involved in lobbying who are in contact with policy-makers. What leeway will they have in decision-making and presenting compromises or fallback positions?

- Provisions for feedback, reassessing the campaign, and dealing with immediate lobbying needs. See point 6 below.

5. Campaign Timeline

Developing a timeline provides a focus on the stages and processes for executing your plan. It's also important for when you'll need resources, particularly the time of staff, volunteers, or members.

The Week-by-Week Schedule

Because each legislative session has its own momentum, you can't plan the lobbying process on a detailed, certain timetable.

But you can set broad time periods for completing activities, such as sending people to Juneau to lobby (if you're based outside the capital), and if you'll hold events, such as a reception for policy-makers and others involved in your campaign.

Set Times for Feedback Sessions

Schedule times during the legislative session when those in your organization involved in the campaign consult to give feedback on what's happening and readjust your lobbying plan, if necessary. These sessions should be organized and directed by your campaign coordinator.

Using the Interim

Much of your preparations and lobbying work can be done in the interim. So your timeline should include:

- Schedule of meetings with policy-makers and others during that time.

- Information sessions for those who'll lobby for you, such as your volunteers.

- A schedule for gathering back-up materials.

(continued . . .)

Planning a
Campaign

BOX 13.2 CONTINUED

6. An Emergency Decision-Making Process

Your plan should include a process for making immediate decisions necessitated by changing circumstances.

These are most likely to occur during the legislative session. They could include: someone or some group working to derail your proposal; one of your key supporters changes their mind; your bill gets stalled in a committee, among other negative developments.

Establish a network, headed by your lobbying coordinator, to facilitate emergency meetings on short notice.

7. Fallback Positions

Your plan needs to include fallback positions. Determine ahead of time how much you are willing to compromise and get less than you want. The major question to answer is:

What would you be willing to accept (if anything) if you can't achieve your major goal or goals?"

The answer will shape your strategy to a large extent. But be careful not to publicize these fallback positions, as decision-makers who get wind of these may hold you to them before you're ready to compromise.

8. Abandoning the Campaign

There may come a point when it's apparent you're not going to get what you want or anything close to it. If you intend to lobby in the future, on your issue or something else, and insist on continuing to lobby on this dead cause, you may alienate policy-makers whose support you'll need down the road.

Reasons for abandoning a campaign include: coalition members backing out; your lobbyists and leaders not doing their job; and missing major opportunities to push your issue, such as not following up at a crucial time.

Again, however, be careful not to publicize the circumstances under which you might abandon your campaign, as it may seriously undermine your lobbying effort.

5. THREE APPROACHES TO DEVELOPING YOUR PLAN

There are many approaches to developing a lobbying plan, and different ways to focus your lobbying effort. Here we outline three possibilities:

- Drawing on previous efforts in Alaska.

- Using experience in other states.

- Working to close your power gap.

These are not mutually exclusive approaches. They can be combined in various ways.

1. Drawing on Previous Efforts in Alaska

You needn't reinvent the wheel. Often, a group or individual will have lobbied on your or a similar issue before, So you can gather existing information as a basis for your plan.

- Search out any existing legislation dealing with your issue. You can get much of the info you need on the legislature's Bill Action and Status Inquiry System (BASIS, see Box 11.7 in Chapter 11 for how to use this system).

- Besides BASIS, legislators' and the governor's websites contain other useful info.

- Contact those who've been involved with or observed lobbying on your issue or related issues in the past. These might be legislators, staffers, lobbyists, association personnel, agency officials, or even journalists. If willing, they can fill you in, and maybe give you advice for lobbying on your issue.

2. Using Experience from Other States

You can find out if your issue has been addressed in another state by contacting a national or regional organization, such as the Council of State Governments (CSG), its western regional office, or the National Conference of State Legislatures (NCSL). You can also search independently on the Internet. Plus, most states have records and archives like BASIS for searching legislative history.

Planning a Campaign

Don't reinvent the wheel—check out what's been done before in Alaska and other states.

Once you've pinned down the state or states and the agency or agencies and legislators that dealt with your issue, most will be helpful if you e-mail or call them. They will likely be more so in their legislative interim than during the legislative session.

3. Working to Close your Power Gap

A third approach is to build your plan around your power gap. This emphasizes the elements of group influence you possess, working to deal with those you're weak on, and accepting that some of them you'll never have in your arsenal of tactics. Box 13.3 is a brief version of the main element of group influence set out in Box 10.1 in section 2 of Chapter 10. There are many ways to use this approach. The following are suggestions to get you started.

An Example

Let's say you're a new group with little experience lobbying. You have minimal financial resources, you don't have a large membership distributed across the state, and at the moment, yours is not a group on which public officials depend.

Looking at the other elements of influence, you could pursue three or four courses of action or a combination immediately and plan to work on some over the long run. Box 13.4, on the next page, sets these out.

Written Materials and Your Lobbying Plan

Whatever approach or combination of approaches you use to develop your plan, you'll need written materials. However thorough your research, it's all be for nothing if these are not presented in a clear and useful way. The next three sections help you develop and present these critical materials.

Planning a Campaign

BOX 13.3
TWELVE FACTORS DETERMINING AN
INTEREST GROUP'S INFLUENCE

1. The degree to which public officials need the group, organization, or coalition's services and resources.

2. Lobbyist-policy maker relations.

3. Whether the group's lobbying focus is primarily defensive or promotional.

4. The extent and strength of opposition groups.

5. The legitimacy of the group and its demands—how the public and public officials view these factors.

6. Group financial resources.

7. The tenure, political, organizational, and managerial skill of group leaders.

8. The political cohesiveness of the membership.

9. Size and geographical distribution of group members.

10. Potential for entering coalitions.

11. Extent of group autonomy in political strategizing.

12. Timing.

6. THE DO'S AND DON'TS OF DEVELOPING AND PRESENTING WRITTEN MATERIALS

The inclination of novices, and even some who've lobbied before, is to provide as much information as they can on their issue. Consequently, sometimes legislators receive impenetrable tomes of information. On occasion, you'll see a witness at a committee hearing pass thick packets of information across the table, met with looks of dismay by committee members.

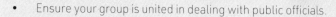

BOX 13.4
DEALING WITH A POWER DEFICIENCY

Immediate Options

- Ensure your group is united in dealing with public officials.

- Work on identifying and dealing with your opposition.

- Focus on your lobbyist-policy-maker relations; and perhaps by having your members or others directly affected by an issue, meet with public officials.

- Exploit the resources you have to the full, such as developing informational materials, attending committee hearings, public hearings, and issue forums, to get your point across.

- You may be able to attract media coverage.

- Join a coalition or work with a group or organization with similar goals.

- You may be able to find a pro bono lobbyist willing to help your lobbying effort.

Over the Long-Term

- Solidify relationship with politicians by developing trust and credibility.

- Work to establish yourself as an expert in your policy area.

- Contribute to campaigns.

- Identify new members or supporters throughout the state.

- If possible, develop a more permanent leadership and institutional memory.

- Try to avoid using a new lobbyist each year. They will likely have a steep learning curve in lobbying. Understandably, using a different lobbyist, especially every year, will trigger caution in the minds of public officials as they deal with yet another unfamiliar face.

- It might be possible to get supporters of your cause to give money to your group.

Planning a Campaign

All public officials have had dozens of experiences of being overwhelmed with written materials. To provide too much information in an initial contact or committee hearing is a big mistake for three reasons:

> *Overwhelming a public official with volumes of material will likely be a detriment to you and getting them to support your issue.*

- Public officials are short of time and won't read it all. This means you won't achieve your goal of informing them in the way you intended.

- They need an overview of what you want them to focus on regarding your issue.

- By inundating them with information, you'll start off on the wrong foot. They'll see you don't understand the basics of lobbying and their needs and constraints. This may color their judgment and undermine your lobbying effort.

Put yourself in their shoes. This will help you see what information they need initially, in subsequent contacts, and how it should be presented. There are five golden rules in providing written information. as set out in Box 13.5 on the next page. The next two sections expand on these points.

An Approach You Should Probably Not Follow

Some lobbyists, particularly the seasoned professionals, will tell you that it's not a good idea to provide too much in writing. Doing so, they say, can pin you down in an ever-changing political environment. This may be the case; but for a small and new group, not well versed in the lobbying business, and not known to public officials, providing appropriate written information will be of great advantage.

Planning a Campaign

BOX 13.5
FIVE GOLDEN RULES FOR PRESENTING
WRITTEN MATERIALS TO PUBLIC OFFICIALS

- All information, whether one page or ten pages, must be formatted in a reader-friendly way. Use numbers for sections, short paragraphs, and bullet points. Avoid long, convoluted sentences. Use simple charts and graphs, if needed.

- In your initial contact, whether in person, by e-mail, phone, or via other means, provide a first contact sheet (FCS). This will be one page long, two at most. See section 7 below for details.

- Anticipate supplementary information you may need at your first meeting, have it available. Provide this only if asked.

- During your meeting or afterwards, you may be asked for more extensive back-up information. Bear in mind the needs of and constraints on public officials when developing and presenting this.

- You'll likely be dealing with several public officials about your issue, in the legislature, governor's office, maybe a state agency. Give each one identical information in your initial contact (including the short summary of your request) to avoid confusion or getting your political wires crossed. Additional information can be geared to each official's request.

7. DEVELOPING A FIRST CONTACT SHEET—FCS

FCS is not a term used by lobbyists or public officials. But it's useful for explaining the extent and sequence of presenting information. In whatever way they refer to the written information they present in their first meeting, in effect, most lobbyists include what's in an FCS.

The Purpose and Content of an FCS

An FCS provides a short, succinct, and very specific explanation of your issue and the various aspects of pursuing it. Box 13.6 lists ten pieces of information for you to include. Your FCS anticipates the questions a public official will likely ask about your issue.

BOX 13.6
TEN POINTS TO COVER IN A
FIRST CONTACT SHEET—FCS

1. This is our request:

2. We are requesting it for this reason:

3. The estimated cost is:

4. A suggested approach to deal with our issue is:

5. We believe you and your constituents/agency/clientele will benefit in the following ways:

In presenting your FCS you may want to split it into two parts.

6. Securing our goals will benefit the state in the following ways:

7. Legislation/regulations existing on this subject, and how our proposal affects this are:

8. Evidence that our proposal will help solve the problem is:

9. So far, we have the following support for our proposal:

10. Those who oppose our goals, their reasons and how we plan to deal with them, are:

Not all public officials will be concerned with all these points; and some will have additional questions. If you're requesting a change in a regulation or something else a state agency can do without involving the legislature or the governor, your FCS will be

Provide only the most pertinent information on your issue in a succinct and reader-friendly form—it's an indispensable part of your lobbying battle.

shorter. You won't need to address all the questions in Box 13.6.

In this and other cases, a lobbyist, particularly one familiar with a public official's needs and preferences, may include other information, and present it in a different sequence than we've done. But, again, we use the example because it includes the major points in the order that public officials are likely to want. You can adapt your FCS to your needs as long as it covers the points in Box 13.6.

A Suggestion about Presenting Your FCS

Although your FCS is short and pithy, covering all ten points, it's a little overwhelming to read—a lot to take in all at once. And you certainly don't want to commit the political sin of overwhelming a public official. To deal with this, besides having your FCS available in its complete form, you can start with the first five points and present points 6-10 only if asked about what they cover. Alternatively, points 6-10 can be provided in follow-up contact.

Exactly what written information you provide in your initial contact, your first face-to-face meeting and follow-up meetings, depend on the preferences of the public official concerned, and the course your meetings take. So you need to be flexible and deal with a each official on their own terms.

Exactly how you present your FCS depends on the information you're asked to provide. Knowing the needs and preferences of those you meet with, and reading the situation during your first contact, will help a lot. As with so much in lobbying, it's a matter of personal judgment and having done your homework to get a feel for those with whom you're dealing.

A Sample FCS

In providing this sample we use the hypothetical U.S. state of North Berne (NB), a politically conservative state in the Midwest. For comparative purposes the hypothetical states of Rancho Verde, a liberal western state, Sullaria, a very conservative southern state, and New Charlotte, a politically moderate northeastern state.

The request in North Berne we consider is that those convicted of a domestic violence offense complete a one-week therapy program. Lobbying for the issue is New-Directions-NB, a small organization advocating for effective approaches to deal with domestic violence. New-Directions-NB has a half-time director, and several volunteers. It's partly funded by a grant from a private donor. The details of the FCS are set out in Box 13.7 on the next page.

In preparing your FCS be sure to include:

- The name of your organization.

- Your name.

- Your contact information—e-mail, phone, mailing address and/or that of your organization.

- The date and the version of your FCS.

- Use numbers for each point (not bullets). This will make for easy reference for you and public officials and avoid confusion.

You'll likely need to modify your FCS as circumstances change. In that case, be sure to put the new date and "Second Version." This will also prevent confusion. And, of course, share it with all those to whom you gave the first version.

8. PROVIDING ADDITIONAL INFORMATION

If you get support for your proposal, you'll likely be asked for information to expand on what's in your FCS.

Information from Other People

The information required might be for you to provide the official with names of people they can consult about your issue. It could be:

Planning a Campaign

BOX 13.7
A SAMPLE FCS

■New—Directions—NB—

From: New-Direction-NB
Name: Debra Barbauer, Board Chairperson
E-mail: DZB5456@gmail.com
Ph: 1-907-494-1595
Address: P.O. Box 3404, Marson, Alaska 99964
Date: September 21, 2019 (first draft of proposal)

1. New-Direction-NB requests:

Legislation to mandate therapy sessions for all those convicted of domestic violence.

2. Reason for Request:

The present policy of prison or probation without counseling or therapy, has not reduced domestic violence. Many of those convicted are repeat offenders.

3. Estimated cost:

Start-up costs $5 million, operating costs $2-3 million per year. Based on figures from Sullaria and New Charlotte, adjusted for population and cost of living; plus estimates from the NB Division of Revenues and Expenditure.

Costs will be offset by savings for police, use of the courts, and prisons.

4. Our suggested approach to deal with the issue:

Legislation, see #1 above.

5. You and your constituents/agency/clientele will benefit because:

It will reduce domestic violence in your district and you'll help address a major and chronic problem in the state.

If you present your FCS in two parts split it here.

6. The Benefit to the state:

According to the National Council Against Domestic Violence (NCADV), North Berne has the third highest rate of domestic violence in the nation—1 in 8 citizens per year; 1 in 6 are abusers two or more times.

The percentage is rising for both first and second offenses. Our proposal will help reduce this number in a way excising laws have not.

7. Legislation/regulations existing and how our proposal affects them:

No existing laws or regulations mandate counseling.

8. Evidence that our proposal will help solve the problem:

According to NCADV, second offenses decreased 30 percent in Rancho Verde and New Charlotte, which have the most extensive programs, and 20 percent in Sullaria, which has a less extensive program.

In all three states, public safety, court, prison, and other related costs for dealing with domestic violence have decreased.

9. Support for our proposal:

So far, 25 groups, organizations, and individuals have expressed support for this proposal. They include:

- North Berne Women's Forum.

- United Tribes of North Berne.

- Children First NB.

- The police and prison guards union.

- The AFL-CIO of North Berne.

- Two former governors, several legislators, and former legislators.

10. The opposition, their reasons, and how we propose dealing with them:

- The Department of Prisons, Department of Health and Public Aid, and the court system, are concerned about increased costs.

- Private prisons fear loss of revenue.

- Some Senators and Representatives are concerned about increasing the budget, and creating more government bureaucracy.

We will work to secure an initial increase in funds for the departments that will administer the program, and plan to show future savings to legislators.

- Someone to verify how the policy worked in other states. This could be a person from another state or an official from an Alaska agency or local government.

- A group leader who can confirm the need for the action based on their previous experience with this or a related issue.

- A person, an "average citizen," other individual or group that will be positively affected by your proposal.

In all these cases, if they agree:

- Be sure to provide them with a copy of your FCS.

- Give them an idea of what you want them to say.

- If they are too busy to do it themselves, and if they're agreeable, put their comments in writing for them.

- Accompany them to the meeting; or, if they prefer to meet the official on their own, ask them to give you a report afterwards.

Get clear instructions from the policy-maker on what additional written information is needed. If you're not told, ask. Then present it in the most appropriate form.

Providing Additional Written Materials

If you're asked for detailed written information, follow similar rules to your FCS in the way it's formatted and presented. Again, the big no-no is not to deluge the official or their staff with information. Box 13.8 sets out key points to bear in mind.

Besides the information you provide, legislators have access to any number of information sources, including the Legislative Research Services (LRS) arm of the Legislative Affairs Agency (LAA). LRS provides independent, objective information and analysis for legislators and their staff. Its specialists will likely have much of the technical information they need on your issue at their fingertips to provide the legislators with whom you're dealing.

TIPS ON PRESENTING ADDITIONAL WRITTEN INFORMATION

- As with your FCS, providing additional written information is an aspect of interpersonal communications—an exercise in human psychology. You want public officials to take note of what you're presenting. And you make it easy to browse for a first look and for a full read. This is particularly the case if it's more than five pages.

- Again, the key is to understand a public official's needs—put yourself in their shoes.

- Don't overwhelm them with information, give them large documents, piles of facts, figures and charts; or, in most circumstances, a public petition containing thousands of names.

- Don't send or give them references to where they can find further information. Put the information in an encapsulated form yourself.

- If your issue involves scientific, professional, legal, or other specialized terms, explain these briefly. Remember, legislators and their staff are generalists and deal with a wide range of issues. You don't want their eyes to glaze over.

- As far as possible, link this additional information to your FCS. This will show how it relates to each point in your FCS and provide a comprehensive view of your request.

- In formatting, avoid small fonts, narrow margins, and pages packed with long paragraphs. This will produce chagrin when a public official starts to review your material. Make it reader-friendly with space on the page. As with your FCS, use numbers for sections or major points. This will make it easier to refer to when presenting the material or you get a call to ask about it. Use bullet points for subsections.

9. PLANNING A LOBBYING VISIT TO JUNEAU

A rough estimate is that about 50 percent of people who lobby don't live in the capital city. How do you overcome this disadvantage if you can only afford to go to Juneau once or twice in the session, or maybe not at all?

The short answer is, unless you have someone on the ground in Juneau, it's difficult to overcome entirely. Those who have a political advocate in Juneau permanently have a distinct advantage. Nevertheless, there are ways to minimize the limitations you may face.

A Lobbying Visit that's Planned for You

Major businesses and groups with extensive resources, such as the mining, construction and utility industries, likely have at least one or two lobbyists in Juneau. They arrange everything for members' visits, and show them how to fit into the lobbying effort.

Similarly, associations such as AML or United Fishermen of Alaska (UFA), bring members to Juneau as part of fly-ins or other events. Arrangements are made by the organization, and typically provide their members an orientation before they start lobbying.

Even if you're part of a planned visit, it's a good idea to know in advance what's involved in lobbying and how to deal with those you'll meet. Much of what you need is in this handbook.

Don't go Lobbying Rogue

An important rule if you're part of a planned lobbying effort is to take guidance from your group's leaders, staff members, or lobbyist. However experienced you are (or think you are) in lobbying, and however well-intentioned, don't go rogue—you must follow and fit into the plan they've developed. If you ignore the leadership's directions and lobby on your own under the guise of the organization, there's a risk that you'll weaken the effectiveness of the lobbying effort by undermining your group's unity

Lobbying for a Small Organizations with Limited Resources

On the other hand, if your group has minimal resources, Box 13.9 offers important tips on planning before you go to Juneau.

Planning a
Campaign

BOX 13.9
BEFORE YOU GO TO JUNEAU

- Build a contact network. It's even more important if you're not on the ground in Juneau.

- Do your planning—the lion's share—during the interim. Develop or expand your contact network, meet or call officials and get others to do so. In the fall, when the budget's being put together, lobby for what you need if your issue involves funding.

- In an election year, work on a campaign and, if you can, contribute money to candidates.

- Make use of legislative and agency staff as much as you can. In many cases, you may not need to meet with legislators and other top officials until you get to Juneau.

- Have your meetings and other things you need to do set up in advance before you go to Juneau. Don't leave things to chance and drop by offices and expect to make appointments. If you do, you may not get to see those you need, and have to go home before they can see you.

- If possible, when you set things up, leave time between appointments to document your meetings, prepare for the next one, and do other things that come up unexpectedly. And try to get early morning meetings, which are less likely to be cancelled than later ones, when legislators can get behind schedule.

- Before you leave home, find out what information you need to send in advance. Those you'll meet with may just want your FCS at this stage, or your FCS and additional information.

- Don't assume once you've talked to people in Juneau that's all you need to do! Follow up with those you met, and constantly monitor the political situation and your issue. Things can change rapidly and you need to be right on top of them.

Planning a Campaign

Consider Finding a Lobbyist

One idea to help overcome your lack of presence on the ground in Juneau is to hire a contract lobbyist. This will help you enormously.

Not all lobbyists charge astronomical fees. You may be able to contract with one for as little as $5,000-$10,000. If you have little or no money, some lobbyists are willing to work pro bono (for free). Some do this because they support a cause, others to be—and appear—responsible citizens. You can find out about possible pro bono opportunities by asking your contacts, including your legislators. The chances of finding someone are slim, but it's worth a try.

But here's two things to bear in mind. It's not seen as appropriate by public officials for certain organizations to hire a contract lobbyist. The reasons are explained in section 3 of Chapter 9. Second, don't hire a lobbyist or have one work pro bono before you've checked them out. Section 4 of Chapter 11 explains what you need and, just as importantly, what you don't need, in a lobbyist.

When's the Best Time to Go to Juneau?

If you're not part of a major lobbying organization and have no one on the ground in Juneau, you'll likely visit the state capital yourself. When's the best time for a visit?

This is not an easy question to answer; but here's two suggestions. These assume you've laid the groundwork for your campaign in the interim. If you haven't, it's likely too late to push your issue and you'll probably be wasting your time.

If You Can Make Two Trips

One trip should be at the beginning of the session to talk to the key players to jog their memories about your issue and get them fully conversant with it. After you return home, keep in touch to see how things are progressing.

These officials will likely be able to advise you on the best time for your second visit. This will probably be when your bill or request is up for some major action, such as before the House Finance Committee, or another point crucial to its successful progress toward passage.

Prepare all your materials, plan your time, and make appointments before going to Juneau.

Schedule
March 9

House Finance 8am
Senator Richter 9:30am
House Convenes 11am
NFIB 1pm
Diane Long 3pm
House State Affairs 4pm
AFN Reception 5:30pm

If things go smoothly, which they rarely do, if possible, make your second visit during the last hectic days of the session. This is when the budget is finalized, and the last round of negotiations between the legislature, the governor, and state agencies take place. A second visit is especially important at the end of the second year of a legislature, after which all bills die.

Only One Visit

This is a judgment call to make with the help of the public officials or others with whom you are dealing in Juneau.

One approach is to go at the beginning of the session and touch base with all the players you've dealt with already, to be sure things are ready to go. Then keep in regular contact.

Alternatively, if you've done your homework, made the necessary contacts in the interim, and have things well under control, you could wait until a crucial decision on your bill or issue is pending. If none of these are necessary, head to Juneau for as long as you can at the end of the session.

Getting Familiar with Downtown Juneau

If you're unfamiliar with the layout of the legislature, and where the major state offices are in Juneau, see Appendices 1 and 2 and maps I and 2 in Appendix 3 (which also show hotels, restaurants, where to park, and places of interest).

Planning a Campaign

THIS CHAPTER COVERS

★ CHAPTER 14 ★

Face-to-Face Meetings with Public Officials

*Don't come to see me about your issue
unless you've done your homework,
and present what you want in a specific,
clear, and concise way.*

—Ramona Barnes,

Speaker, Alaska House of Representatives,

1993-95

Fundamental to lobbying is meeting with public officials to lobby them directly. The way you do this, how you deal with their reactions to the meeting, and the factual and political information you provide, will be a major factor in shaping the degree of success of your campaign. This chapter provides tips on the do's and don'ts on this crucial tactic of lobbying.

> *Remember—to deal with a public official effectively, as much as possible, put yourself in their shoes. Know where they're coming from professionally and personally, and deal with them accordingly.*

1. WHEN'S THE BEST TIME TO MEET WITH PUBLIC OFFICIALS?

Many novices don't think about or focus on lobbying until the legislature is in session. Certainly, you'll need to meet with legislators, their staff, and administration officials during the session to promote your issue and keep it active in their minds. But the work of the legislature, legislators, and, of course, the work of the governor and administrative agencies, doesn't begin and end with the session. They all operate year-round.

A lot of government activity takes place in the eight or so months when the legislature is not in session—the interim. Consequently, lobbying doesn't begin and end with the session either—it's a 365-days-a-year operation. In fact, the interim is the best time to deal with most legislators and other government officials. Several reasons to do so are set out in Box 14.1.

Exactly When to Approach Public Officials in the Interim

Use the interim to lay the groundwork for your campaign.

During the interim, you can likely meet with most agency people, and staff in the governor's office at most times from May to December. The situation is a little different with legislators.

If it's Not an Election Year

In years with no election, once the session is over, legislators and agency people are all trying to recover. Many legislators and their staff are away for the summer, and often hard to reach.

Most legislators begin to focus on the upcoming session between Labor Day and Thanksgiving. This is typically a productive time to meet with them. After that, they're busy with the holidays and preparing to move to Juneau for the session.

In an Election Year

Things are less certain in election years. This is particularly so for House members, who all serve two-year terms, and the half of the senate seats up for election; and for the governor and his or her staff in a gubernatorial election year.

Even those politicians with safe seats will be consumed with the election, helping colleagues with their campaigns. Many won't focus on the upcoming session until after election day; even later for those

Face-to-Face Meetings

BOX 14.1
GOOD REASONS TO USE THE INTERIM

The Interim is the Formative Period of Much Policy-Making

The interim is when many key decisions are made that will affect what happens in the session and beyond. These include:

- Putting the budget together, which involves receiving input from a wide-range of sources.

- Individual legislators and the majority and minority organizations are working on what they plan to accomplish: the bills they want to introduce, and prioritizing other activities for the session.

- The governor and his or her staff are working on the administration's goals for the session.

- Agency personnel are developing their plans for the session, and working on many other tasks, such as writing regulations.

The Work of the Legislature Continues

During the interim, various legislative committees hold hearings and discussions of all types. This is also when special committees that may have been set up in the session, for instance, on an aspect of fisheries, education, or public safety, have most of their meetings.

This is the time to both find out how these meetings may affect your organization or issue, and work to get your perspectives included in their decisions.

Public Officials have More Time

During the session, public officials are running crazy with work. Legislators are dealing with a host of people, and their staff are trying to juggle those who want their boss's time and their time too. The same is true for the governor's office. Agency personnel are also dealing with the legislature, often on politically-sensitive issues.

As a result, all these people have much less time to spend with you, if at all. If you do get an appointment, it's likely to be a short one.

By contrast, in the interim most public officials have more time, particularly legislators who are at home. They're much more likely to be able to meet with you. Plus, if you need to contact them more than once, they're likely to be available. *(continued ...)*

Face-to-Face Meetings

BOX 14.1 CONTINUED

You also won't surprise anyone when you turn up during the session having dealt with them in the interim. They'll remember you and your issue, and you'll be off to a faster start.

You'll Have the Time to Develop Your Lobbying Plans

You have more time during the interim to:

- Plan the details of your upcoming campaign. Run ideas past others; meet with public officials (or deal with them by e-mail, phone, social media, and maybe over Skype); conduct research, and prepare written materials.

- Deal with your members or clients. Fill them in on what's coming up in the session; get their input; and perhaps give them a short course or a workshop on lobbying.

- Touch base and build relations with members of the minority. While the bulk of your time should be spent dealing with those who can help you most, you also have time to cultivate relationships with those who may be members of a future majority.

---

who go on vacation immediately after the election. Though they'll likely be around for the weeks before Christmas as they begin to focus on the session.

In election years, a good approach is to contact officials in June or July to see when you might meet between then and Christmas.

2. THE MOST EFFECTIVE WAYS TO GET YOUR MESSAGE ACROSS

What are the most effective ways to interact with public officials, get your point across and keep it on their mind? Should you seek direct contact, or use indirect contact, such as editorials or a rally? The answer depends on the stage of your lobbying efforts, your reason for contacting them, and the preferences of the public officials concerned.

Face-to-Face Meetings

The Preferences of Individual Public Officials

Regardless of which public official you meet with and when, each is different in how they approach their job. This includes:

- The way they use their staff.

- If they are elected officials or mid-level or senior agency personnel.

- How they prefer to receive information.

- How they prioritize their time.

For instance, some public officials are big picture people who use their staff to get the details on issues and prepare overview reports. Others are detail-oriented and want to be in on all aspects of issues.

Virtually all want written material, but some, particularly those who are lawyers, want extensive written information in advance of meetings. Some prefer oral briefings on first contact, while others rely more heavily on social media. You can glean a lot of this information from your contacts.

All this requires dealing with individual public officials on their own terms. It involves political judgment—yet another reason lobbying is an art and not a science.

General Preferences on Contact

All's fair in the legislative game, and public officials expect to be contacted in all sorts of ways—personal meetings, phone calls, e-mails, letters, POMs, social media, mass petitions, and so on—as people work to get their issues considered. But not all of these are equally effective forms of contact.

If you ask public officials, particularly legislators, what they see as the most effective ways to make an initial contact, they list the approaches set out in Box 14.2, on the next page, more or less in order. These approaches are not mutually exclusive. They should be

Face-to-Face Meetings

BOX 14.2
LEVELS OF EFFECTIVENESS OF WAYS OF CONTACTING PUBLIC OFFICIALS

Public officials most often gauge their response to those lobbying them by the effort they expend in that contact. The more effort put in, the more individualized, positive, and quick their response is likely to be, and vice versa. Consequently, the effectiveness of a contact depends, in large part, on how individualized is the message—a personal contact or mass impersonal lobbying.

Generally, the most effective forms of contact are:

- A personal visit with the public official or their staff. These can be especially effective in the interim.

- A phone call.

- Letters, particularly if written by an individual geared to particular aspects of the issue.

- An e-mail, various types of social media, or a POM directed to a policy-maker. The problem with e-mail is that most elected officials get inundated with them and yours could go into their Spam folder. Even though staff check e-mails regularly, it could take a while for them to respond. Similarly with a POM or a social media message. You're better off trying to arrange a personal meeting or making a phone call.

The following forms of contact can also be effective:

- Committee hearings. If you've not met some of the committee members, this gives you a way for them to get to know you and your issue. The best way to make an initial contact with members of a legislative committee, board or commission, and how to do an effective presentation, is covered in the next section and in section 6.

- A brown bag—a presentation by a group in the legislature. This gets the group and its issue before legislators and staff for when you need to meet with them personally.

- To have a legislator recognize your group in the gallery during a House or Senate floor session. Again, this can be useful to bring your group and issue to the attention of legislators you might need in the future. Such recognition is particularly valuable for groups from out of town making brief visits.

- Having a person they know and trust contact an official about your issue; or taking that person to your first meeting.

Lobbying en masse: (usually) less effective methods of contact.

Any mass impersonal contact, such as hundreds of e-mails, letters, POMs, melting down their phones with endless calls, and mass petitions.

- This type of contact shows little effort by the senders. Such impersonal contact is a sure sign of an orchestrated, boilerplate campaign. In an overworked office, the senders will likely be the last to get a response, if at all.

- Lobbying overkill may also annoy those being inundated with messages. It may color their view of your organization as it shows you lack understanding of the problems they face and the basics of lobbying.

- Such contact is not always frowned upon, however. A well-planned lobbying effort involving several group members, with individualized contact, such as a fly-in, a group meeting with a public official in the interim, turning up at a town hall or issue session, can be effective. Also, having a well-developed petition can be useful in presenting back-up on your issue.

used in combination, and the right combination for the public officials you contact based on your homework.

In developing your lobbying plan, you need to know the most effective and less effective methods of contact. This is particularly important if you have a small operation and want to maximize your limited resources to the fullest.

As might be expected, the most effective contact is a one-on-one, direct personal interaction or message between the lobbyist and the public official. By contrast, the more impersonal the contact, the less effective it is likely to be.

Face-to-Face Meetings

3. GETTING YOUR ACT TOGETHER BEFORE A MEETING

Even if you've done all your homework and have all you need, it's still a good idea to take ten minutes before a meeting to review your material. If you have three or four meetings or more in a day, and maybe a committee hearing, you likely won't remember all you need without doing some reviewing first. One of the cardinal sins of lobbying is not to be prepared and waste a public official's time (and yours, too).

If you're meeting a public official you've not met before, it's particularly important to be prepared to make a good impression.

Keep on top of things—know the course of your bill and where it's at currently, who's for and against it, how many votes you have in the House and Senate.

Otherwise, if you're not prepared you might be dismissed as not serious about what you want, and the official may be reluctant to work with you. Box 14.3 sets out five important things to do before a first meeting.

Be on time. Remember, with all the demands on them, a shortage of time is a major problem for public officials. Not only is it courteous to be prompt, it'll ensure you can present your case in full, as you'll have all the time you were promised. Otherwise you'll be rushed and maybe flustered.

Don't be surprised if the public official is late, especially during the session. Urgent matters needing immediate attention interfere with schedules all the time. Be understanding and gracious. Reschedule or meet with a staffer. Smile.

4. YOUR FIRST FACE-TO-FACE MEETING

When you meet someone for the first time, particularly in a professional situation, whether consciously or subconsciously, there's a combination of interest and caution. This is especially the case with public

BOX ·14.3
PREPARING FOR A FIRST MEETING WITH A PUBLIC OFFICIAL

Know Details about the Official

This is one aspect of the information you should have gathered as set out in section 9 of Chapter 11 as part of your research. Review that section.

One additional piece of information that's very useful is to find out the colleagues the official is close to professionally or personally, and those they don't get along with. This helps you anticipate their reactions when you explain the pros and cons of your proposal, the solution you propose, and particularly the legislators and others who support or oppose what you want.

Organize Your Materials

Check before you leave home or the office that you have all your written materials.

Before the meeting, make sure you have these materials ready, in order, easily accessible in your bag or folder. Have your first contact sheet (FCS) on top, and your supplemental materials under that, together with any materials you want to leave.

Think Over Your Goal for the Meeting

Remind yourself exactly what you want to get across in the meeting and what you want to get out of it. Practice your first pitch and make it as short as you can. Again, a good guide to the length of your pitch, is the time it takes to ride from the ground floor to the fifth floor in the Capitol elevator. If you can, practice it on a colleague or friend.

Be Prepared for the Likely Dynamics of the Meeting

In a first meeting, the official will be cautious, sizing you up and figuring you out. They'll also likely have information on you in addition to what you've given them. This will likely include: if you're registered to vote or not; how often you vote; your party declaration (or no party); and when you registered to vote.

(continued . . .)

BOX 14.1 *CONTINUED*

For the most part, if you're dealing with politicians or appointed agency people, they'll likely see things from a transactional perspective, and feel you out on what you will and will not accept to address your issue. If they can't, or won't support you, take it with grace. An initial rejection may not be a final decision. But if you're impolite and react badly, it will most likely become their final decision.

Before a Committee Hearing

Before you present your testimony, write down your remarks. Your FCS is a good guide for this. Practice your presentation beforehand. Again, practice it on a colleague or a friend.

Try to memorize a lot of your remarks. Then you can look at the committee members and not just read from your script. This will set a positive atmosphere for the rest of your testimony.

Be sure to touch base with committee staff at least 24 hours before any public hearing to be sure they have everything they need from you in the format required. There's more on the importance of committee staff in section 6 below.

As a division director and the target of lobbying, I appreciate those who know exactly what they want, are well-informed, low-key, and respect my time.

Face-to-Face Meetings

officials, particularly politicians and their staff. If they don't know you, or even if they do, but haven't dealt with you in a political situation, they'll likely be very cautious.

This caution is part of their mindset given the nature of politics with its uncertainties and consequent need for trust and confidentiality. The official will also wonder how well informed you are and how much you understand about the way things operate in politics.

With all this caution, as far as you can, put them at ease. An effective way to do this is showing you've done your homework and understand their situations as public officials.

They'll have the advantage in the meeting because they hold the political marbles and dealt with people like you hundreds of times. This means they'll likely direct the meeting. But you should work to strike a balance between your needs and their reactions. Don't be intimidated, especially if they don't support your issue. Box 14.4 provides guidelines on how to approach the meeting and the subjects to cover.

BOX 14.4
TEN TIPS FOR MEETING WITH PUBLIC OFFICIALS

1. Engage in a Minimum of Small Talk

You'll exchange pleasantries when you first meet, perhaps many if you know each other. But remember, you likely have only ten minutes or so with a legislator, staffer, or someone from the governor's office (maybe longer with an agency official). So keep small talk short—get to the point.

If you spend too much time in pleasantries you'll use up valuable time, fail to get your key points over, and won't be able to respond to questions adequately. Be the one to conclude the meeting, with a "thank you." If the public official gets up and walks you to the door, you've stayed too long and maybe worn out your welcome.

2. Make Things as Straightforward and Uncomplicated as you Can

Raise only your major issue, two at the most if they're related. Stick to this issue so you don't complicate things and confuse the official. Don't raise an unrelated issue that's important to you and know is of concern to the public official. It will sidetrack you and your major goal of the meeting may be lost.

3. Present Your First Contact Sheet—FCS

If you haven't already done so in a previous contact, present your FCS. Let them read it and then offer to provide clarification. Likely the official will have questions.

(continued . . .)

BOX 14.4 *CONTINUED*

4. If Necessary, Present the Second Half of Your FCS and Offer to Provide More Information

If the questions they ask are covered in the second part of your FCS, provide it, but expand on the points only if asked questions.

You'll likely be asked for additional information. If not, offer to provide it. Explain what you have and that you'll get it to them that day, or in the next couple of days.

5. Present Both Sides of the Issue

It's important for your credibility that, in your materials and your conversation, you present both sides of the issue. Your homework will have told you which of the official's, friends or colleagues who support or oppose your position. Don't insult opponents only to learn they are close to that public official. Dissect and counter opponents' arguments factually and dispassionately.

6. Offer a Solution

You will have outlined this in your FCS. Supplement it with solutions used in similar situations, such as how your proposal worked in other states. Also, offer suggestions on what you might do to help in this solution; suggest a possible strategy if you can. Ask the public official's advice on what else you should do.

7. Don't be Sidetracked

Sometimes, if a public official doesn't support your issue but won't tell you directly, or just wants to avoid dealing with it, they may try to sidetrack you by bringing up other issues or go back to small talk. Don't let this happen—come back to your issue and focus them on it.

8. Be Direct if You Can't Meet their Demands

On occasion, a public official may stipulate one or more conditions before they'll help you. If you can meet these, that's good. If not, or if you need to check back with your organization first, tell them directly. Even if you have to say "sorry, can't go there," don't count this public official out on your issue. Circumstances change.

9. Get a Commitment—There Must be a Resolution to the Meeting

Don't be left hanging at the end of the meeting. There must be a resolution—what you and the official agreed or disagreed on, and what to do next, unless it's a "can't go there" situation on your part.

Some officials will tell you directly if they can't support you. Others won't be direct. They'll say something like, "let me take this under advisement," "we'll talk later on this," or "thanks for coming by," among other vague statements.

If they tell you they're on the other side, ask if they'll be neutral or actively oppose you. If they say they'll be neutral, you've got to hope they keep their word.

If they are part of the active opposition, you have to take this into account, and try to deal with it as you pursue your objective. Exactly how to do so depends on a host of factors. You need to use your political acumen, and perhaps get advice from your contacts or other public officials.

But try hard to get a clear and specific resolution to the meeting. Be sure to write this down and make other notes on the meeting for your records.

10. Follow Up with a Letter, E-mail, Text, or other Communication

This serves three purposes:

- To thank the official for their time and concern.

- An opportunity to confirm in a very brief overview what you understand was decided in the meeting, particularly the outcome.

- Another chance to provide information and to emphasize you are willing to meet with them again.

A letter serves best. It shows you're serious about your issue and intend to pursue it with all seriousness and energy. Electronic communications are ephemeral and less effective than a tangible letter.

After the Meeting: What the Public Official is Likely Thinking

When you've left the meeting, even if they know you, but especially if they've not met you before, they'll ask themselves several question. This is particularly true of politicians and their staff, but

Face-to-Face Meetings

also of bureaucrats. Box 14.5 sets out several of these questions. They are not the only ones they'll likely consider, but are among the most important.

BOX 14.5
LIKELY THOUGHTS PUBLIC OFFICIALS WILL HAVE AFTER MEETING WITH A LOBBYIST

- How do I view the person I've just met?

- Will the bill be high profile, attract a lot of attention, or will it be low profile and allow me to work more freely to secure it?

- Do the advocates have a realistic assessment of the policy and budget implications of the bill? How will it affect existing laws and impacting the interests affected by the bill (state agencies, local government, etc.)?

- Will their bill achieve its goals as they claim?

- Who is the bill's sponsor? Who are the co-cosponsors?

- Can I work with the committee chairs and Rules chair to get this bill through?

- How might my constituents feel about this bill? Will most of them care about it, or have little concern?

- How are other legislators likely to vote?

- Does the bill have a chance to pass?

- How close is the vote likely to be?

- Will my vote matter?

- If I vote for the bill, will it hurt me or help me when I stand for re-election?

- The big question: Do I want to use my political capital on this issue—cash in some of my chits?

5. FOLLOW UP CONTACT AND THE NEED TO GET A DECISION

Having had your first meeting, you'll know the best ways to contact each public official in a follow-up. They, or their staff, will likely tell you if and when to follow up, depending on what they need. Plus, you'll have a feel for how and in what form the office wants to receive additional information.

> To help get a public official to consider helping you, don't just present your issue—suggest a way to deal with it.

You'll also have gotten an idea of the questions and concerns the official might have from your first meeting. Some of the answers will be in the second part of your FCS, if you didn't provide it in your first meeting. Plus, to supplement this, you should have done your homework. Check with the staff after a few days to see if, in addition to what you've already provided, they need particular information before your follow-up meeting. Or if no follow-up meeting was arranged, this is the time to make one. If they hem and haw about making you an appointment, it's an indication that you likely won't get the support of their boss.

If you do have a follow-up meeting, as you're likely to be asked more in-depth questions than in your first one, prepare thoroughly. This includes having your written materials in a succinct and reader-friendly form (as explained in Chapter 13, sections 7, 8 and 9), and presenting it in the way preferred by the official.

Get a Decision—Pro or Con

If you didn't get a firm "yes" or "no" decision in your first contact, you need to get one in a follow-up. Even after reading your materials and thinking things over, many public officials won't want to commit to supporting you. If your lobbying effort involves a bill, they may support the concept, but want to reserve judgment until the final text and the proposal is moving through the process.

Face-to-Face Meetings

If you're new to lobbying and haven't dealt face-to-face with a politician, staffer or agency person before, you'll likely feel nervous, even intimidated. You're not alone—novices often feel this way. Most public officials realize this, and will put you at ease.

While this is a normal approach on the part of many public officials, both elected and appointed, if they are key to your campaign, you need a decision up or down. Indecisiveness on their part may be for many reasons, including those set out earlier in Box 14.5. But the fact is they are waffling and you should count them as a "maybe" or a "no" on your issue. All the same, check back at some point to see if they've made a more definite decision.

6. COMMITTEE HEARINGS

Committee meetings are held in the afternoon and in the early morning before the House and Senate floor sessions (though committees meet at all times of the day and night in the last days of the session, particularly the finance committees). To make the best impression at a hearing, find out what information the committee needs and the protocol in presenting testimony. First, here's a reminder on the role of the committee chair.

The Chair

Few chairs would ever admit it, but they are a "dictator" on all aspects of the committee's operation. Perhaps their major power is deciding which bills assigned to their committee will be considered. If, for whatever reason, the chair chooses not to hear a bill, it is effectively dead. An exception is when the caucus leadership, the governor, an influential interest group, or a powerful individual, brings pressures on them to hear the bill.

Most chairs control their committee sessions tightly. They decide how often the committee will meet, control how long witnesses have to testify, direct the discussion among committee members, and decide when a vote will be held on a bill. Committee members can challenge the chair's decisions, but they rarely succeed.

Before the Hearing—the Crucial Role of the Committee Aide

Each legislative committee has a staff person assigned to it, usually one of the committee chair's staff. At the direction of the chair, committee staff arrange the schedule of the committee, work with those who will testify, and put together the packets of information for committee members.

In many ways, committee aides are the gatekeepers of the committee for their boss. Some even have influence on what bills are heard and when. For these and other reasons, committee staff will be invaluable to you and your lobbying effort. Box 14.6, on the next page, explains how valuable they can be.

Check out how things Operate before you Testify

It's a good idea to attend a few committee hearings before you give testimony to see how they operate, particularly those you'll be dealing with. You'll get a feel for the dynamics of their operation.

Given all that's on their mind, many public officials won't know or remember the specifics of your issue and what you're requesting. So when meeting with them face-to-face, or giving committee testimony, be sure to state your issue right up front.

Committee Hearing Protocol

Committee hearings follow a strict protocol. As do most state legislatures, they more or less follow the rules set out in *Mason's*

BOX 14.6
THE VALUE OF COMMITTEE STAFF AS CONTACTS

No one knows their bosses, the committee chairs, and other committee members, better than committee aides. They can give you necessary instructions to follow in hearings and all sorts of useful information. Some have put together a sheet, some even a booklet, with info on procedure and what those testifying should know and do, that they'll give you. This information includes:

- If their boss wants a hearing choreographed in a certain way. For instance, a committee chair who strongly supports a bill may want as little testimony and discussion as possible to prevent opposing arguments from gaining attention. Or, a chair may want to kill the bill. In that case, they may want a lot of testimony, which will cause it to be held over for another hearing. This second hearing may never take place—and the bill will likely die. A committee aide may or may not be willing to share this political information with you.

- In what format their boss and committee members prefer written material. This may be broad guidelines; or as detailed as the size of

Manual of Legislative Procedure (commonly referred to as *Mason's Manual*) and not *Robert's Rules of Order*. Though committee chairs are often less diligent in following these procedures compared to House and Senate floor sessions, where they are followed strictly. All questions from committee members and your replies are addressed through the chair. So the procedure goes like this:

When recognized by the chair, committee member Representative Brown asks:

"Madam chair, I would like to ask Mr. Hamilton why they haven't included the cost of maintenance in their proposal for the harbor extension?"

Mr. Hamilton answers:

"Thank you for that question, Madam Chair, from Representative Brown. Representative Brown, through the chair, we did not include this because…."

Face-to-Face
Meetings

the font and the amount of white space on each page. At whatever level they specify these details, follow them to the letter.

- Whether the chair wants all the materials beforehand or just an outline, with the rest presented and distributed during the meeting. Aides can tell you if the chair prefers to be given additional materials at the beginning or end of your testimony.

- The personalities, likes and dislikes, and the ways their bosses and committee members operate and interact.

- How much time you have for testimony.

- Feedback after the hearing, including if you need to provide further information, and if you're invited or even expected to give further testimony at a future hearing.

Cultivate committee staff. Besides following their instructions, take note of their insights, especially if you're a novice and haven't given testimony before.

If you don't follow the committee aides' advice and think you know better, your testimony may be received poorly. Not only that, you may get on their wrong side, receive a cool reception, or alienate these potential allies, and get less help—or even obstruction—from them in the future.

If the chair wants to give you more time than you've been allocated, they'll do so. The indication that your time is up is when the chair thanks you for your testimony.

Generally, while initial testimony is limited in time, questioning witnesses by committee members can go on as long as the chair is willing to allow. Other than committee members, no one at the meeting who's not giving testimony can ask a question or make a comment.

A Word of Caution

Sometimes the tenor of a hearing becomes relaxed, with even some humor exchanged. Don't take this as a cue to discard the formal procedure, and, for example, start to address members directly.

Keep to the formal rules. If you don't, you're likely to be pulled up short. This could destroy your composure and the strength or your testimony; not to mention that the committee members may get a negative impression of you.

7. CASUAL ENCOUNTERS

One of the advantages of living in Alaska is everyone has ready access to politicians and public officials of all types. Even though

few Alaskans visit the legislature or the governor's office, they are likely to run into those they've elected in the grocery store, at a restaurant, at the gas station, or at a Fourth of July parade. In these chance meetings, many people feel it's appropriate to give the public official their opinion on issues or ask for favors.

Buttonholing a public official in these situations may be fine for a constituent or other member of the public, but lobbyists or others involved in an advocacy effort need to be cautious. The reasons are explained in Box 14.7

It's a different matter if they broach the subject of your issue. This may well happen if you run into them at a legislative reception put on by an interest group; and, of course, if you have a reception for them. In these situations, you can go into things as much as they want. But it's still a good idea to keep the interchange short and be the one to say: "Well, I know you're busy, so I'll let you go and see you on Wednesday of next week" (or something like that). Don't wear out your welcome.

As with so many aspects of dealing with public officials, the rule of thumb is: "Put yourself in their shoes." Ask yourself: "Would I like to be approached by a lobbyist, even a citizen lobbyist, when I'm in a hurry to buy food to cook for friends coming over for dinner?" Or have someone come up to you when you're trying to relax with your

Face-to-Face Meetings

BOX 14.7
BE CAUTIOUS IN DEALING WITH
PUBLIC OFFICIALS IN CASUAL ENCOUNTERS

They Have a Personal as well as a Public Life

Certainly, it was their choice to run for office or take a job in an agency and, at least for elected politicians, be in a fish bowl and easily recognized.

But like all of us, they have lives outside their job, with all that entails from day-to-day. They need space to do all the things they have to do, including going to the grocery store and buying gas.

Don't Talk Shop

If you've met with them and are on their radar with a course of action decided upon, or even if you haven't met them yet but plan to do so soon, you should not start up a conversation to push your issue. They may set this as both inappropriate or overkill; though they likely won't tell you this directly.

If you plan to make an appointment with them, you're better off contacting their staff who know their schedule, which the official may not considering all their commitments. In either case, using this meeting as an opportunity to lobby might give them bad vibes about you or even annoy them.

Will they Remember Your Issue?

Although your issue is in the front of your mind and you know its ins and outs, the public official has scores of things to deal with, so they may not remember the details of your issue. You've surprised them, caught them off guard, and you'll need to explain things in less than ideal circumstances when they've got other things on their mind. This likely won't endear them to you, either.

Just Say "Hi"

In these situations, it's best to just greet them, remind them of who you are, and why they might remember you. Engage in a minimum of pleasantries and move on.

Face-to-Face
Meetings

spouse and enjoy a meal in a restaurant? Or be approached when watching your kids playing baseball or basketball?

When in doubt, err on the side of caution.

8. WHAT TO AVOID IN DEALING WITH PUBLIC OFFICIALS

Equally as important as how to approach public officials in a positive way, is what not to do when dealing with them. Remember, it takes a long time to build up trust and develop a good relationship with a public official. But you can destroy all your efforts in just a minute—even less—by making an offensive comment or approaching them in an inappropriate way.

I get in to see them, make my pitch, and get out. There's no camping on doorsteps or long-term haranguing involved.

As a result, they and their staff may not take you seriously or even avoid you. But again, being politicians, worried about their reputations, and probably the next election, they likely won't tell you. You'll be left wondering why you aren't getting through to them.

Box 14.8 lists the major no-no's or political sins to avoid. Several have been mentioned before, but it's useful to put them in one list.

BOX 14.8
FIFTEEN NO-NO'S WHEN DEALING WITH PUBLIC OFFICIALS

- Lying, dishonesty, or misrepresentation, such as: telling a legislator a bill has no opposition when it does; not explaining opposing arguments; or having a hidden agenda. You'll most likely be found out and may destroy their trust in you.

- Threaten them by saying: you'll tell people not to vote for them; or in the case of an agency official, you'll complain about them. This includes aggressive behavior, such as shouting and getting angry.

- Going on the attack when a legislator won't support your issue, or actively opposes it. In this situation, sometimes a group will attempt to villainize a legislator. This will often have the opposite of the desired effect.

- Displaying arrogance by saying or insinuating that you're brighter than they are, they are seriously misguided, and don't know what they're talking about.

- Saying that, as a member of the public who elected them, "they work for you!"

- Blindsiding and undermining a legislator or agency person by first contacting the governor or getting a media story about your issue intended to pressure them.

- Not knowing exactly what you want, not being prepared, or having poorly researched material. You'll waste their time and yours.

- Giving public officials masses of material when you first contact or meet them. Again, use your FCS and provide more information only if requested.

- Engaging in lobbying overkill by having crowds of members turn up at their office, inundating them with e-mails, burning up their phones with masses of calls, among other annoying things.

- Button-holing them in a Capitol corridor, state office, in the grocery store, or in a restaurant and insisting they listen to you. It's a different matter if they approach you.

- Dropping by their office without an appointment. This serves neither their interests nor yours, as they'll not be prepared to deal with your issue.

- Not appreciating their time constraints, such as staying too long in a meeting.

- Dismissing, ignoring, and mistreating, members of their staff. This may eventually be avenged, even by the seemingly lowliest staffer.

- Turning up late for a meeting.

- Not returning a phone call or e-mails, or failing to provide additional information when requested.

Face-to-Face Meetings

THIS CHAPTER COVERS

1. Seeing the Big Picture before You Lobby

2. Unguarded Talk Can Sink a Lobbying Campaign

3. Planning Your Daily and Weekly Schedule

4. Briefing Your Members before they Lobby

5. Modifying Your Proposal

6. Attending Floor Sessions

7. Making Notes after a Meeting

8. A Reminder on Follow-ups and Timing

9. If Things Aren't Going Well

10. The End Game: Closing out the Legislative Session

11. Reflecting on Your Lobbying Experience

★ CHAPTER 15 ★

In the Political Trenches: Your Day-to-Day Lobbying Effort

As you lobby day-to-day,
remember that legislators are elected by and represent their
constituents, not you, your organization, or your clients.

—Dennis DeWitt,

DeWitt & DeWitt, LLC,

Government Relations Consulting

This chapter brings together key points covered so far, with several new ones, to provide a guide to what's needed as you lobby day-to-day.

Many who lobby in Juneau, particularly contract lobbyists, may approach things differently than covered here. And you certainly don't have to follow it all to the letter. As you gain experience, you'll develop your own way of going about lobbying.

That said, in whatever way a lobbyist approaches their job, they'll be involved in most, if not all, aspects of lobbying explained in this chapter.

1. SEEING THE BIG PICTURE BEFORE YOU LOBBY

Before you begin lobbying, take time to step back and look at the big picture. Mull over what you'll need to do and remind yourself that you must deal with the fluid nature of lobbying, and how you might approach it. The following five factors are particularly important to consider.

Multi-Tasking: Coordinating the Various tasks in Your Lobbying Effort

You need to be prepared to manage multiple tasks simultaneously. This is more so if you're a one-person operation, but it's true of any lobbyist representing a large organization. Among the most important tasks to coordinate during the session are:

- Dealing with the legislature, one or more state agencies, the governor's office, and groups you're working with.

- Monitoring developments that may affect your issue.

- Gathering, organizing, and appropriately presenting supplementary information requested by policy makers.

- Coordinating lobbying by your group members.

- Keeping records and reporting back to your campaign coordinator.

- Getting information and advice from your contact network.

Keeping Perspective and Being Realistic

You can be passionate about your issue, but keep things in perspective. Bear in mind:

- Your issue is only one of many a public official is dealing with.

- No one has a monopoly on truth; realize some policy-makers will disagree with you—be prepared to deal with it.

- In most cases, the policy process is slow and frustrating. You are unlikely to see your issue dealt with in one legislative session, or a regulation changed immediately on request.

- Almost certainly, at some point, you'll have to compromise on your original goal.

- All this means that you must look at your issue and your lobbying effort as objectively as possible. Make practical decisions realistically, not in an emotional way, which will cloud your judgment.

Be Organized

With all these aspects involved in your lobbying effort you need to be organized. This enables you to access information quickly when needed and, as far as you can, identify the challenges you'll face. The best time to organize things is before the session begins; you'll likely be too rushed for most of the legislative session and won't be able to put everything together.

A politician who tells you "no" today, may be your ally tomorrow.

Certainly, given the fluidity of politics, you can't plan everything precisely. But you can organize some aspects of your campaign and anticipate others. You can, for example:

- Prepare your written materials.

- Make initial contacts with the public officials you'll need.

- If you've not done so already or it's a new administration, familiarize yourself with key officials (and they with you) in the legislature, the governor's office, and state agencies.

- You should be able to anticipate your opposition, how the present state of the budget might affect you, and several aspects of the upcoming legislative session.

The Likely Character of the Upcoming Legislative Session

In some way or another, the likely character of the upcoming session will affect your lobbying effort—especially the strategies and tactics you'll use. No two legislative sessions are the same; never assume the dynamics of the last one will be the same as the upcoming session.

After any election, but especially when there's a new governor, there'll be new power dynamics between the majority caucuses in the House and Senate and the governor, driven, in part, by the new governor's agenda. Plus. with many new members, and likely a new leadership, there'll be new relationships between the majority and minority caucuses. Every year there's a new budget which often produces a contrast between the first and second sessions. You need to get a feel for all these and assess what they might mean for you.

Ask yourself how the new power structure will affect you:

- Who are the new leaders? What do you know about them, if anything?

- What about the newly elected legislators, how are they likely to fit in? Will they be useful or not to your cause?

You can glean some of this information from media reports and, to some extent, social media. But you'll need to get inside information and insights from those in the know. This is yet another reason to build an extensive network of contacts.

Balancing Structure with Flexibility

It's important to have some structure day-to-day as you campaign; but the inevitable unexpected developments will require you to adjust. Some will be easy to deal with, like a change in the time of a committee meeting. Others will be more serious, such as one of your members presenting a message to a public official at odds with the position of your group.

Because of changes that require attention, particularly at the end of the session, you need to be prepared to deal with them at any time. Likely, these will occur when you least expect them to.

2. UNGUARDED TALK AND COMMENTS CAN SINK A LOBBYING CAMPAIGN

The need for discretion by all lobbyists, applies not only to keeping confidences, but also not voicing personal opinions about people, or trading in rumors that turn out to be false. Making such mistakes will come back to haunt you.

Alaska's Small Political World

Alaska's political world is the size of an average high school with all its intricate relationships. There are probably fewer than a thousand people actively involved in state politics as all or part of their job, or other aspect of their life. Only five hundred or so are involved in politics all year round; and less than a hundred who have major political influence.

Even among the thousand, some have personal relationships and know many others by name. Among the five hundred—legislators, their staffs, the governor and his or her staff, senior administrative officials, lobbyists, interest group personnel, and local government leaders—particularly the movers and shakers, almost everyone knows most of the others. Those they don't know personally they know by reputation, or can find out about through their web of political contacts.

Many Alaskans have long histories, extending back to the days when they first came to the state, or were childhood friends. Others have close friends, even though they may be on opposite sides of the political fence. And, of course, there are likes and dislikes among many people, sometimes very bad blood for past political slights.

The Political Rumor Mill and Political Telegraph Systems

The necessity of confidentiality in settling policy disputes, with those involved keeping their cards close to their chest, leads to speculation about what's happening or likely to happen in a transaction.

Plus, there are rumors about people's professional and personal lives that are common in any workplace. All this is grist for a massive rumor mill.

The walls in the Capitol have ears. A rumor can travel from the ground floor to the fifth floor faster than you can get there on the elevator or using the stairs. Not only that, every restaurant, bar, hotel lobby, and the airport in Juneau has its own telegraph system. This is also true of the Anchorage and Fairbanks airports, even the Alaska Airlines C and D concourses, and the N terminal in the Seattle airport.

Don't be naive and think most of your legislative contacts will keep your confidences—they won't.

Keep Tight Lips

The major lesson of all this is: You never know who's listening and how they relate to whom you're talking about. Ears all over the state and beyond almost certainly mean whatever you say will get back to the person you talked about. If it's negative, you'll likely pay for it. Box 15.1 offers some cautions about what you say as you go about lobbying.

Damage Control

It's not much consolation, but if you do screw up, you won't be the first. Virtually everyone in politics has done this at some time. Most have weathered the storm that followed. In many cases, this is because they had leverage and power, or were indispensable to others in the system.

You likely won't have a power base to draw on, so you need to apologize. Don't let is fester in the mind of the target of your misdeed. And don't make all sorts of excuses—just come clean and admit it, the quicker the better. Learn from your mistake and hope it works out for the best.

BOX 15.1
AVOIDING UNGUARDED TALK

⚠ **CAUTION**

Be careful about:

- What you say.

- Where you say it.

- When you say it.

- To whom you say it.

To avoid putting your foot in it:

- Be overly careful not to share confidences with people you don't know.

- Don't offer opinions of people, particularly bad-mouth them.

- Even though it's tempting, don't pass on rumors. There are many political gossip-mongers in Juneau. Find out who they are and take their information with circumspection.

- Be particularly wary of giving your opinions to the media. Not that they're out to get you. Even though a journalist turns in a story relaying exactly what you said, it could get edited and come out as an insult and not a compliment to the person you commented on.

3. PLANNING YOUR DAILY AND WEEKLY SCHEDULE

You'll benefit a lot from developing a daily and weekly schedule. Having a routine helps in following your lobbying plan, executing the multi-tasking it involves, and avoiding failing to do essential things.

Regular Tasks

- Get the legislative schedule for the coming week and the next day. These are available from the documents room on the ground floor of the Capitol and on the legislature's website. The daily schedule is not available until the night before.

- Get the schedule of committee hearings you need to attend. If you are giving testimony, be sure to communicate with the committee aide beforehand.

- Allocate a time to update your campaign coordinator, group members, and clients.

Scheduling Meetings

If you've not dealt with public officials before, it's important to bear some things in mind in scheduling a meeting, particularly if you need to schedule several in a day. Box 15.2 provides some tips.

Rep. Carter - Tuesday 8:30am
Sen. McCarthy - Wed. 8:45am
Director Mitchell - Friday 10am

BOX 15.2
TIPS ON SCHEDULING MEETINGS

- If you need to deal with your issue in detail:

  O Whether this is a first meeting or follow-up, and your meetings are schedule for 15-20 minutes or so, if you have the choice, don't schedule more than eight, ten at the most, in a day.

  O If you over-schedule, you'll likely get frazzled as you run from meeting to meeting. Plus, you won't have time to read your notes thoroughly before a meeting or take good notes afterwards.

- On the other hand, if you're in town for only a few days, and are just making the rounds to introduce yourself, you'll want to fit in as many meetings as you can.

- If you are part of a fly-in or other organized group, your group leader or lobbyist will likely have set up the meeting schedule for you.

- Try to avoid back-to-back meetings. Legislators often get behind schedule. So if you schedule two or more meetings back-to-back, and the first legislator is late, it will mess up your entire schedule.

- Similiarly, get early morning appointments. Mid-morning or afternoon meetings are frequently cancelled as caucus business or other urgent matters push officials behind schedule.

Dealing with Cancelled Meetings and Schedule Changes

Appointments with legislators and staff are sometimes canceled, and committee hearings rescheduled. Inevitably this will happen to you. This is often the result of the tight schedule and unforeseen circumstances that's part of being a public official.

If this happens, keep your cool. However exasperating it may be, don't say something like, "but I had an appointment," or "this is very annoying." It may alienate those who are the subject of your

> *Canceling and rescheduling appointments is a fact of legislative life—so get used to it.*

wrath. If you've been stood up, your meeting will be rescheduled, as will a cancelled committee hearing.

4. BRIEFING YOUR MEMBERS BEFORE THEY LOBBY

Using one or more of your group members or a constituent to put a face on an issue can be a valuable technique in making a positive and lasting impression on a public official.

Unfortunately, as explained in section 4 of Chapter 12, covering strategies and tactics, this can backfire if it's not coordinated to fit your campaign. Box 15.3, on the next page, provides reminders on how to try and avoid these problems.

5. MODIFYING YOUR PROPOSAL

> *Your bill is likely to be changed—amended—by every committee that considers it. Dealing with this, and perhaps modifying your goal, is where the skill of a lobbyist comes in.*

At some point along the journey of your issue, you'll undoubtedly have to compromise, modify what you want, and be willing to take less. Exactly how much you're able and willing to compromise

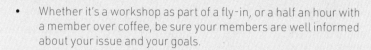

BOX 15.3
PREPPING YOUR MEMBERS BEFORE THEY LOBBY

- Whether it's a workshop as part of a fly-in, or a half an hour with a member over coffee, be sure your members are well informed about your issue and your goals.

- Impress upon them the need for a single message on your issue, and the potential problem of lack of unity in that message.

- If they're a novice, explain:

  o The basics of dealing with public officials.

  o How to get their points over succinctly.

  o They should deal with only your major issue, two others at most.

  o The importance of respecting the official's time—keeping the meeting short.

  o They need to be courteous even when an official disagrees with your organization's position on an issue.

  o The importance of thanking the official for their time.

- Explain that, although you want them to advocate strongly on your issue, and they can be passionate about it, they can undermine the effectiveness of their effort if they push too hard.

- In most situations, impress upon your members to meet only those public officials important to advancing your cause.

- Meet with your members afterwards for a report on what they did and the reactions they got. This is an essential part of your lobbying coordination process. It'll give you a heads-up on likely damage control you'll need to do with the public officials with whom they met.

depends on the forces you are dealing with, and the fallback position you've set out in your lobbying plan.

As you're faced with the need to compromise, keep in mind the points set out in Box 15.4. In the process of negotiating a compromise,

BOX 15.4
REMINDERS ON NEGOTIATING AND COMPROMISING

- Be open-minded, willing to compromise, and flexible; try to see your issue dispassionately.

- Even though you are pushing as hard as you can for your cause, try to put yourself in the shoes of those with whom you are negotiating. It'll put things in perspective as you work with them. Balance this with keeping the following points in mind.

- Some of those you'll be dealing with will be old hands at political negotiations. Don't be intimidated, but be cautious.

- Political negotiations often involve posturing, sending up trial balloons, playing chicken, and sometimes making exaggerated or false claims. Approach these situations with a healthy skepticism.

- However congenial and casual the negotiations might be, don't let that lull you into making decisions you'll regret. Remember—this is a power game.

- In a process involving power and transactions, success largely depends on how many political chits you've accumulated. Without chits, you can't offer benefits in return for favorable consideration, and your chances of success will be slim.

- As you compromise, you'll likely have to agree to some things you'd not anticipated. Be mentally prepared for this.

- Negotiations may be concluded quickly, especially when there's time pressure at the end of the legislative session. Or they can take a long time for a variety of reasons, such as political posturing, or because a participant in the negotiations needs to check with their organization or client on a proposal. The latter situation can be frustrating. Don't get upset or express your ire—go with the flow.

remember different political operatives—politicians, bureaucrats, lobbyists, and group leaders—have different styles, approaches, needs, and goals, both in general and in specific circumstances. To know the styles of different people, you need to do your homework,

BOX 15.5
DIFFERENT STYLES AND FACTORS SHAPING BARGAINING

These styles are not mutually exclusive. Policy-makers come to the negotiating table with one or a combination of them:

- Facilitators (pejoratively called "fixers"), who see things entirely in transactional terms and broker deals between opposing sides. Their skill is a form of street smarts.

- Loyal caucus members, heeding constraints imposed by their caucus.

- Politicians with their constituents and contributors foremost in mind, in most cases, but not in other situations.

- Personally ambitious politicians, focusing on political advantage or advancement to higher office.

- Career politicians, putting re-election above all else.

- Ideologues, driven by a strongly-held set of views on the role of government.

- Single issue politicians, driven by one overriding issue, such as cutting the budget, or some personal pet project.

including getting information from people in your contact network. The motives behind most prominent negotiating styles are set out in Box 15.5.

6. ATTENDING FLOOR SESSIONS

Some days you'll want to attend House and Senate floor sessions, especially if you have a bill up for a vote. To help make sense of who's involved and what's going on, this section covers the logistics, etiquette, procedure and politics of sessions.

House and Senate sessions begin between 10AM. and 11AM.

depending on the time in the session and how much business is to be done. The start of floor sessions is indicated by several cycles of bells ringing and tunes playing in the Capitol and adjacent buildings.

The Layout and Major Officers of the Chambers

Each chamber has two public galleries. The steps to these are to the left and right of the doors into the chamber.

The Senate has 20 members, the House 40. You can get a seating chart for both houses from the documents room or from the legislature's website. Each member's desk has three buttons: a green one for voting "yes" on bills or other procedural provisions; a red one for voting "no"; and a blue one for calling a page (the "gofers" of the legislature). The blue button is no longer used; members typically summon pages by raising notes they'd like passed to other members.

In front of each chamber is a podium where the President of the Senate or Speaker of the House presides over the body. To the President's or Speaker's left sit the major administrative officials of the respective houses and their staffs, the Secretary of the Senate, or the Chief Clerk of the House. To the presiding officers' right sit the Sergeant at Arms and the Assistant Sergeant at Arms, who keep order in the body and direct the pages.

On either side of the front of each chamber are large electronic boards that display the members' names, short titles of the items under immediate consideration, and all votes.

Crews stand with television cameras on both sides of the podium. Commercial television crew members at the presiding officers' right, the crew of Gavel Alaska on the left. Two tables at the back of the chambers are reserved for members of the press, both electronic and print. Members of the various caucuses' press staff are frequently on the floor photographing the proceedings.

Etiquette and the Operations of Floor Sessions

There is a strict etiquette followed in floor session. The major rules are set out in Box 15.6 on the next page.

BOX 15.6
ETIQUETTE DURING HOUSE AND SENATE FLOOR SESSIONS

Members of the public cannot:

- Enter either chamber.

- Pass notes or attempt to speak to legislators or anyone else across the rail from the gallery to the floor, except when the body is "at ease" and a member approaches you.

- Take drinks (including coffee) or food into the galleries. Smoking is prohibited throughout the Capitol.

- Use a flash camera.

- Talk loudly or engage in other disrupted behavior.

Legislators cannot:

- Address other members directly, either in asking questions or answering them. All discourse must go through the presiding officer.

- Pass notes directly to one another—they must use a page.

Introductions of people in the galleries

- Those introduced by a member rise when recognized.

- Only former members of the legislature may speak when introduced in the gallery.

- The value of an introduction to a group, especially one from out of town, is covered in section 6 of Chapter 12, on specific group tactics.

Operation of Floor Sessions

Floor sessions are highly choreographed by the majority in each house, aided by the presiding officer's considerable power to direct the proceedings. The leadership almost never brings a bill to the floor without having enough votes to pass it. All bills scheduled for floor sessions are considered, but to varying degrees. Except for floor amendments, floor action rarely affects the substance of legislation.

The Consideration of Bills

When a bill reaches the floor for final action, the Secretary or Clerk reads the title. The presiding officer recognizes the bill's sponsor; and the other legislators involved in the case of bills with multiple sponsors and/or co-sponsors. Then the designated floor manager (chosen by the majority caucus), presents the bill, briefly explaining what it is intended to accomplish, and then debate begins.

Floor Strategies

A time-honored adage is that, when a caucus has enough votes to pass a measure, it votes. If it doesn't have the votes, it talks.

Floor debate is often where minority caucus members talk and talk and talk. They raise questions about a bill's value and appropriateness, and sometimes question its cost. The majority must allow all members who wish to speak

As in virtually all aspects of law-making, in floor sessions the minority is the most vocal, but has very little influence.

on the bill to do so. When they've all spoken, the majority calls for a vote. The bill inevitably passes over the minority's objections.

Whenever the presiding officer deems it necessary, he or she calls a brief "at ease" (a break in the proceeding), which is rarely brief. These "at eases" are off the record. They allow the bodies to clarify procedural or parliamentary details, caucuses to straighten out strategic moves, or even entire caucuses to leave the chamber for private discussion.

Debate may be perfunctory or nonexistent on popular measures. Although there can be much discussion and sometimes grandstanding on broadly popular, bipartisan bills, as legislators seek to

BOX 15.7
PROCEDURE IN HOUSE AND
SENATE FLOOR DEBATES

- Amendments must be written and usually prepared before floor debate. Most legislators have amendments prepared by the Legal Services Division to be sure they reflect their intent. All amendments are considered as long as they are presented in the correct form.

- For strategic purposes, caucuses typically keep their amendments under cover until the floor session.

- Amendments go to the House Clerk or Senate Secretary to be recorded as part of the debate. They are copied and the Sergeant at Arms directs the pages to distribute them to all Members.

- After being proposed, each amendment is debated and voted on, unless withdrawn by the sponsor.

- When the vote is held, all members must vote "yes" or "no" if they are present. No abstentions are allowed.

- Sometimes "friendly amendments" are proposed. These are usually intended to improve a bill and non-controversial. For example, a friendly amendment might add an effective date to a bill that did not include one in its original form. Typically, these amendments are presented with concurrence of the bill's sponsor.

- At any time, a member can request a vote on a bill—known as "calling for the question." If there's no objection, the vote takes place. If any member objects, debate continues.

- On complex measures, such as the budget, debate can go on for hours, even for days. In many cases, the minority proposes scores of budget amendments, all of which are invariably voted down by the majority. Eventually, once all the minority's amendments have been considered, or due to exhaustion, the majority and minority agree to end debate and vote on the bill.

associate themselves with favorable measures. On bills where there's disagreement between majority and minority caucuses, amendments are allowed, but rarely proposed by majority members. The minority proposes most amendments to legislation, in a process set out in Box 15.7.

Going through the Motions

In effect, floor action, while required by the state constitution, is typically a mere formality, little more than political theater. With the majority caucuses firmly in charge, the end of the story of virtually every bill is known from the start. Still, sometimes along the way, the antics in the chambers can be entertaining.

7. MAKING NOTES AFTER A MEETING

You'll have no problem remembering what was said and decided in a meeting. Right? Wrong! However good your memory, with all the meetings and contacts you'll have, your recollections may not serve you well, especially when there's a dispute over what "really happened" in a meeting.

It's essential that you make notes immediately after all contacts with policy makers and others involved in your lobbying effort. It's tedious, many people put if off or don't do it at all. You'll regret it when you need specifics on a meeting.

Get into the habit of making notes not only after a personal meeting but for phone calls, too. Whether on your laptop, by hand, or a voice recording, you need to do it in some form. For e-mails and social media posts, keep a special file on your computer.

There are several good reasons for making notes. We've identified some before. Box 15.8, on the next page, brings these together and adds other reasons.

BOX 15.8
REASONS TO DOCUMENT MEETINGS

- There's a paper trail and not just oral recollections that can differ between people, and become a "he said, she said" standoff over what happened in a meeting.

- You can send your notes, or the main points on the outcome of a meeting, to public officials to confirm what happened and was decided.

- Use your notes to refresh your memory before follow-up meetings.

- Notes are useful to keep your lobbying coordinator, and others in your organization or business, up-to-date on the lobbying effort.

- Your notes can be used to draft newsletters to your group members.

- Most important of all, notes are a record of your lobbying efforts and their outcome over time. The information they provide is a useful source for modifying your lobbying plan, or developing new ones.

8. A REMINDER ON FOLLOW-UPS AND TIMING

As follow-up and timing can make the difference between success and failure, here's a recap of important things to do as you lobby day-to-day.

The Best Time to Present Your Message in the Session

The first time you present your message should not be during the legislative session. It should be done long before—during the interim. Contact in the session should be follow-ups to get things moving as the legislature and the administration gear up for action.

But one conversation or one meeting with a public official is not enough. If you have one meeting and leave it at that, your issue will almost certainly get lost in the piles of things the official is monitoring. This is particularly the case if your contact comes early in the session. Even if it's not been buried, your issue or proposed law will have likely gone through many changes. You must make contact to adjust or even come up with a new proposal.

Best Time to Follow-Up

Follow-up should be when policy makers are most open to your message. This will be at a crucial time when a decision is about to be made on your issue; or when your participation in a meeting is essential to convey your point of view.

That said, because your issue may get buried, drop by for a minute or two at regular intervals to check with staff that things are progressing smoothly. Some people use gestures, such as delivering cookies or candy, to keep their issues in the public official's mind. Most importantly, the end of the session is the crucial time to maintain contact and be available.

One of the toughest judgments a lobbyist has to make is the most effective times to follow up. Making the right judgment can bring success, making the wrong one, or not following up at all, can lead to failure.

It's a fine line between making necessary contact and becoming a pest. You don't want to wear out your welcome, earn a reputation for being a zealot, use overkill by getting your members to flood an office with messages, or annoyingly button-hole a politician when they're hurrying to a meeting. Striking this balance takes political savvy and experience. Again, lobbying is an art, not a science.

9. IF THINGS AREN'T GOING WELL

You've put your heart and soul into lobbying for your issue. You've covered all the bases in the legislature, the governor's office, and state agencies, and you've adjusted your goal (compromised) as necessary.

But things are just not working out. You're not alone. Depending on the year, and particularly the budget situation, only 10–15 percent of bills become law.

Making a Tough Decision

Whatever the reason, you're at a critical point. You're faced with a crucial decision. Do you throw in the towel or go on?

If you've planned well, this situation will not come as a surprise. You'll have included the possibility in your lobbying plan; one of the decisions you've anticipated as your effort takes its twists and turns. In this case, it may not be a hard decision, particularly if you've reached the point when you feel you can't compromise anymore. You'll pull the plug.

Continuing Your Lobbying Effort

Deciding in other situations may not be as easy. Many people, especially those lobbying for the first time who are particularly passionate about their issue, may not want to waste all the effort they've put in, and can't bring themselves to throw in the towel.

If there's any chance you can salvage the situation, you should try, but only if you see clearly what you need to do, and have a good chance of turning things around. The chances are, though, if things are really bogged down, and largely out of your control, you won't be successful.

The Downside

If you decide to continue, consider the major downside.

If you plan to lobby next session or sometime in the future, you risk alienating those you'll need down the road. Pounding on a dead issue will only make you appear lacking in political savvy and the realities of lobbying. Public officials may not take you seriously as you continue to push your present issue, and when you return next session to lobby on it again, or lobby on another issue.

As many of these officials will be part of your contact network, you also risk losing important sources of information. If the word gets around that you're unrealistic about achieving your goals, some of those you've relied on, such as other lobbyists and personnel in lobbying organizations, may also be reluctant to deal with you again.

Think Long-Term

To avoid losing your grip, think long-term. Look at your role as a lobbyist and the issue you are advocating as a process of building

> *A lobbyist should think long-term and not fight a losing battle and tank their reputation.*

a foundation this year, next year, and the years after that. Show political judgment in making the decision. Show you have the skill of a lobbyist, weighing the pros and cons of continuing your campaign, or gracefully putting an end to it.

10. THE END GAME: CLOSING OUT THE LEGISLATIVE SESSION

The last week to ten days of the session is frenzied. Things appear chaotic as everyone works to get things done and leave town.

If your bill is part of the adjournment package, you may not know it, but there are telltale hints. If a bill that's been languishing in its first committee of referral, suddenly sees quick movement toward the end of session, such as perfunctory committee hearings, or even motions to waive a bill from a committee, it may have become a majority priority, even a "must-have." If you find out that your measure is part of this final scramble, there are important things to bear in mind and do. Box 15.9, on the next page, lists the major tasks.

Rapidly Changing Schedules and Long Hours

As negotiations heat up, things can change at a moment's notice. The normal legislative schedule goes out the window. Committee

BOX 15.9
A CHECKLIST FOR THE END OF THE SESSION

If your bill is included in the adjournment package, you need to:

- Monitor the bill's progress closely.

- Touch base with the sponsor and co-sponsors (if any) to get their advice on what you need to do to get the bill through.

- Stay in touch with caucus staff and follow through immediately on all their suggestions and instructions.

- It may be necessary to contact the Speaker and President's office, or perhaps the Finance Committee staff, depending on your sponsor's recommendation.

- Do a vote count to be sure you have at least 21 votes in the House and 11 in the Senate.

- Stay in regular contact with your lobbying coordinator and others involved in your campaign. These will include your coalition members if you are part of a joint effort, to make changes in your original goals, and decide on compromises (if compromise is possible).

- Be prepared to act unilaterally. Given how quickly things develop during these last days, it may not be possible to discuss every step with your group or client. Make sure your organization's leaders, clients, or members, agree to you making decisions on your own, if necessary. This is essential because it's one of the most common situations in which lobbyists and their organizations get their wires crossed.

hearings and floor sessions may take place at any time and often go into the early hours of the morning. Everyone is scurrying around as deals are made. The halls of the Capitol fill with people lobbying on their issues. Lobbyists virtually camp out. You'll see many of them gathered in the House and Senate galleries, outside the entrances to the chambers, and the two Finance Committee rooms, to get a chance to lobby legislators as final decisions are made.

If your time to lobby is limited or you're from out of town, this is the time to be around to watch all these developments and react accordingly.

Your Bill May Get Lost in the Scramble

Even though both the legislature and the governor want the "must haves" in their respective adjournment packages, both sides realize the need to compromise, to cooperate on closing out the budget and the session. This means that, of necessity, some bills get amended extensively, others sacrificed in the final negotiations. Many bills don't receive hearings in the final floor sessions. This isn't a problem if it's the end of the first legislative session; if it's the second session, all unconsidered bills die.

You and your organization must be prepared for your bill to fall by the wayside, too. If you don't have an "in" with the leadership or other influential legislators, there's not much you can do to save it.

The Role of the Governor

If your bill clears the legislative hurdle, you now have to wait on the governor to sign it, veto it, let it become law without a signature, or line item veto or reduce any appropriation in your bill. This is a stage where you need to be extra diligent and on top of the situation.

If your bill is non-controversial or has bipartisan support, you'll likely have no problem. If it has attracted opposition for whatever reason, or includes a major cost, you must work to be sure it gets signed. This might involve working with your legislator, and/or other supporters, to lobby the governor and those advising him or her. Sometimes, getting your membership to contact the governor's office can help, but this must be done skillfully to avoid overkill.

"It's Not Over 'til It's Over"

When the governor signs the bill, this will be the end of your effort for the moment. But if your bill needs regulations written

BOX 15.10
FACTORS TO CONSIDER IN REFLECTING ON YOUR LOBBYING CAMPAIGN

- Look at the big picture: What were the crucial factors in your success or failure?

- Delve deeper: What particularly about these factors made the difference and why?

- Even if you were successful, what needs improving next time?

- If things didn't work out, was it due to an aspect of your lobbying plan, mixed messages sent to legislators, a problem with timing, or something beyond your control?

- If you were unsuccessful, can you correct the problem or problems? Or do you need to rethink your approach in a major way next time?

- If the second session is still to come, reflect on how things went, and how to approach the second session.

- What one thing came out of this experience you didn't know before, didn't take into consideration, anticipate, or otherwise learned?

- Was it an experience that you enjoyed? Do you have the enthusiasm and political smarts to be a lobbyist? Do you want to do it again?

- If you didn't like the personal contact with public officials, the wheeling-and-dealing, the frustrations, and other essential aspects of being a lobbyist, is there some other aspect of an advocacy campaign that would suit you better? This could be:

  o Being a campaign coordinator/campaign manager.

  o Research.

  o Putting together materials for the lobbying effort.

  o Helping to monitor political developments.

  o Doing PR work, among other tasks.

  o Or do you just want to get out of political advocacy altogether?

before it goes into effect, you'll have to monitor this process to be sure your new law is
implemented as intended. Depending on the
priority the department gives or doesn't give
these regulations, this could be a short or long
process. It may involve more lobbying.

The important message is: "It's not over 'til
it's over." Constant monitoring of the situation is needed.

11. REFLECTING ON YOUR LOBBYING EXPERIENCE

After the legislative session is over, the regulations for your bill
have been written, and you have distance from your campaign, it's
worth taking time to reflect on your experience. Whether you were
successful, got only some of what you wanted, or your campaign
bombed completely, this is an important exercise. If you've been lobbying for a while, you've likely done this before. If you haven't, spend
an hour or more going over what you did, and what you'd do the
same or differently next time.

Box 15.10 sets out questions and factors to consider. In doing so,
besides your own or organization's reflections, get an assessment of
your performance from those you dealt with during your campaign,
or others familiar with lobbying. It will give you a valuable perspective and likely identify things you wouldn't have thought of on your
own.

THIS CHAPTER COVERS

1. Ten Fundamentals of the Lobbyist's Mindset

2. Ten Essential Lobbying Tactics

3. Ten Cautions about Lobbying

4. A Check List

5. Now Get Practical Experience

★ CHAPTER 16 ★

A Recap of the Fundamentals of Lobbying

*Effective lobbying involves getting
the right message on the right issue
to the right people in the right form
at the right time.*

—Wes Coyner,

Contract Lobbyist,

Coyner Associates

Since the overview of lobbying in Chapter 1, we've seen that political advocacy requires a host of decisions and judgments, often making a lobbying campaign complex. Yet, repeatedly, we've returned to the key points of lobbying in Bob Manners's quote at the head of that chapter—contacts, trust, information, management, and compromise.

In expanding on these points throughout the book, we can now encapsulate the factors that are essential for effective lobbying. These are identified above by the late Wes Coyner, one of the most effective and respective Alaska lobbyists of the 1980s and "90s.

Combining these two perspectives:

Effective lobbying is built on contacts, trust, information, management, and compromise, and working these to get the right message on the right issue to the right people in the right form at the right time.

By reducing lobbying to these essentials, this chapter summarizes the key aspects of political advocacy covered in this book.

Our approach is to consider thirty fundamentals of lobbying and divide them into three sections, each covering ten points. Section 1 looks at the essentials in approaching lobbying—the mindset it takes to think like a lobbyist. Then, sections 2 and 3 identify the key tactics to use and those about which to be cautious.

1. TEN FUNDAMENTALS OF THE LOBBYIST'S MINDSET

Consciously or subconsciously, everyone is familiar with what it takes to be a lobbyist. At base, it involves being a student of human nature and understanding how to communicate effectively.

That said, being an effective lobbyist requires developing a political mindset. This skill is essential to deal with politicians in the ever-changing environment of politics, where relationships are built on mutual benefit involving transactions and compromise.

> *Despite sometimes having rocks thrown at them, lobbyists are a crucial part of the policy system.*

This is not everyone's cup of tea. Many people just can't or don't want to think this way or be involved in politics. But if you're not certain, or want to know how to think like a lobbyist, and what it takes to be effective, the following ten fundamentals will start you on the right road.

1. Suppress Negative Attitudes about Politicians and Lobbying

Even though you may have such negative attitudes, you can't let them come through in your contact with politicians and other public officials. They have all the political marbles, and you need their cooperation. Focus on your goal and treat them with respect and courtesy.

If you can't do this, you shouldn't engage in lobbying—it'll lead to certain failure.

2. Think Politically

The previous point is an aspect of thinking politically—to have the savvy to deal with the political system on its own terms. This involves:

- Figuring out who's got the power to help you.

- Learning how to deal with policy makers one-on-one.

- Being able to understand the political ramifications of a situation beyond the obvious.

- A willingness to compromise.

Again, if you can't think this way, lobbying is not for you.

3. Lobbying is a Personal Relationships Industry

Successful lobbying is a product of good personal relationships between the lobbyist and public officials and their staff.

Personal relationships are also the key to building a contact network that includes public officials, their staff, lobbyists, group leaders, and journalists, among others.

Building relationships takes time. It requires establishing trust and credibility, and understanding how to deal with each policy maker as an individual. Without these assets and abilities, a lobbyist won't last long.

4. Lobbying is also an Information Business

The major aspect of a lobbyist's job is providing information to policy-makers. This includes factual and technical information:

- What you are specifically requesting and why.

- Providing supporting material to back up your case.

An important part of a lobbyist's job is educating public officials.

- Explaining the pros of your issue and why those who oppose it are misguided.

- Offering a solution to your request.

Many lobbyists also provide political information on the status of various developments in the legislative process, as well as likely developments based on their sources and personal observations.

5. Give Policy-makers a Reason to Help You

Like politics in general, part of lobbying involves some mutual benefit to all involved. In this transactional environment, those you lobby need to derive some benefit from helping you. They may be willing to help because you:

- Have an issue they see as worthy and advantageous to them.

- Are a constituent.

- Supported them in an election, either financially or by working on their campaign.

- Can get information or make a contact they need.

Providing a public official with some benefit will help to cement the relationship between the two of you. This is another important aspect of thinking and acting politically.

6. Group Unity is Essential for Success

An interest group can't be successful if it doesn't convey a united front. If the group is divided, politicians and bureaucrats will be reluctant to act for fear of alienating some group members. Public officials won't move forward with a proposal if they can't argue to their colleagues that an issue is fully supported by a group.

Ensuring unity is a major role of lobbyists and group leaders. Any disagreements must be worked out in private and a consensus established. If this is not possible, the lobbying effort should be shelved until agreement can be reached.

7. A Lobbying Plan is also Essential

Lobbying campaigns that operate by the seats of their pants usually fail. You need a plan before you start lobbying. Without a detailed plan, your advocacy campaign will be unfocused, its major goals not pursued through the most efficient strategies and tactics.

A plan provides the big picture of the campaign and how all the pieces fit together. It should also include procedures on how to adjust the plan as circumstances change. This increases the ability to react to developments rapidly and refocus the campaign.

8. Don't Fall in Love with Your Issue

You can be committed to your issue and passionate about it, but don't let it cloud your political judgment—don't fall in love with your issue. If you do, like being smitten in a romantic relationship, you'll be totally engrossed, it'll dominate your thinking, and may prevent you from making balanced decisions.

Step back and realistically view your issue in ways to promote it effectively. This includes:

- Not getting upset with those who oppose it, particularly if they are politicians.

- Realizing that you will need to adapt your strategy as circumstances change.

- Being willing to compromise; even abandoning your effort if the situation looks hopeless.

If you fall in love with your issue, those you deal with will have control over you and what you do to promote your cause. This prevents you from making one of the most important decisions in lobbying. This is when to say: "Sorry, I can't go there, I can't do that,

30 Lobbying Fundamentals

I've got to leave you," when a politician wants something you find unpalatable in order to get their support.

By being inextricably tied to your issue, you'll appear a poor political advocate, and politicians may avoid you.

9. Think Long-term

Whether you have a one-time issue and then plan to disappear from the lobbying scene, or are promoting an ongoing issue, you need to think long term.

You are unlikely to achieve success in one legislative session or even two sessions. Take this into consideration in planning your lobbying effort.

- Build relationships. Don't destroy them because you don't get what you want immediately.

- If necessary, recognize when you need to abandon your effort and try again next year.

There are no permanent friends or permanent enemies in politics. The person who's your opponent today may be your ally tomorrow. So don't burn any political bridges.

- A long-term mindset is even more important if you plan to lobby on a continual basis. Not only do you need to take lobbying on your current issue into consideration, but allow for the inevitable need to accommodate changing circumstances down the road.

10. The Necessity for Compromise

Compromise is an essential, ever-present, and fundamental aspect of the policy process.

- It's instinctive to politicians, as their way of operating is most often transactional.

- They operate this way because they can't get all they'd like, so are willing to give up something to get part of what they want. They expect others to do the same.

- The need for compromise is why politics is a business involving intense competition, hardball negotiations, and cutting deals.

- To be successful in this environment, those involved must build up political chits to cash in when really needed.

If you're not willing to compromise, not only will you likely get no piece of the pie rather than some of it, you'll show you don't understand the basics of policy making. Politicians will likely dismiss you as politically naïve, because you don't understand how to resolve a contentious issue.

Understanding the need to compromise is probably the most important aspect of thinking politically. As a novice, however distasteful you might find compromising, it's part of not falling in love with your issue.

2. TEN ESSENTIAL LOBBYING TACTICS

Moving to the specifics, the ten essential lobbying tactics set out below, are the ones most often identified by those involved in the policy process. These people include: legislators and their staff; governors and their staff; department and agency personnel, including legislative liaisons; contract, in-house, and volunteer lobbyists; and political journalists.

1. Clearly Define Your Goal and Present it in the Right Form

The best way to get the ball rolling on your issue is to present a clear statement of your request and your goal. Summarize it on one sheet of paper, or in a short e-mail. This should include:

- What you want.

Each public official is a unique human being with their own way of approaching their job. Get inside their mind, know their operating style, their constraints and their needs. Do what you can to help them deal with their problems.

- Why you want it.

- How much it will cost.

- How it will affect the policy-maker with whom you're dealing, especially how it may affect their constituents, if at all.

To prevent confusion between the public officials dealing with your issue, use the same short description for all of them.

Don't overload a public official with mounds of information in your first contact. You can provide supplementary material when it's requested.

2. Be Well Prepared—Do Your Homework

To provide this clear and concise statement and develop backup information, be organized and well prepared to convince politicians to take you seriously as a lobbyist. Doing your homework is essential.

In fact, most of what's involved in a campaign—50 percent or more—is not lobbying, but doing all the prep work, including:

- Research and analysis.

- Planning your campaign.

- Preparing materials.

- Perhaps bringing your members up to speed on your lobbying effort, and how they can help.

3. Figure out the Most Effective Form of Personal Contact

There are many ways to get a message across to a policy-maker. You can lobby them on your own or use your members. Once you've laid the groundwork, you could get a prominent person or another legislator to help promote your issue.

Most politicians like to hear from group members or those directly affected by an issue. This can make an even greater impact if children are involved.

Every public official is different in how they like information presented. Your job is to find out how, and work to organize your lobbying effort accordingly.

4. Present Your Issue to the Right People

There are key people who can help you: in the legislature, in the governor's office and, depending on your issue, in one or more state agencies. Find out who they are.

In most situations, don't waste time with those who can't help you. So, it's pointless to visit all 60 legislators. Many won't be interested in your issue or can't or won't help you. You'll be wasting your time and theirs.

5. Start Lower Down and Work up the Chain of Authority

To give yourself maximum flexibility, and adapt your approach based on sound advice, first deal with a staffer in the legislature, a special assistant in the governor's office, or a mid-level manager in a state agency.

If you start at the top—with a legislator, the governor, or a commissioner—their approach to your issue may be colored by their perspective, more so than a staffer or agency person. Plus, they'll likely be too busy, and pass your request down to the person who can best handle it.

In your initial contact, find the person who can help you most. This is likely not the governor, a legislator, or a commissioner.

When it's passed down, it'll likely be with instructions on how to deal with it. This limits the options of the person dealing with your issue, and thus your available options. The specifics of what you want may also get garbled as it goes down the chain. Not only that, the person who must deal with your issue may be miffed because you didn't come to them first.

If you start with the right person, there will probably be a point where the top dog steps in. By then, those dealing with your issue will be fully conversant with it, and can clearly inform their boss about your needs.

6. Explain Both Sides of Your Issue

For public officials to trust and see you as a credible lobbyist, you must present both sides of your issue. Obviously, you'll explain why yours is the best course to take and that your opponents are misguided or plain wrong.

This will alert a public official to the potential opposition, so they won't be blindsided when someone gives them a dissenting opinion. If you present only your side, they'll be very unhappy and may withdraw their support.

This means looking at the big picture of your situation, and being able to see the other side—"not loving your issue to death."

7. Propose a Solution

Don't just explain your issue—propose a solution. If you don't, the public official will likely ask you. You'll come across as not having thought things through, and not on top of your issue. This may color their view of you, and how much they're willing to push your issue. You don't have to have the entire solution. But you need to suggest some options and possible strategies and tactics. Then, the official has something to react to and may offer advice on whether this is the best course, or if it needs modifying and how.

8. Make Notes on all Meetings

In any day or week, you'll have several meetings. Even if you think you'll remember what happened in each one, most likely you won't. Write it down.

Make notes after the meeting; better still, in the meeting, if it's appropriate. Keeping detailed notes is essential for three reasons:

- You'll have a clear reminder of what occurred for when you meet with that official the next time.

- To provide a report to your organization or clients.

- Most importantly, by sending a version of your notes, you can confirm the substance of your meeting with a public official, or other person with whom you met.

9. Plan During the Interim

Lobbying is a year-round activity. It doesn't stop when the legislative session ends and begin again when it comes back for the next session.

Groups do a lot of planning for their upcoming lobbying effort during the interim (late April/early May thru mid-January), long before the session begins. During these months, you have more time and much less pressure on you. Legislators and state agency officials also have more time, and it's much easier to get an appointment than in the legislative session.

10. The Importance of Timing

As you plan and implement your campaign, timing is important in a host of ways. Your message will be less effective, even lost, if it's not delivered to a policy maker when most appropriate. Poor timing can seriously undermine your campaign, in some cases ruin it.

Besides contacting public officials when they have the most time, good timing includes:

- Knowing the right political environment to push an issue. For instance, you're not likely to get a positive reception if your issue requires major funding in a time of low state revenues.

- Making contacts at the best time in the session and following up (don't assume one contact is enough).

- Making contact when a key decision is coming up in a committee or on the floor of the House or Senate.

3. TEN CAUTIONS ABOUT LOBBYING

Many people coming to lobbying for the first time bring ideas about the best tactics and how to use them. Some are good ideas; many are misconceptions or just plain wrong. Plus, there are pitfalls of which a novice will be unaware.

For both novices and those who've not done as well as they'd liked in lobbying, dealing with these misconceptions, avoiding the pitfalls, is as important as knowing the right things to do. Accordingly, this section raises cautions about ten tactics and other aspects of lobbying.

> *I frequently tell my members: "We have no enemies in the legislature—only people we don't agree with."*

1. Lobbying Involves More than the Legislature

Depending on your issue, you may or may not need to lobby the legislature.

On the one hand, if you have an issue that can only be dealt with by a new law, an amendment to an existing one, or want to block a proposal, you need to deal with more than the legislature. You'll also have to lobby the governor's office, and the state agency with authority over the issue. All this must be incorporated in your lobbying plan.

On the other hand, if you want to change a regulation or have a law applied in a certain way, contact the appropriate department or agency. If they are not very receptive, you may want to contact your legislator for help.

2. Choose Your Lobbyist Carefully

If you have the choice, the person who lobbies for you should have some specific personality traits.

Besides being willing to do their homework and having a mind for detail, they should be patient and not easily riled, especially when told "no" or, on occasion, are a punching bag for a public official. Your lobbyist doesn't have to be a glad-hander, but needs good people skills.

If you're hiring a contract lobbyist, don't be overawed because you recognize their name or they make big bucks. Contract lobbyists range from the excellent to the mediocre to the poor and lazy. Ask around and find one who fits your group and your issues.

3. Remember that Politicians Represent their Constituents

This is obvious, but important to emphasize: foremost in the minds of elected officials, particularly legislators, but also many agency personnel, are their constituents. This is their driving force, in many cases the major factor influencing their actions.

Always keep this in mind and gear your request and proposal to show how it will benefit their constituents or clientele, if you can. This is another aspect of giving public officials a reason to help you.

4. Ignore Legislative Staff at Your Peril

Staff can be a valuable part of your contact network. Once they get to know and trust you, staffers can help you get to their legislator.

They can also be great source of information, both factual and political, including details about those you'll need to deal with.

If you ignore staff or, worse still, dismiss them, they can make your life very difficult. Though likely you'll never know it, but be left wondering why things aren't working out the way you'd planned. Not only that, if they have a mind to, they can get back at you in the future.

5. Make an Appointment—Don't Drop in

All politicians and agency staff have more work than they can handle, and people are always asking for their time. If you drop by without an appointment, you likely won't be able to see them. Some may even get annoyed that you expected their time without making prior arrangements.

Make an appointment. Then you'll have a slot of time to make your pitch, as opposed to a hurried minute when you drop by, if you can catch them. If they need to cancel your appointment they'll be sure to reschedule.

6. Overkill Can Kill Your Chance of Success

Good lobbyists work to keep their goals in the minds of those they are lobbying. They do this without engaging in overkill, camping on the doorsteps of these public officials, flooding them with e-mails, phone calls, and unleashing scores of visits from clients or members.

By contrast, the novice often has one conversation or meeting and leaves it at that. Then they may resort to overkill. They inundate public officials with messages, or stage a protest or rally on the Capitol steps, occupy a hallway or an office, when a simple follow-up meeting would have accomplished their goal.

It's important to strike a balance between pushing your issue and being a persistent nuisance.

You may even kill your bill if you arrange for too many people to testify at a committee hearing. This will prevent a decision being made on your legislation. The bill may be held over for another hearing, a hearing that may never be scheduled.

In general, overkill can alienate legislators and their staff as well as agency personnel—something you want to avoid at all costs.

7. Don't go Rogue if You're Not Your Group's Lobbyist

If you're part of an interest group or organization, but not the lobbyist, never contact a public official unless you've worked out the details with your organization's lobbyist.

You shouldn't lobby on your own unless you're asked and been given clear guidelines on what to do. Even if you have a contact who might help your group's lobbying effort, talk to your leadership before meeting with the official and, if possible, get one of your organization's staff to accompany you.

The reason is that you likely won't be up to speed on recent developments, the status of an issue and the political dynamics involved. Even if you are, there's the risk that you'll convey a different message than the leadership would. This mixed message can confuse legislators or their staff. It will undermine the unity of the message, reduce its impact, and perhaps weaken the lobbying effort.

8. When Your Bill is Passed, that May Not be the End of It

If your lobbying focus is to pass a bill, as opposed to killing one or changing a regulation, follow through to the very end of the process. Your work may not be over when the governor signs your bill. It may need regulations written before being implemented.

If the bill was passed over the objection of an agency and the governor didn't veto it, or even if supported by all concerned, you need to be diligent. There are several legitimate reasons why an agency might delay drafting the regulations. If it's so inclined, an agency can drag this process out for months, even years. Monitor these developments, and step in where necessary, including using your members, or get help from public officials who supported the bill.

If the opposition to your bill is strong from some quarters, there may be a future attempt to amend or repeal it. This means your lobbying effort will continue.

9. Know When to Quit

As only about 20 percent, often less, of bills become law, there's an 80 percent chance you won't get what you want. If you're opposing a bill or other proposal, the chance of success is higher, but still far from certain. The likelihood is that your bill will be stalled at some point in the process

In this case, unless you have a good chance of salvaging the situation, at some point you need to decide whether to continue lobbying or call it a day.

If the situation is hopeless and you keep pounding away, you'll almost certainly diminish your chances for success in the next session, and you may get a reputation for lacking political savvy. This will be particularly detrimental if you plan to lobby on a continual basis. Step back, think long-term, not just for the moment, and make a realistic decision.

10. Don't Take Things Personally, and Dealing with a Screw-Up

Sometimes tempers get frayed in the intensity of politics, especially when things aren't going right for a legislator, staffer, or agency person.

In the heat of the moment, tensions occasionally cause emotional outbursts of exasperation, sometimes anger. Often this is directed at a lobbyist who is being too persistent or demanding or clashes with a legislator or staffer for some other reason.

Generally, these incidents are not personal and are forgotten soon after, because they were something said in the heat of the moment. Even if the memory lingers, because in politics your "enemy" today may be your "friend" tomorrow, these incidents don't usually affect relationships long-term.

If you're the target of an outburst, as unpleasant and unsettling at the time, it's unlikely to be personal. Pick yourself up and don't lose sight of your goal.

Dealing with a Screw-Up

Almost all interest group leaders and lobbyists who've been around for a while, have stories about mistakes they've made when lobbying. It happened because they were in a rush, hadn't done their homework and tried to wing it, were stressed out, or lost their cool. It's not surprising, then, that novices sometimes make mistakes.

Like the professionals, if you make a mistake inadvertently and you realize it, if it's not too egregious, most public officials will accept your apology. The important thing is to apologize and not let it fester in the mind of the official you may have annoyed or offended.

4. A CHECK LIST

Now you know how to think like a lobbyist, and the do's and the don'ts of political advocacy, it's useful to have all 30 points in a short list.

This is set out in Box 16.1 on the next page. Use it as a quick reminder before you meet with a public official. You can also use it to provide a short information session or a more extensive workshop for your members or clients.

5. NOW GET PRACTICAL EXPERIENCE

To the novice, perhaps even those with some experience, all the information in this handbook may be a little overwhelming. Although we've taken a practical approach to lobbying, obviously these pages can't provide the hands-on experience of organizing and implementing an actual campaign.

BOX 16.1
THIRTY KEY ELEMENTS OF LOBBYING

1. Ten Fundamentals of the Lobbyist's Mindset

1. Suppress negative attitudes about politicians and lobbying.
2. Think politically.
3. Lobbying is a personal relationships industry.
4. Lobbying is also an information business.
5. Give policy-makers a reason to help you.
6. Group unity is essential for success.
7. A lobbying plan is also essential.
8. Don't fall in love with your issue.
9. Think long-term.
10. The necessity for compromise.

2. Ten Essential Lobbying Tactics

1. Clearly define your goal and present it in the right form.
2. Be well prepared—do your homework.
3. Figure out the most effective form of personal contact.
4. Present your issue to the right people.
5. Start lower down and work up the chain of authority.
6. Explain both sides of your issue.
7. Propose a solution.
8. Make notes on all meetings .
9. Plan during the interim.
10. The importance of timing.

3. Ten Cautions about Lobbying

1. Lobbying involves more than the legislature.
2. Choose your lobbyist carefully.
3. Remember that politicians represent their constituents .
4. Ignore legislative staff at your peril.
5. Make an appointment—don't drop in.
6. Overkill can kill your chance of success.
7. Don't go rogue if you're not your group's lobbyist.
8. When your bill is passed, that may not be the end of it.
9. Know when to quit.
10. Don't take things personally, and dealing with a screw-up.

For the novice, getting hands-on experience will help answer many of the open questions raised in this handbook. Likely these include what strategies and tactics work best for your organization, and which public officials want what information in what form.

Most of all, practical experience will enable you to cut your own style in organizing a campaign and lobbying in the way that best suits you. This is because, at bottom, lobbying is a matter or judgment and personal style.

All this said, as pointed out in the "Truth in Advertising" section of the introduction, while this

Lobbying comes down to hard work, knowing your issue, and maintaining your credibility, even if it means losing on your issue.

handbook cannot guarantee you success in your lobbying effort, it explains the factors that can lead to success. As important, or maybe more so, it identifies the things to avoid that may sink your campaign. But whether you're a novice, someone with a little experience, or a seasoned pro, lobbying is a never-ending learning experience.

30 Lobbying Fundamentals

★ APPENDIX 1 ★

A Tour of Alaska's State Capitol Building

The Capitol building opened in 1931. Originally the Juneau federal building, when Alaska achieved statehood in 1959 it became the state Capitol. It's one of the few state capitols without a dome.

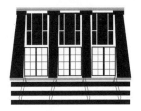

THE CAPITOL BUILDING AS OF FALL 2019

This tour was written in fall 2019. So bear the following in mind when visiting the capitol:

- Renovations and reconfiguring of the building mean that changes in location of offices, committee rooms, and other facilities, occur from time to time.

- The locations of legislators' offices change after each two-year legislative election. This is a result of changes in the leadership, and the composition of the majority and minority in the House and Senate.

You can get a list of legislators' offices from the documents room on the ground floor. This is also available on the legislature's website (http://akleg.gov/publications.php): and posted throughout the capitol, as is the location of committee rooms.

LOCATION AND LAYOUT

The Capitol is located between 4th and 5th and Main and Seward Streets in downtown Juneau. The front entrance is on 4th Street.

- There are five full floors, plus a bottom floor that is a half floor (no back entrance) because the Capitol is built into a hill.

- On the first floor are side entrances (on Main and Seward) and a back entrance from the parking lot, off 5fh Street, where legislators and administration officials have reserved parking.

- Floors 1 thru 5 are shaped like a "U," with the front entrance of the building forming the bottom of the "U."

ROOM NUMBERING

Rooms in the Capitol are not numbered consecutively, with, for example, room 411 next to room 412.

- Standing at the front of the Capitol, looking up the steps, rooms on the left-hand side—the Gastineau Channel or water side—have odd numbers, 209, 415, etc.

- Rooms on the right-hand side, the mountain side of the building, have even numbers, 422, 426, etc.

- As you climb the stairs or leave the elevator, odd-numbered offices are on your right, even ones on your left.

THE FLOOR LAYOUT

The Ground (half) Floor

When you walk up the steps into the lobby, you'll find an information booth, and the elevators straight ahead to the left.

- Rooms on this floor are numbered with single or double digits, 6, 12, etc. They do not have "G" in front of them to signify the ground floor; but there is a "G" button in the elevator.

- To your left are a few legislators' offices and the building manager's office.

- To the right is the documents room where, as well as a list of legislators and their committee assignments, you can get bills, the House and Senate Journals, the House and Senate Calendars, the weekly schedule of committee meetings, as well as other useful materials.

> Gavel Alaska *coverage of floor sessions and committee hearings is on TV screens throughout the capitol and in the lounge in the Stewart Annex.*

- If you keep going around the corner, you'll see more legislators' offices, the press room, and a committee room.

The First Floor

Here you'll find several legislators' offices and some committee rooms.

- As indicated above, this is the floor with the two side entrances and the back entrance to the building.

- As you leave the elevator or come onto the floor from the stairs, to your left is a large vintage photograph of the members of one of the territorial legislatures.

The Second Floor

The House and Senate chambers, committee rooms, and legislators' offices, including those of the legislative leadership, are on this floor.

- The Senate chamber is on the Channel side, the House chamber on the mountain side.

- Each chamber has two public galleries, one to the left and one to the right of the entrance to each chamber.

Capitol Tour

The House galleries are the Warren A. Taylor gallery to the left, named for a former member; and the Elizabeth A. Peratrovich gallery to the right, named for a prominent Alaska Native leader.

The Senate galleries, both named for former senators, are the Senator Ziegler gallery to the left, and the Senator Groh gallery to the right.

Capitol Tour

- The public is not allowed on the floor of the chambers when the bodies are in session, to pass notes or speak to legislators from the galleries.

The legislative lounge and dining room are on the Channel side, just to the right as you enter the floor. Only legislators, former legislators, pages (to deliver messages to legislators), and lounge staff can enter. But you can order food from a menu outside the door.

You can get a seating chart for the House and Senate chambers from the document room on the ground floor, or from the legislature's website.

On the mountain side is the sky bridge to the Thomas Stewart Building. See below for details on this building.

The Third Floor

This is where the governor and the lieutenant governor are located. The governor's office is on the mountain side, the lieutenant governor's on the Channel side.

The Fourth Floor

Here, there are legislators' offices and committee rooms.

The Fifth (top) Floor

Here you'll find legislators' offices, plus the all-important Senate and House Finance Committee rooms.

- The Senate room is on the mountain side, the House room on the Channel side.

- As with all committee rooms, there are chairs for observing committee sessions.

If you visit a committee room when there's no meeting in progress, don't sit in a chair at the committee table. These are off limits at all times for anyone who's not a legislator.

THE THOMAS B. STEWART BUILDING CAPITOL ANNEX

Usually called the Stewart Building or Stewart Annex, it was opened in 2010. It's named after Thomas "Tom" B. Stewart, the Secretary to the Alaska Constitutional Convention (1955-56), and a Superior Court judge.

- It's located across from the Capitol building on the mountain side, at the corner of 4th and Seward Streets.

- You can enter at the front door and from the second floor of the Capitol.

- No legislators have their main office here, but some majority members have extra office space where some legislative staff are located.

- As well as other offices and conference rooms, there's a public lounge where visitors can watch Gavel Alaska.

- There's also a day-care center.

- And a kitchen for staff (which can only be opened with a key).

PUBLIC AND VIDEO TOURS OF THE CAPITOL

Public tours are available, but only in summer.

There are also several video tours. One particularly good one is on the website of Alaska Political Advocacy Strategies (APAS) at: http://www.akpoliticaladvocacy.com/

For others, type in "Alaska State Capitol tour" on Google, and several will pop up.

Capitol
Tour

★ APPENDIX 2 ★

Locating State Offices, Lobbying Groups, and Lobbyists in Juneau

Like the tour of the Capitol in Appendix 1, this tour was written in fall 2019. Bear this in mind, and check current addresses and locations.

STATE OFFICE BUILDINGS

Map 1 in Appendix 3, shows government buildings in downtown Juneau. Have it with you when you take this tour.

Getting Your Bearings

To get your bearings, stand at the front of the Capitol at the corner of 4th and Main Streets (about 25 yards to the right of the steps as you leave the Capitol). Have your back to the building, looking downhill toward the harbor.

The State Court Building

Right across the street, #3 on the map, is the Dimond Court Building (yes, no "a" in Dimond), with its sloping glass roof (though the main offices of the Alaska State Court System are in Anchorage). In this building are courtrooms, the Attorney General's office, and the Juneau offices of the Alaska Supreme Court, located on the eighth (top) floor.

You'll need to pass through security screening to enter. The only other government building you'll need to do this is at the federal building, if you want to go to federal offices (though there's no screening for the Post Office located here). The federal building is about half a mile from the legislature, #9 on the map.

The Stewart Annex and the Terry Miller Building

Fifty yards or so to your left, across Seward Street, number #2 on the map, is the Stewart Annex, explained in Appendix 1. Behind the Capitol building (so not visible to you) on 5th Street, is the Terry Miller Legislative Office Building, #1 on the map (named for a former lieutenant governor). It's used for legislative administrative offices, including the Legislative Affairs Agency (LAA).

The Alaska State Office Building—SOB

Now, look to your right, across Main Street, another 50 yards or so, and you'll see steps. These lead to the Alaska State Office Building (known as the SOB), #5 on the map. It houses several state departments including: the Departments of Administration, Revenue, and Commerce and Community Development. There's an information booth just inside the door and a directory lists where offices are located.

As the SOB is built into a hill, when you go up the steps into the building, you're on the eighth floor. There's also an entrance on Willoughby Avenue on the Channel side, across from the Juneau Convention Center (#36 on map 4—places of interest). There's another office location directory inside the entrance.

Three State Office Buildings on Main Street

Still looking to the right, before the steps to the SOB, is an older building, the original Alaska State Office Building constructed in the 1950s (#4 on the map). It's now known as the Alaska Office Building, occupied mainly by the Alaska Department of Health and Social Services (DHSS).

Directly down the hill is a building of eight floors with rounded corners (#6 on the map). This is the Court Plaza Building, but known in Juneau as the "Spam Can." Two of the agencies it houses are the Office of Management and Budget (OMB), and the Alaska Public Offices Commission (APOC). A directory is posted at the entrance.

Across the street from the Spam Can, going toward the mountain, at 3rd and Main, is the State of Alaska Community Building (#7 on map 1). Locals often refer to it as the old Coast Guard building. It houses the Department of Public Safety, and the Public Defender's Office.

Other State Offices

The Department of Natural Resources and Department of Environmental Conservation, are located at 400 and 410 Willoughby Avenue respectively, across from the back of the SOB and next to the Twilight Café (#34 on map 3).

Other government offices are scattered throughout Juneau.

The Department of Education and the Permanent Fund Corporation are housed in the Goldbelt Building, about half a mile from the Capitol near the federal building. The Department of Fish and Game and the Department of Labor are two blocks from the Goldbelt building across Egan Drive near the Douglas Island bridge (on the south side). The Department of Corrections is located in the town of Douglas, two miles south of the bridge.

Other offices are located at various places "out the road." Juneauites identify places by the number of miles they are from downtown (the road goes 42 miles and then ends). The Department of Transportation's main office is at 3 mile and its Southeast regional office at 7 mile. The airport is at 9 mile "out the road."

Alaska Directory of State Officials

You can find the location of all state departments and their divisions in Juneau (and throughout the state), and other state agencies, together with their major personnel, in the *Alaska*

The Alaska Directory of State Officials (DOSO) is an invaluable source for getting contact info on all state agencies and elected and appointed officials.

Locating State Offices

Directory of State Officials (sometimes referred to as DOSO). It's available in hard copy from the documents room in the Capitol, and online at: http://w3.akleg.gov/pubs/doso.php. See the section on "Information on Public Officials" in Appendix 4 for more details.

LOBBYING GROUPS AND LOBBYISTS

Many interest groups, organizations, and lobbyists have offices scattered throughout downtown, some a little way from the Capitol.

These include: The National Education Association (NEA-Alaska),

the state K-12 employees union; the Alaska Municipal League (AML); United Fishermen of Alaska (UFA); the Alaska Hospital and Nursing Home Association; the University of Alaska; and the National Federation of Independent Business (NFIB). Many of the large groups and organizations also have offices in Anchorage.

Virtually all have websites with contact information and a list of their personnel.

★ APPENDIX 3 ★

Maps for Locating Places in Downtown Juneau

This appendix includes four maps of downtown Juneau. They'll be particularly useful if you are among the 50 percent or so of those who come to lobby from outside the capital city.

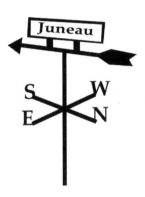

Map 1, showing government offices in downtown, can be used together with the descriptions and locations of these offices in Appendix 2.

Map 2 shows hotels, Map 3 restaurants and food stores, Map 4 places of interest. The locations on the maps are numbered 1 thru 44, running consecutively from map 1 thru Map 4.

Most places you'll need to find are within four or five blocks of the Capitol building; others are just a 10-15 minute walk away.

Parking

As shown on each map, there are two large parking garages. Plus, you can park on most streets in the downtown area, although open spaces can be hard to find during the legislative session.

Taxis, Uber, and Lyft

Taxis arrive pretty promptly after being called. Uber and Lyft also operate in Juneau. It costs about half as much using Uber or Lyft to get from the airport to downtown than in a cab, about $10-12 versus $20.

Buses

Buses go from the transit center down the hill from the Capitol at the corner of Egan Drive and Main Street (#44 on Map 4). The bus will take you to the restaurants and food stores on Willoughby Avenue, to the federal building, and to and from the airport. Be sure to get the Express bus if you're going to the airport.

Juneau
Maps

Government Buildings

MAP 1

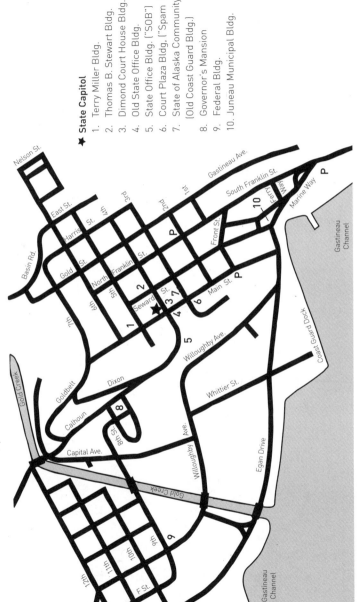

★ **State Capitol**

1. Terry Miller Bldg.
2. Thomas B. Stewart Bldg.
3. Dimond Court House Bldg.
4. Old State Office Bldg.
5. State Office Bldg. ("SOB")
6. Court Plaza Bldg. ("Spam Can")
7. State of Alaska Community Bldg.
   (Old Coast Guard Bldg.)
8. Governor's Mansion
9. Federal Bldg.
10. Juneau Municipal Bldg.

Juneau Maps

Source: Developed by the author.

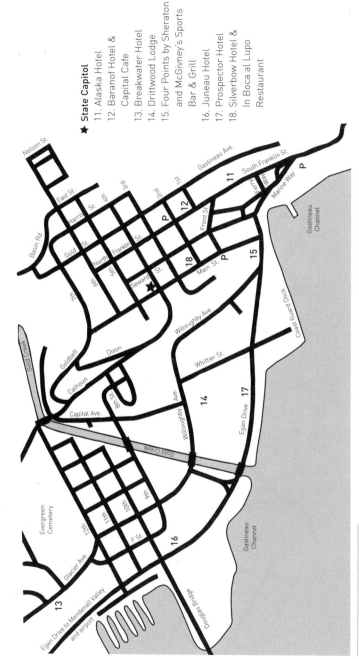

★ **State Capitol**
11. Alaska Hotel
12. Baranof Hotel & Capital Cafe
13. Breakwater Hotel
14. Driftwood Lodge
15. Four Points by Sheraton and McGivney's Sports Bar & Grill
16. Juneau Hotel
17. Prospector Hotel
18. Silverbow Hotel & In Boca al Lupo Restaurant

Juneau Maps

MAP 2
Hotels

Source: Developed by the author.

MAP 3

Restaurants and Food Stores

★ **State Capitol**
19. El Sombrero
20. Hangar On the Wharf
21. Heritage Coffee House
22. IGA Grocery Store
23. Home Liquor & Deli
24. Little Tokyo
25. Rainbow Foods
26. Pizza places
27. The Rookery Café
28. The Capital Cafe &
    Bubble Room Lounge
29. Saffron Indian Comfort Cuisine
30. Sandpiper Cafe
31. Salt Restaurant
32. The Tacueria
33. Twilight Cafe
34. V's Cellar Door
35. Subway

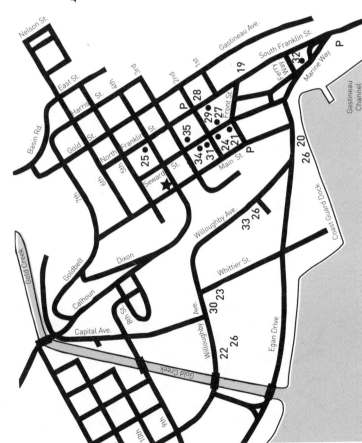

Juneau Maps

Source: Developed by the author.

MAP 4

Places of Interest, Parking, and Transit Terminal

★ **State Capitol**

36. Centennial Hall
    (Convention Center)
37. Juneau Arts and
    Humanities Bldg.
38. Juneau City Museum
39. Russian Orthodox
    Church
40. State Library
    and Museum
41. Sealaska Bldg.
42. Andrew Hope Bldg.
    (ANB Hall)
43. Swimming Pool
44. Transit Terminal
P Parking Garages

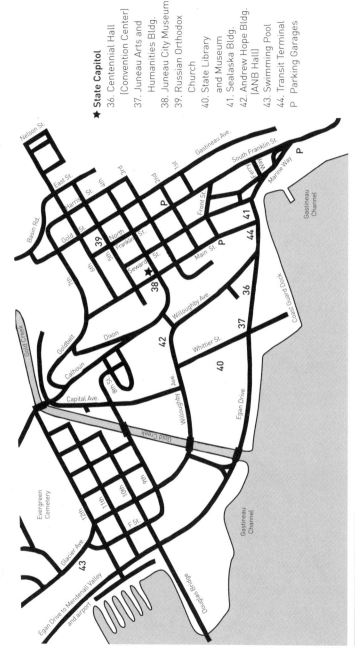

Source: Developed by the author.

★ APPENDIX 4 ★

Getting More Information

This list of further information includes:

- Printed Sources on Alaska Political and Government

- Gavel Alaska and Other Media Sources

- Newsletters, Blogs, and Policy Institutes

- Lobbying Groups and Organizations

- Information on Public Officials

- State Agencies and their Personnel

- BASIS—Bill Action and Status Inquiry System

- State Government Websites

- The State Budget

- Books on Lobbying

Printed Sources on Alaska Politics and Government

Gordon Harrison, *Alaska's Constitution; A Citizen's Guide,* Fifth
Edition (Juneau, AK: Alaska Legislative Affairs Agency, 2012).

 Can also be read on-line at: www.ltgov.state.ak.us/
constitution.php. An excellent explanation of the
Articles of the Constitution, and its amendments. It
includes: background to each Article; court decisions
that have affected the document; and the present-day
operation and political implications of the Constitution.

Clive S. Thomas, ed., *Alaska Politics and Public Policy: The Dynamics of Beliefs, Institutions, Personalities and Power* (University of Alaska Press, 2016).

The most comprehensive book to date on Alaska politics. It covers virtually all aspects of state politics and government as well as the major areas of public policy.

Clive. S. Thomas, "Alaska." In Donald P. Haider-Markel, ed., *Political Encyclopedia of U.S. States and Regions,* 2 Volumes (Washington, D.C.: C. Q. Press, 2008), Volume 1, pp. 353-64.

A good overview of the basics of Alaska politics.

Handbook on Alaska State Government (Legislative Affairs Agency, 2011).

This can be downloaded in pdf from the Legislature's website at: http://w3.legis.state.ak.us/pubs/pubs.php. It's a useful but purely descriptive explanation of the organization of state government. It doesn't include any aspects of state politics.

Gavel Alaska and Other Media Sources

Public television provides live and recorded coverage of the Alaska legislature, including: committee meetings; Senate and House floor sessions; press conferences; and other legislative events.

It also covers: oral arguments before the Alaska Supreme Court; administration press conferences and briefings; general government activities; and other meetings about legislative issues of interest.

Most legislative and administration offices have Gavel Alaska on constantly. Or watch it in the public lounge in the Stewart building.

360 North

This is a public affairs channel on Alaska public television. The most widely distributed television channel in Alaska, it provides

Getting More Info

coverage of Alaska government and public affairs, documentaries, and activities of the Alaska Native community, among other topics.

The Alaska Public Radio Network—APRN

APRN has some programming covering public affairs, including Alaska News Nightly, on weekdays. The network has a reporter in Juneau, and uses reporters from its member stations statewide to cover some politics. APRN's weekly programs, Talk of Alaska and Alaska Insight (not aired in the summer), often deal with current topics in Alaska politics and government as well as social issues.

Newspapers

Alaska's major newspaper, the *Anchorage Daily News* (adn.com), can also be read on-line by subscription. It also publishes an Alaska politics blog. From 2013–17, this paper was the *Alaska Dispatch News*.

The *Fairbanks Daily News-Miner* and the *Juneau Empire* are also useful. Local newspapers include:

- *Mat-Su Valley Frontiersman*

- *Ketchikan Daily News*

- *Kodiak Daily Mirror*

- *Kenai Peninsula Clarion*

- *Sitka Sentinel*

- *Homer Tribune*

- *Bristol Bay Times*

- *Arctic Sounder*

All are also available on-line.

Getting
More Info

Newsletters, Blogs, and Policy Institutes

To get an idea of the variety of these sources, Google "Alaska politics," "Alaska government" or "Alaska political issues" and you'll get many leads.

Newsletters

Most interest groups and organizations have newsletters available on-line. Some can only be accessed by members; but to publicize their issues, some will give you access to their newsletter, or put you on their mailing list.

The Democrats and Republicans, also have newsletters.

A subscription newsletter, *Bradners' Legislative Digest*, which includes information and opinion, is published every four of five days during the legislative session, less frequently in the interim. It covers major legislation and issues as they unfold during the session, including a list of the status of bills.

Occasionally the *Digest* does special editions on policy issues, such as education, health, and the Permanent Fund.

The subscription (as of 2019) is $475.00 a year: e-mail: timbradner@pobox.alaska.net

Blogs

There are several blogs covering Alaska politics. These are mostly free, but vary in quality and reliability. Some are ideologically biased. Plus, they come and go, as most are one-person operations.

Those which have been around for a while include:

- *The Midnight Sun*—http://midnightsunak.com/

- *The Mudflats*—http://www.themudflats.net/

- *Alaska Politics and Elections*—http://apeonline.org/

- *Must Read Alaska*—http://mustreadalaska.com/

- *Alaska Politics & Blogs Daily*—https://paper.li/f-1499994092#/

- *The Alaska Landmine*—https://alaskalandmine.com/

> **Be wary of the information in political blogs and from policy institutes. Find out their political slant—if any—and use them accordingly.**

As of fall 2019, *The Midnight Sun* is by far the best blog on Alaska politics. It presents comprehensive, in-depth coverage, and is (more or less) up-to-date. *Must Read Alaska* is very conservative, opinionated, and sometimes pushes conspiracy theories.

While not a blog, another useful website is that of a private political consulting firm, Alaska Political Advocacy Strategies (APAS, http://www.akpoliticaladvocacy.com/). It contains information about Alaska politics, including a video tour of the Capitol building.

Policy Institutes

There are a few policy institutes in Alaska that can be useful sources of political and policy information. These include:

- The Institute of Social and Economic Research (ISER—www.iser.uaa.alaska.edu) at the University of Alaska Anchorage. It's the most objective source of factual and policy information.

- Commonwealth North (www.commonwealthnorth.org) with a general Alaska polity focus.

- The Institute of the North (http://www.institutenorth.org) dealing with Arctic as well as other issues.

- The Alaska Policy Forum (www.alaskapolicyforum.org), with a conservative/libertarian viewpoint.

Getting More Info

Lobbying Groups and Organizations

The Internet is your best bet here. Virtually all interest groups have websites where you can find information, including their staff, and often the organization's positions on issues.

Major organizations, like the Association of Alaska School Boards (AASB), the Alaska Municipal League (AML), and the Alaska State Chamber of Commerce (ASCC), have extensive websites that often go into depth on issues.

Information on Public Officials

Legislators and their Staff

A list of the locations of their offices and committee assignments is available from the documents room on the ground floor of the Capitol, and on the legislature's website. This website also has a pdf listing legislators' districts, phones, e-mails, mailing addresses, and the names of their staff. There is also a booklet published for each legislature that includes most of this information.

Each legislator has a website that usually provides personal information and their positions on various issues. Most also use Facebook, Twitter, and other social media platforms.

The Governor, their Staff, and Senior Agency Personnel

Information on the governor and his or her policy issues, and reports on the status of these issues, are available on the governor's website.

Other than contact information, it's harder to find personal and professional information on the governor's staff, commissioners, deputy commissioners, and members of boards and commissions. One place to look is agency websites where some information on their top officials is available. A list of commissioners and their contact information is at: http://alaska.gov/commlist.html.

Most of this information on key public officials is factual and tells little about the personalities, political style, likes and dislikes, the best way to approach and deal with them, etc. The best source for getting this info is to be part of a contact network.

State Agencies and their Personnel

An indispensable source for this information is the Alaska *Directory of State Officials* (often referred to as DOSO). It includes:

- Contact information and committee assignments of legislators, but not a listing of their staff.

- Contact information for: the governor's and lieutenant governor's office in Juneau and around the state: a list of special assistants; and personnel in the Office of Management and Budget (OMB).

- A list of all state department, their divisions and location, including contact information for the commissioner, deputy commissioner, and division directors.

- Contact information for most boards and commissions.

- The location of the 23 Legislative Information Offices (LIOs) around the state with their contact details.

- Contact information for the state court system, the University of Alaska, and the state's Congressional delegation.

The DOSO is updated every year or so, but the updates often lag behind changes in elected and appointed officials. Bear this in mind when using it. The Directory is available in hard copy from the documents room in the Capitol, and on-line at: http://w3.akleg.gov/pubs/doso.php

BASIS—Bill Action and Status Inquiry System

BASIS is the legislature's Internet site with an extensive database for researching bills. An outline of the range of information available and how to use BASIS, is

You'll definitely want to become familiar with BASIS for tracking current bills and researching past legislation.

provided in Box 11.7 in Chapter 11 covering campaign management. More extensive information and a tutorial on using BASIS can be download at: https://akleg.gov/docs/pdf/basis.pdf

State Government Websites

In addition to the websites already mentioned, five other sites provide a treasure trove of information.

The Official Alaska State Website

Besides general information on the legislature, the governor's office, all state departments, and other agencies, here you'll find a directory of all state employees: http://alaska.gov/.

All social media sites used by various parts of state government, particularly state agencies, are at: http://alaska.gov/socialmedia.html

In addition, the Alaska Department of Administration's Division of General Services website provides a link to all state facilities. It's at: http://doa.alaska.gov/dgs/facilities/

The Legislature's Website

This contains masses of information. Particularly useful is the website of the Legislative Affairs Agency (LAA), the public information arm of the legislature. The site contains many useful items that you can download, including, how to read a bill's history, and a glossary of legislative terms.

You can access the site at: http://akleg.gov/publications.php/

Getting More Info

The Office of Management and Budget—OMB

Includes information on the current budget and past budgets. It also has a list of staff and the parts of the budget they cover. There are publications to download, including a glossary of budget

The legislature's website contains a mine of information, much of which you can download.

terms, and a guide to understanding the budget process (see below under State Budget). OMB's website is at: https://www.omb.alaska.gov//

The Alaska Public Offices Commission—APOC

APOC administers campaign financial disclosures, public official financial disclosures (formerly conflict of interest provisions), legislative financial disclosures, and lobbying regulations.

Their website has a list of lobbyists, what they get paid, the businesses and organizations they represent, and information on who's required to register as a lobbyist. Go to: http://doa.alaska.gov/apoc/

The Division of Elections

Contains the results of all state elections—for the legislature, governor, judges, ballot propositions, and Congress. It also has an extensive archive of information. It's at: http://www.elections.alaska.gov/

The State Budget

"Understanding Alaska's State Budget: The Process and its Political Dynamics." Chapter 19 in, Clive S. Thomas, ed,, *Alaska Politics and Public Policy.* See above for full details.

Budget Terms/Glossary (Alaska Office of Management and Budget, 2018).https://www.omb.alaska.gov/html/informationreports/budget-terminology.html

Budgeting 101 (Alaska Office of Management and Budget, 2005/06).

Alaska Legislative Budget Handbook: For Legislators and Legislative Staff—The Swiss Army Knife of Budget Handbooks (Alaska Legislature, Division of Legislative Finance, 2018), http://www.legfin.akleg.gov/Other/SwissArmyKnife14.pdf

Getting
More Info

Books on Lobbying

General Guides

Deanna R. Gelak, *Lobbying and Advocacy* (Alexandria, VA: TheCapital.Net, Inc., 2008).

Barry Hessenlus, *Hardball Lobbying for Nonprofits: Real Advocacy for Nonprofits in the New Century* (New York: Palgrave, 2007).

Amanda Knief, *The Citizen Lobbyist: A How-to Manual for Making Your Voice Heard in Government* (Durham, NC: Pitchstone Publishing, 2013).

Judith C. Meredith, *Lobbying on a Shoestring* (Dover, MA: Auburn House Publishing, 1989).

State, Local Government and Political Advocacy in Washington, D.C.

Marcia Avner, *The Lobbying and Advocacy Handbook for Nonprofit Organizations: Shaping Public Policy at the State and Local Level* (St. Paul, Minn.: Amherst H. Wilder Foundation, 2002).

Bradford Fitch, *Citizen's Handbook to Influencing Elected Officials: Citizen Advocacy in State Legislatures and Congress* (Alexandria, VA: TheCapital.Net, Inc., 2010).

Robert L. Guyer, *Guide to State Legislative Lobbying,* Revised Edition (Gainesville, FL: Engineering The Law, 2003).

Greg Rushford, *How Washington Really Works for Dummies* (Hoboken, NJ: John Wiley & Sons, Inc,, 2012).

In addition, the Foraker Group (which provides aid to non-profit organizations and Native groups) as well as many associations and lobby groups, have lobbying guides for newcomers. Most will provide you a copy on request.

★ APPENDIX 5 ★

Acknowledgments and List of Interviews

ACKNOWLEDGMENTS

I owe special thanks to Krista West, Production Editor, and Nate Bauer, Director & Acquisitions Editor, at the University of Alaska Press. Amber Granados was a wizard in developing graphics. Ten people were especially helpful in reviewing the manuscript as I wrote this book. They were:

- Johnny Ellis, who served in the Alaska House and Senate for 30 years.

- Ron Clarke, who has over thirty years of experience in many aspects of state government, including: as a special assistant in the governor's office; a legislative aide; a deputy division director; and as a lobbyist.

- Michelle Bonnet Hale, is a former division director and deputy director in the Alaska Department of Environmental Conservation (DEC). In 2018 she was elected to the Juneau Municipal Assembly.

- George Ascott, is one of the longest-serving staffers in the Alaska legislature. He has also worked in the governor's office.

- Rynnieva Moss, is also one of the longest-serving staff in the Alaska legislature, with a broad range of experiences as a personal aide and committee staffer.

- Glenn Wright, is an associate professor of political science at the University of Alaska in Juneau, and the director of the University's Statewide Legislative Internship Program.

- Weston Eiler worked as a staffer in the Alaska legislature for 10 years, and now helps manage government relations for the University of Alaska.

- Tom Brice, is a former Alaska legislator and lobbyist.

- Dennis DeWitt, has been a legislative aide, a senior official in a federal agency, an in-house lobbyist and a contract lobbyist.

- Darwin Peterson, has been a legislative aide for many years, and served as Governor Walker's legislative director.

LIST OF INTERVIEWS

Over the past 40 years, I've interviewed and closely observed over 150 lobbyists in 15 countries, as well as another 100 or more public officials, journalists, and political observers, to get their perspectives on lobbying.

Political practitioners emphasize what's important in lobbying from their vantage point in the policy process. So it's important to get many perspectives to provide a comprehensive picture of the various aspects of lobbying.

Well over half of these interviews were conducted in Alaska between 1980 and 2019. The list below includes most of those in the state who shared their experiences with me or who I observed operating in state politics. The list also includes some practitioners from out of state who were particularly helpful.

Some of those listed appear more than once. This is because they've held more than one position in government, politics or a related field, and so have viewed lobbying from different angles.

Thanks & Interviews

Lobbyists and Legislative Liaisons

Tom Brice
Beth Capell (California)
Wendy Chamberlain
Ginny Chitwood
Ron Clarke
Bob Cooksey
Wes Coyner
Stanley Crossick (Brussels)
Kent Dawson
Dennis DeWitt
Bob Evans
Gordon Evans
Macaela Fowler
Ray Gillespie

Norm Gorsuch
Joe Hayes
Melanie Lesh
Sharon Macklin
Bob Manners
Kevin C. Ritchie
Brian Rogers
Carl Rose
Thor Stacey
Mary Sattler
Carl Shepro
Arthur Snowden
Kate Troll
Norm Wooten

Legislators

Ramona Barnes
Mike Bradner
Tom Brice
Kay Brown
John Coghill
Harry Crawford
Mike Davis
Harriet Drummond
Mike Doogan
Jim Duncan
Dennis Egan
Johnny Ellis
Kim Elton
Victor Fischer
Berta Gardner
Lyda Green
Max Gruenberg

David Guttenberg
Joe Hayes
Bill Hudson
Loren Leman
Beth Kerttula
Mike Miller (Juneau)
Mike Navarre
Brian Rogers
Mary Sattler
John Sackett
Paul Seaton
Arliss Sturgulewski
John Torgerson
Fran Ulmer
Peggy Wilson
Bill Wielechowski
Bob Ziegler

Thanks &
Interviews

Legislative Staff

George Ascott
Nancy Barnes
Marla Berg
Chris Birdsall
Sandy Burd
Ron Clarke
Pat Cunningham
Katie Drennan
Allison Elgee
Cecile Elliott
Johnny Ellis
Kim Elton
Louie Flores

Cheryl Frasca
Max Gifford
Jesse Kiehl
Rynnieva Moss
Mike Scott
Jomo Stewart
Roxanne Stewart
Mike Young

Governors and Lieutenant Governors

Cecil Andrus (Idaho)
Jerry Brown (California)
Jack Coghill
Jay Hammond
Walter J. Hickel

Tony Knowles
Terry Miller
Bill Sheffield
Fran Ulmer

Governor's Staff

George Ascott
Ron Clarke
Allison Elgee
Richard Fineberg
Cheryl Frasca
Gordon Harrison

Bob King
Karen Rehfeld
Darwin Peterson
Nancy Bear Usera
Malcolm B. Roberts
Fran Ulmer

State Agency Personnel

Bob Arnold
Rick Barrier
Jeff Berliner
Michelle Bonnet Hale
Bruce Botelho
Britteny Cioni-Hayward
Ron Clarke
Billy Connor
Jerry Covey
Allison Elgee
Micaela Fowler
Leslie Houston
Bernice M. Joseph
John W. Katz

Norma Lang
Mary Lou Madden
Byron Mallott
Mike Navarre
Bill Noll
Emil Notti
Jeffery C. Ottesen
Fred Pardy
Karen Perdue
Karen Rehfeld
Arthur Snowden
Naomi Stockdale
Laura Savatgy
Mike Young

Journalists

Mike Bradner
Tim Bradner
Dave Donaldson
Mike Doogan
John Creely

Alexandra Gutierrez
Stan Jones
Dan Joling
Bill McAllister
Ralph Thomas

Other Political Practitioners and Observers

Douglas Barry
Susan Burke
Bud Carpeneti
Cornell W. Clayton
Delores Dinneen

Richard Elgar
Lois N. Epstein
Gregg Erickson
LeJane Ferguson
Scott Goldsmith

Thanks & Interviews

Gordon S. Harrison
Ronald J. Hrebenar
Gunnar Knapp
Tanyce M. Lang
John Lepore
Conor McGrath
Joan Messner
Malcolm B. Roberts

Ceceile Richter
Jay Rabinowitz
Elizabeth Selfridge
Thomas B. Stewart
Jeffrey Weinberg
Carol A. Winton
Venus Zink

In interviewing lobbyists around the world, it's clear that the basics of lobbying are the same from Alaska to Washington, D.C. to Austria to Japan. The differences result mainly from the politics in each country.

Thanks & Interviews